AF322954

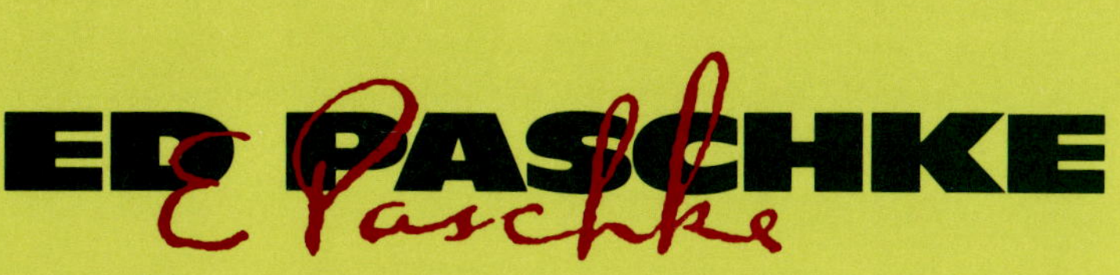

With the compliments of the Ameritech Foundation

ED PASCHKE

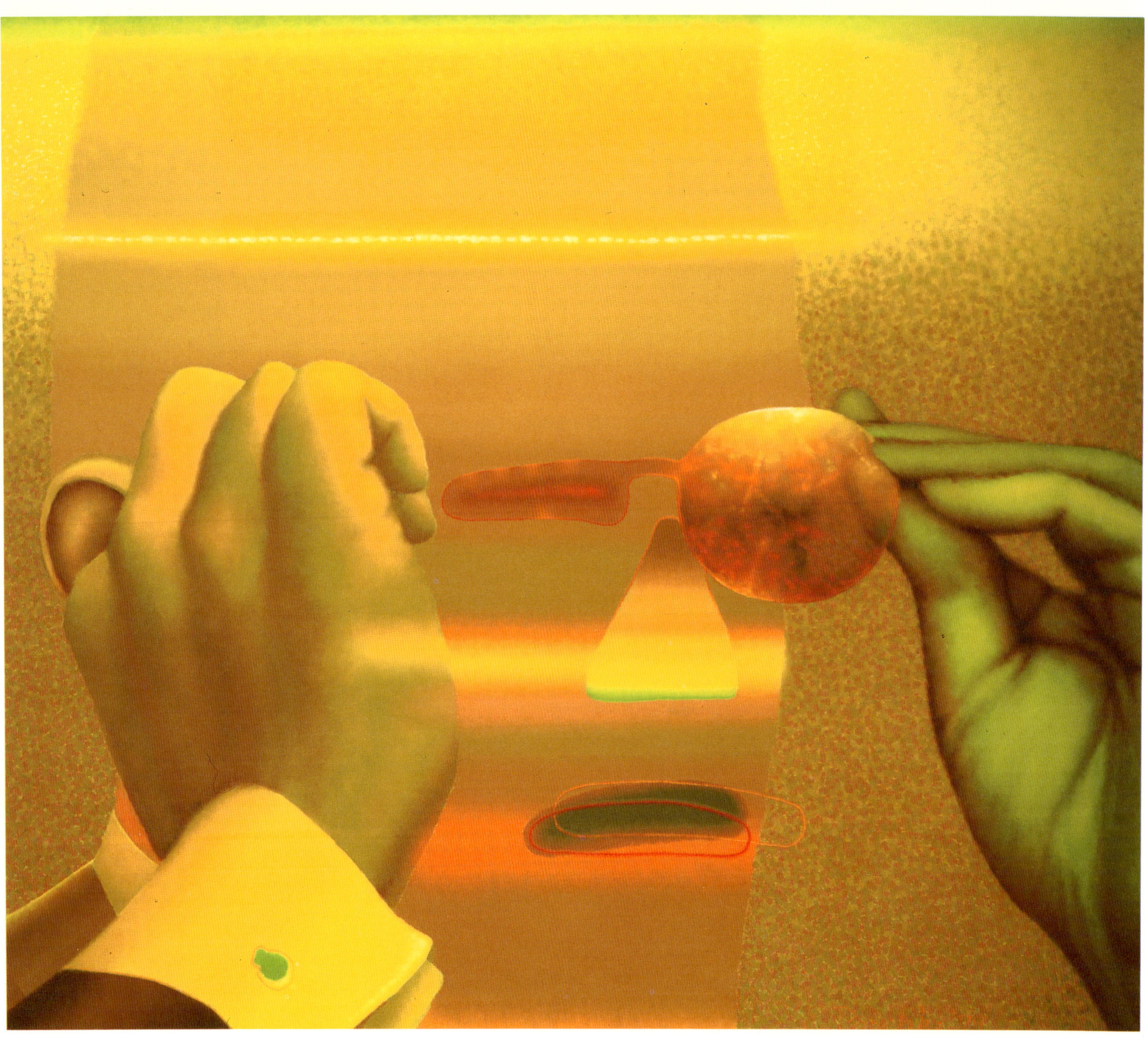

27
AMBROSIA, 1979

BY NEAL BENEZRA

WITH CONTRIBUTIONS BY DENNIS ADRIAN,
CAROL SCHREIBER, AND JOHN YAU

ED PASCHKE

HUDSON HILLS PRESS, NEW YORK

THE ART INSTITUTE OF CHICAGO

FIRST EDITION

© 1990 by The Art Institute of Chicago

Co-published by *The Art Institute of Chicago*, Michigan Avenue at Adams Street, Chicago, Illinois 60603; and Hudson Hills Press, Inc., Suite 1308, 230 Fifth Avenue, New York, NY 10001-7704.

Distributed in the United States, its territories and possessions, Canada, Mexico, and Central and South America by Rizzoli International Publications, Inc.
Distributed in Japan by Yohan (Western Publications Distribution Agency).

LIBRARY OF CONGRESS CATALOGUING-IN-PUBLICATION DATA

Benezra, Neal David, 1953–
    Ed Paschke/by Neal Benezra with contributions by Dennis
    Adrian and John Yau.—1st ed.
        p.   cm.
    Includes bibliographical references.
    1. Paschke, Ed—Criticism and interpretation.   I. Adrian, Dennis,
    1937– . II. Yau, John, 1950– .   III. Title.
    ND237.P2522A4   1990
    759.13—dc20   89-28252
                                                   CIP

HUDSON HILLS PRESS

Editor and Publisher: Paul Anbinder
Senior Editor: Virginia Wageman
Indexer: Gisela S. Knight
Designer: Binns & Lubin/Betty Binns
Composition: U.S. Lithograph, typographers
Manufactured in Japan by Toppan Printing Company

THE ART INSTITUTE OF CHICAGO

Editor: Terry Ann R. Neff
Executive Director of Publications: Susan F. Rossen
Production Manager: Katherine A. Houck

ISBN: 0-86559-084-2 (alk. paper)

Frontispiece: *Ambrosia*, 1979

Cover illustration: *Matinee*, 1987

This book is dedicated by The Art Institute of
Chicago and Ed Paschke to the memory of
Carol Schreiber (1944–1989), whose tireless efforts
and unwavering support on behalf of the artist
and his career will always be appreciated and
never forgotten.

CONTENTS

LIST OF PLATES   8

FOREWORD   9
JAMES N. WOOD

ACKNOWLEDGMENTS   11
NEAL BENEZRA

ED PASCHKE: TWENTY-FIVE YEARS OF CONFRONTATION   15
NEAL BENEZRA

COLORPLATES   43

THE SELF AS SUBJECT, THE SUBJECTED SELF: THE PAINTINGS OF ED PASCHKE   107
JOHN YAU

A CONVERSATION WITH ED PASCHKE   115
DENNIS ADRIAN

CATALOGUE OF THE EXHIBITION   123

DOCUMENTATION   129
CAROL SCHREIBER
Chronology, 129; One-Person Exhibitions, 134; Selected Group Exhibitions, 135;
Selected Bibliography, 141; Documentation for Text Illustrations/Photograph Credits, 150

INDEX   153

PLATES

1	*Purple Ritual, 1967*	44
2	*Amor, 1968*	45
3	*Dos Criados, 1968*	46
4	*Accordion Man, 1969*	47
5	*Mid American, 1969*	48
6	*Ramrod, 1969*	49
7	*Hophead, 1970*	50
8	*Pink Lady, 1970*	51
9	*Hairy Shoes, 1971*	52
10	*Bag Boots, 1972*	53
11	*Francine, 1973*	54
12	*Jeanine, 1973*	55
13	*Joella, 1973*	56
14	*Lucy, 1973*	57
15	*Rufus, 1974*	58
16	*Armondo, 1975*	59
17	*Red Sweeney, 1975*	60
18	*Machino, 1976*	61
19	*Sabreena, 1976*	62
20	*Dominant Nurse, 1977*	63

21	*Mandrix, 1977*	64
22	*Melon-Lamé, 1977*	65
23	*Metal de Bleu, 1977*	66
24	*Terminale, 1977*	67
25	*Cho Chan, 1978*	68
26	*Duro-Verde, 1978*	69
27	*Ambrosia, 1979*	70
28	*Fumar, 1979*	71
29	*Strangulita, 1979*	72
30	*Nervosa, 1980*	73
31	*Violencia, 1980*	74
32	*L'Impression, 1981*	75
33	*Televismo, 1981*	76–77
34	*Bibutsu, 1982*	78
35	*Fernsehen, 1982*	79
36	*Mechanique, 1982*	80–81
37	*Der Tanz, 1982*	82
38	*Bahamas, 1983*	83
39	*Le Sac, 1983*	84
40	*Towanda, 1983*	85

41	*Vosostros, 1983*	86
42	*Afrique, 1984*	87
43	*Electalady, 1984*	88
44	*Malibu, 1984*	89
45	*Caliente, 1985*	90
46	*Frio, 1985*	91
47	*Troika, 1985*	92–93
48	*Pazzo, 1986*	94
49	*Prima Vere, 1986*	95
50	*Purisma, 1986*	96
51	*Cosmetica, 1987*	97
52	*Libredo, 1987*	98
53	*Matinee, 1987*	99
54	*Papal Lunacy, 1987*	100
55	*Pedifem, 1987*	101
56	*Blackstone, 1988*	102
57	*Negrette, 1988*	103
58	*Santa Caballo, 1988*	104
59	*Yin and Yang, 1988*	105

FOREWORD

FOREWORD

Since its inception in 1879, The Art Institute of Chicago and its collections and exhibitions have provided an essential resource for students enrolled at the School of the Art Institute. Despite the extraordinary number and quality of the artists who have matriculated here, only a select few have subsequently been honored with a one-person exhibition at the Art Institute: Ivan Albright, Georgia O'Keeffe, Claes Oldenburg, H. C. Westermann, and Grant Wood. We are pleased to be able to place Ed Paschke's work and career into this context and to honor him with this major exhibition, which will also present his work in Paris and Dallas.

There has long been a strong interest in Paschke's work in Europe, and the exhibition has benefited in a fundamental way from the long-standing enthusiasm for Paschke's painting of Jean-Hubert Martin, Director of the Musée National d'Art Moderne, Paris. To Mr. Martin and Richard R. Brettell, Director of the Dallas Museum of Art and previously Searle Curator of European Painting here at the Art Institute, where he followed Paschke's development with interest, go our gratitude for joining in the presentation of this exhibition.

We are deeply indebted to the Ameritech Foundation and The Henry Luce Foundation for their crucial and very generous support of this project. Finally, we owe a special debt to all the lenders, without whose sacrifice exhibitions such as this would not be possible.

JAMES N. WOOD
DIRECTOR

One of the great pleasures that attends the arrival of a new curatorial colleague is a fresh exchange of aesthetic enthusiasms. Soon after the arrival of Charles F. Stuckey as Curator of 20th-Century Painting and Sculpture in September 1988, we recognized a long-standing, mutual admiration for the work of Ed Paschke; from these conversations the present exhibition evolved. I am very grateful to Charlie, as I am to Director James N. Wood for his great enthusiasm and support. I am pleased, as well, that our enthusiasm is shared by my colleagues Jean-Pierre Bordaz and Paul-Hervé Parsy, Curators, Musée National d'Art Moderne, and Sue Graze, Curator of Contemporary Art, Dallas Museum of Art.

Beyond the quality of Paschke's paintings, the artist's heritage as a Chicago-based artist, educated at The School of The Art Institute of Chicago, and nourished by the museum and its exhibitions, has made this project a labor of love for a great many individuals within the institution. I am particularly indebted to Larry Ter Molen, Vice-President for Development and Public Relations, as well as Linda Noyle and Mary Jane Keitel, of his department, for their extraordinary efforts on behalf of this exhibition. Robert E. Mars, Vice-President for Administrative Affairs, Katharine C. Lee, Deputy Director, Mary Solt, Associate Registrar, Eileen Harakal,

Executive Director of Public Affairs, Barbara Scharres, Director of the Film Center of the School of the Art Institute, and Yutaka Mino, Curator of Chinese and Japanese Art, have all lent their efforts toward the exhibition. I owe a special debt to Dorothy Schroeder, Assistant to the Director, for her always wise counsel.

We have documented this exhibition in two parallel ways, and I am thankful to a number of individuals who have committed themselves to these twin endeavors. The catalogue contains a thoughtful essay by John Yau and an interview with the artist conducted by Dennis Adrian, and I am grateful to both of them. Dennis Adrian deserves our special gratitude for his long-standing role as a champion of Ed Paschke through his work as both critic and art historian. The book itself is the work of the Department of Publications, Susan F. Rossen, Executive Director, and Terry Ann R. Neff, Katherine Houck, Cris Ligenza, and Susan Snodgrass of her staff. Given Ed Paschke's interest in new forms of media and technology, it seemed appropriate, if not necessary, to explore new methods with which to interpret his work for the public. The state-of-the-art video disc that accompanies this exhibition was directed by James Sheldon, Curator of Photography at the Addison Gallery of American Art, and produced by

John Kent Lydecker, Executive Director, Museum Education, and Alan Newman, Executive Director, Photographic Services, assisted by John Manning of the School of the Art Institute.

In my own Department of 20th-Century Painting and Sculpture, I am pleased to acknowledge Courtney Donnell, Eddi Wolk, Elizabeth Leitgen, Thomas Berry, James Pogozelski, Judith Cizek, Mary Murphy, and Carole Tormollan. I am indebted to the late Carol Schreiber, my assistant for this exhibition, whose master's thesis in art history for the School of the Art Institute is devoted to Paschke, whose assistance has been indispensable, and to whom this book is dedicated.

My debt to Ed Paschke's longtime dealers is of particular consequence. Phyllis Kind, William H. Bengtson, Ron Jagger, David Russick, and Alexa Reimer of the Phyllis Kind Gallery, New York and Chicago; and Darthea Speyer and Isabelle Vassart of the Galerie Darthea Speyer, Paris, have all been unfailingly helpful and hospitable. In addition, I am grateful to Mary McIsaac, School of the Art Institute; I. Michael Danoff, former Director, and Alice M. Piron, Librarian, Museum of Contemporary Art, Chicago; Barbara Saniie and Catherine Zurybida of the Hyde Park Art Center; and Art Paul, former Art Director for *Playboy*, and Barbara Hoffman of that magazine. To all, my heartfelt thanks.

Surely of greatest consequence is my debt to Ed Paschke himself. The artist has been a constant source of wisdom, intelligence, information, and restraint throughout the preparation of this exhibition. It is indeed a blessing for any curator working in the field of contemporary art to become closely acquainted with an important artist who also happens to be a wonderful individual; this exhibition has afforded me such an opportunity.

NEAL BENEZRA
CURATOR
DEPARTMENT OF 20TH-CENTURY
PAINTING AND SCULPTURE

ED PASCHKE

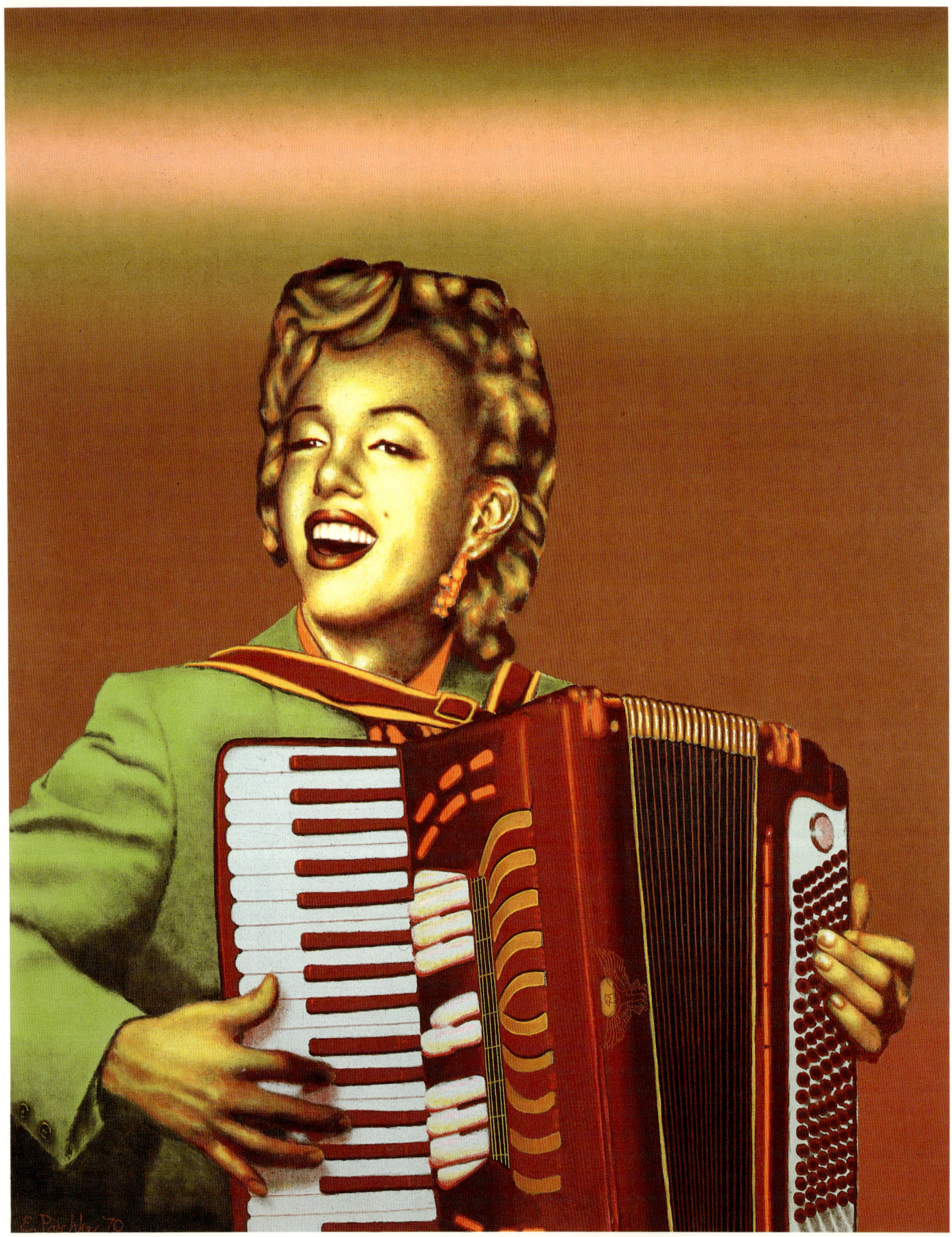

PINK LADY, 1970

Ed Paschke has spent the past twenty-five years creating paintings that confront social and cultural values. In the process, he has consistently explored media-based imagery for the sources of his commentary. Among his most persistent and compelling motifs has been the woman performer, and one figure who appears in both Paschke's early and his more recent work is Marilyn Monroe. Among the early paintings of this most celebrated of American sex symbols is *Pink Lady* (1970) (cat. no. 8). Although the painting presents a characteristic publicity image of Monroe smiling, she is dressed in a man's green sports coat and, even more surprisingly, she carries a large accordion that she plays with considerable gusto. In making a painting such as this, Paschke employed an opaque projector in order to transpose the image from an existing reproduction to his canvas and thereby juxtapose a number of dissimilar images. In this case, Paschke took a movie-magazine image of Monroe and grafted it to a music-trade advertisement showing a man playing an accordion (fig. 1).

On one level, *Pink Lady* challenges our notions of popular images and their appearance in works of art. Marilyn Monroe, for example, has been a subject for artists since Willem de Kooning painted the actress in 1954 (fig. 2). At the

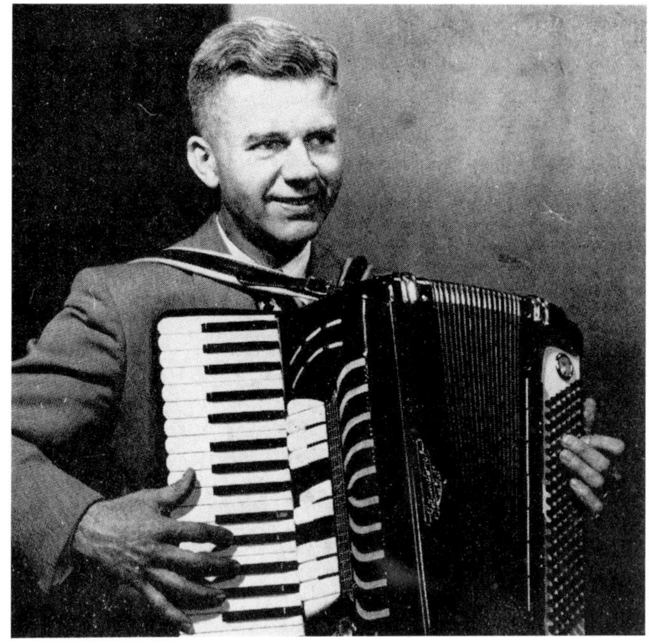

FIG. 1
UNIDENTIFIED PHOTOGRAPH USED BY THE ARTIST

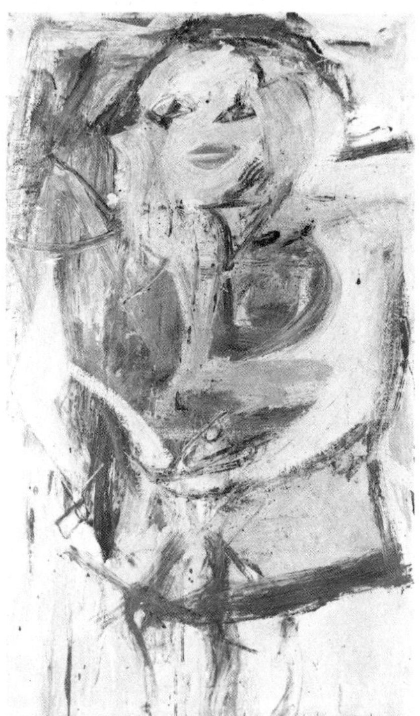

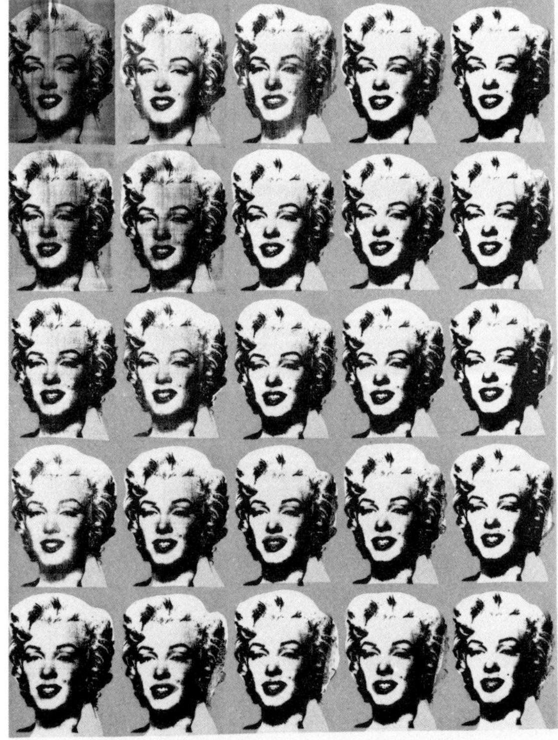

time of her death in 1962, Monroe became a subject for countless Pop artists; most prominent among the resulting images are Andy Warhol's serial portraits (see fig. 3).[1] Because of her constant representation in the media as well as in works of art, Monroe came to personify a timeless, though stereotypical, object of the public's obsession with sexuality and glamour.

Rather than placing Monroe on her accustomed public pedestal, as did de Kooning and Warhol, in *Pink Lady* Ed Paschke reduced the actress to a curiosity. Beyond leveling an American icon and endowing her with altogether mundane if surprising attributes, Paschke subverted the public figure in additional ways. A theme common to the artist's early painting is the intentional confusion and transformation of sexual identity: men and women are joined one to another and simultaneously assume contrasting attributes. Although this is most explicit in other paintings, the willful placement of Monroe's face and hands on an undistinguished male body and suit of clothing introduces Paschke's pleasure in transforming the conventional in surprising, if not shocking, ways.

In the nearly two decades separating *Pink Lady* and *Pazzo* (1986) (cat. no. 48), Paschke's interests shifted from print to electronic media, and a dazzling array of waves and flashes similar to those found in television and video now fill his paintings. Heads, radically fragmented by one another and the frame, have now largely replaced the naturalistic full figures of the earlier work. In *Pazzo*, fields of extraordinarily brilliant color serve to mask the face, with lips and eyes alone suggesting likeness and human presence beneath the electronic overlay. So complete is Paschke's transformation of the individual that, although we may correctly recognize Marilyn Monroe in the figure at the right, her identity is subsumed in the surrounding theatrical spectacle.[2] Once again, Paschke has distinguished himself from artists like Warhol and James Rosenquist, who, even in their most extreme depictions of Monroe, still celebrated the actress in both image and title (see fig. 4). In contrast, Paschke here manipulated a less obvious image of Monroe and aggressively sheathed and fractured it virtually beyond recognition, and then combined it with other similarly violated likenesses. Unlike *Pink Lady*, which

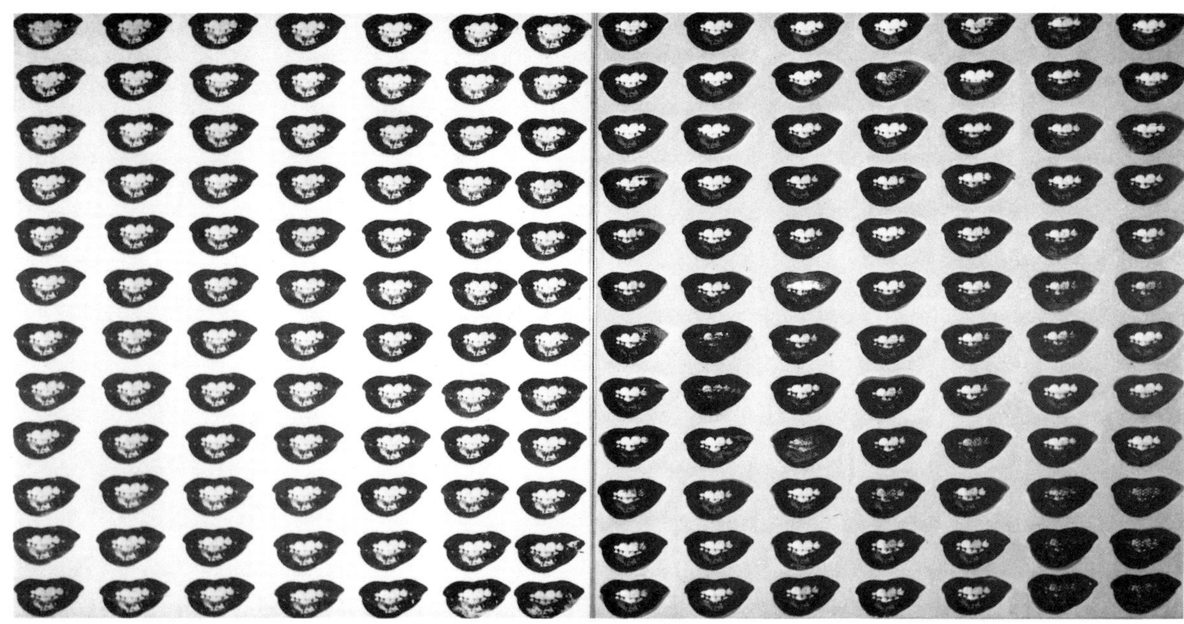

levels Monroe, *Pazzo* bespeaks the artist's sweeping critique of the media itself and its role in minimalizing, and occasionally even brutalizing, the individual.

Pink Lady and *Pazzo* bracket the changes that Ed Paschke's work has undergone during the last twenty-five years, while simultaneously demonstrating the remarkable consistency of his intention and vision. Underlying all of Paschke's work is a fascination with media. This interest is not unique, as artists such as Warhol and Robert Rauschenberg, among many others, championed the introduction of public images into works of art. What distinguishes Paschke, beyond his shift from print to electronic imagery, is his obsession both with less accessible media forms and with the manner in which the individual is ultimately transformed by the images one sees on a daily basis. For Paschke, the media conveys not only the rhythms of mundane public life but also our private obsessions and darker, repressed fascinations. In contrast with Pop Art's willing and often optimistic embrace of contemporary culture, Ed Paschke has adopted an outsider's stance, submerging himself in a world of shadows and exploring the dark underside of American values as well as our popular culture.

The sensibility that Ed Paschke brings to works like *Pink Lady* and *Pazzo* is the product of both the extraordinary range of experience that the artist accumulated in his youth and Chicago's artistic climate after World War II. Chicago had long been a center for American literature and architecture, but it was not until the conclusion of World War II that painters and sculptors became important contributors to the city's

cultural life.[3] In the late 1940s many veterans, mature in years and by wartime experience, settled in Chicago and lent the art community an unusual intensity. Indeed, debates over both aesthetics and exhibition opportunities were frequent and heated during this period, and The Art Institute of Chicago's then-annual "Chicago and Vicinity" exhibitions were the focus of such discussions. In the absence of commercial galleries, this event provided local artists with their sole meaningful opportunity to exhibit. When, in 1947, the museum banned student work from the show, a protest movement formed, and "Momentum" became the title for a series of open exhibitions that continued into the early 1960s. These shows, held at various locations in the city and juried through the years by Alfred Barr, Clement Greenberg, Betty Parsons, Sidney Janis, Jackson Pollock, Robert Motherwell, and Josef Albers, among numerous others, were subsequently the locus of aesthetic debate in the postwar artists' community.

Despite the predominance of jurors from New York, in its early years "Momentum" was dominated by Chicago's first generation of Imagist artists: Cosmo Campoli, George Cohen, Leon Golub, and June Leaf, among others.[4] Theirs was a hybrid style influenced by the Surrealist works that were so avidly collected privately in the city, by the extraordinary collection of tribal arts housed in the city's Field Museum of Natural History, and, more generally, by the European expressionist tradition, particularly as represented by Jean Dubuffet. His work, which synthesized Western and tribal forms in a body of powerful expressionist paintings and sculpture, was much in evidence in Chicago, and a major painting, *Jules Supervielle grand portrait mythe* (1947) (fig. 5)

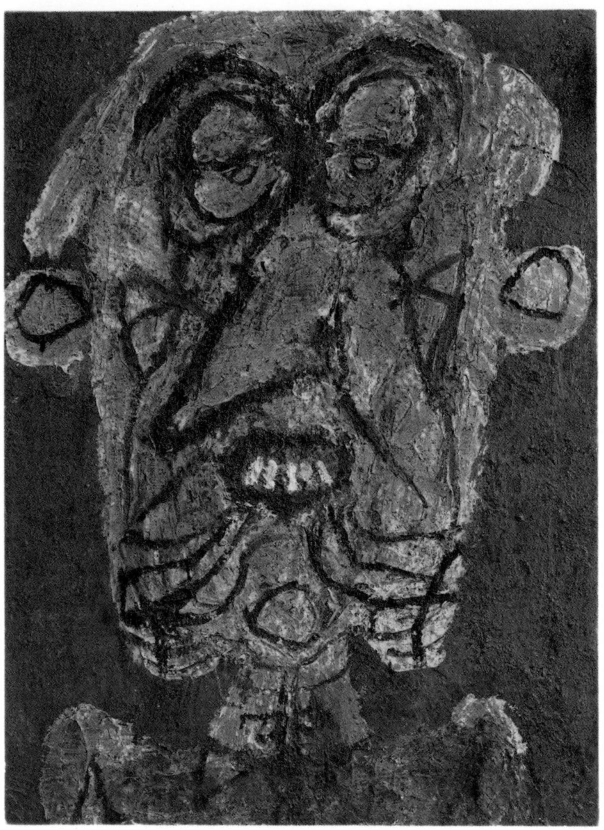

entered the Art Institute's collection in 1950. The presence of a work such as this, as well as Dubuffet's exhibition at The Arts Club of Chicago in 1951–52 and an accompanying lecture by the artist, "Anti-Cultural Positions," delivered on December 20, 1951, lent credence to the direct, soul-baring, generally figurative expressionism that younger artists such as Golub and Cohen were attempting. In his talk Dubuffet encouraged artists to ignore Western concepts of beauty and replace them with nontraditional values—"instinct, passion, mood, violence, madness."[5] For Dubuffet:

This idea of beauty [is] a meager and not very ingenious invention, and especially not very encouraging for man . . . on the contrary if he becomes aware that there is no ugly object or ugly person in the world and that beauty does not exist anywhere, but that any object is able to become for any man a way of fascination and illumination, he will have made a good catch.[6]

Dubuffet stressed that artists could best overcome this obsession with beauty by looking anew at daily life: "For myself, I aim for an art which would be in immediate connection with daily life, an art which would start from the daily life, and would be a very direct and very sincere expression of our real life and our real moods."[7]

Artists such as Cohen and Golub attended Dubuffet's lecture, and printed texts circulated in the city, confirming notions already in the air in Chicago concerning the existential status of the artist in modern society.[8] Golub, Cohen, Seymour Rosofsky, and others were making art in an attempt to cope with the psychological fallout of World War II. Evidence of this is found in Cohen's *Emblem for an Unknown Nation #1* (1954) (fig. 6), one of the most compelling paintings of the period. A Surrealist pictograph of anatomical fragments composed in mock resemblance of a flag, this painting demonstrates the tragic fallacy of mankind's nationalist aspirations. Figurative imagery predominated at the time, and Golub's *Head I* (1958) (fig. 7) typifies the tendency. Golub's work of the period—frontal figures based on classical Greek sculpture that have been fragmented as if devastated by combat—characterizes these artists' response to post–World War II civilization. With their primitivizing, generally figurative subject matter and self-conscious subjectivism, Chicago artists established a position for themselves outside the mainstream of New York School abstraction in the 1950s.

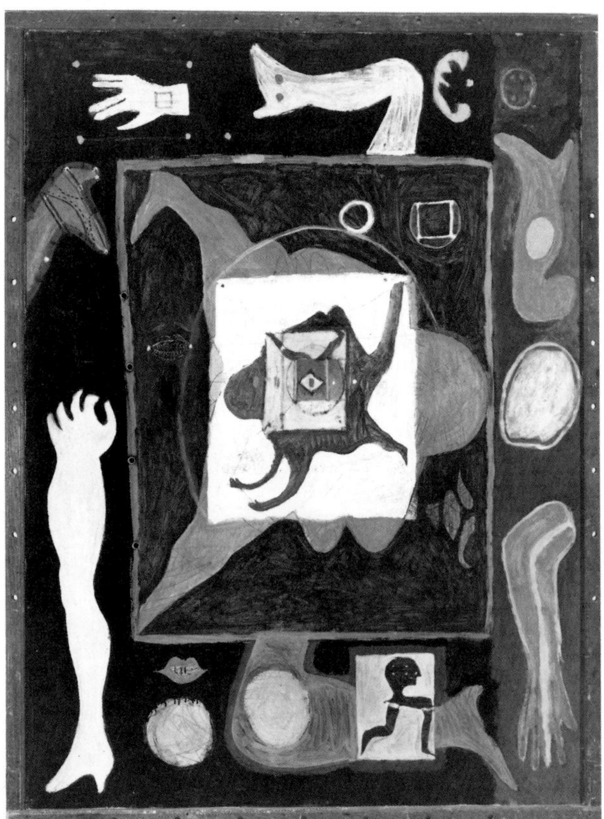

In sum, Imagism, the prevailing Chicago aesthetic—a Surrealist-influenced, highly personal, and expressive attitude in which figurative imagery dominated—was clearly in place by the late 1950s. Although this approach was in no way binding nor absolute, with artists of as distinct temperament and attitude as Golub, H. C. Westermann, and Claes Oldenburg all finding nourishment for several years in Chicago, Imagism was certainly the dominant direction. Perhaps more important than any particular shared aesthetic was the defiant sense of independence that Chicago's artists cultivated, as well as a belief in the humanistic power of art apart from established formal and social norms.

It was this environment that Ed Paschke entered in the fall of 1957. Born in 1939 to Polish-Catholic parents, as a child Paschke had lived at various times in Chicago and its northwest suburbs. He drew as a youngster and developed a particular interest in animation and cartoons, at one time even submitting a portfolio of drawings to Walt Disney. Paschke developed an obsession with urban life at an early age; even as a teenager he found the suburbs stifling in comparison with the rich street life of Chicago. A loner by nature, Paschke indulged his interest in art and the city and, following graduation from high school in 1957, he enrolled in the degree program in drawing, painting, and illustration at The School of The Art Institute of Chicago.[9]

The institutional home of the Imagist tradition, the School of the Art Institute had provided education to Golub, Cohen, Oldenburg, and Westermann. Its dominant teachers of the late 1950s—Kathleen Blackshear and Whitney Halstead—stressed the outsider, non-Western tradition (to be studied at the Field Museum) as well as Dubuffet's *art brut* and popular culture. Nonetheless, the school was also open to more formally oriented course work, which Paschke undertook with Isobel Steele MacKinnon and John Fabion, as well as commercial art, which Paschke studied with a gifted and flamboyant young graphic designer named Leroy Niemann. Paschke was naturally inclined toward representational imagery; while in high school he had developed

the capacity to be a relatively good mimic, and that was all I really knew how to do when I began art school. And it was almost a taboo to be dealing with things in a somewhat representational way. So I became kind of schizophrenic in the sense that during

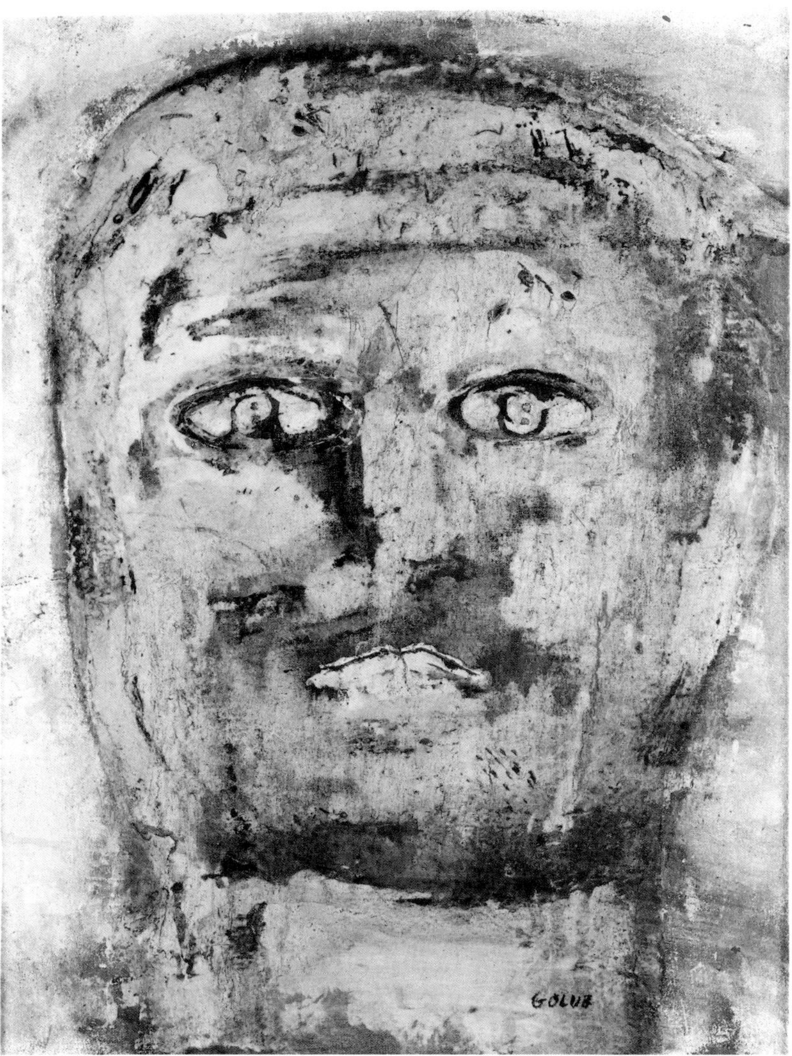

FIG. 7
LEON GOLUB (AMERICAN, B. 1922)
HEAD I, 1958

school I was learning how to paint based on certain principles of Abstract, Gestalt, Expressionism and all that. But in private, at home at night, I was drawn towards things that had more of a content-oriented approach.[10]

The Hans Hofmann–derived training, which Paschke received as an undergraduate studying composition and color, emphasized balanced figure-ground relationships and the im-

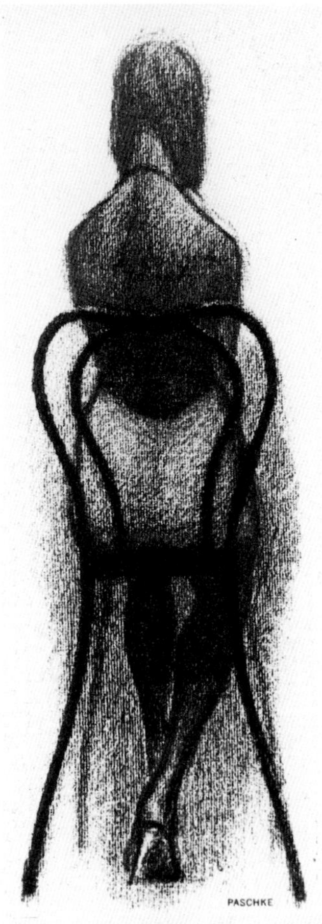

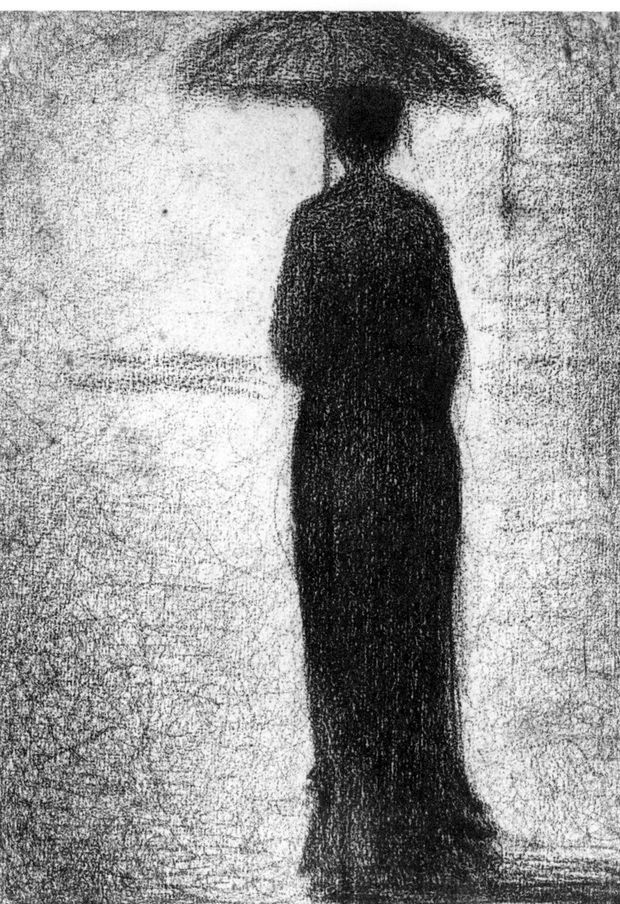

FIG. 8
ED PASCHKE (AMERICAN, B. 1939)
**UNTITLED ILLUSTRATION FOR "QUEEN DIDO,"
A MEMOIR BY BEN HECHT, 1962**

FIG. 9
GEORGES SEURAT (FRENCH, 1859–1891)
**WOMAN WITH A PARASOL, SEEN FROM THE
BACK, C. 1882–84**

portance of the flattened picture plane. Although at that time he rejected formalist theory as "dry, abstract concepts,"[11] this approach would provide an important basis for his work beginning in the late 1970s.

In addition to the education he received in the classroom, Paschke was also able to see a number of important special exhibitions while an undergraduate. Particularly important were the Art Institute's regular American Exhibitions, which introduced him to current works by established and emerging artists: Richard Lindner (62nd American Exhibition, 1957); Leon Golub, Jack Levine, and H. C. Westermann (63rd American Exhibition, 1959–60); Bruce Conner, Stuart Davis, Jasper Johns, Robert Rauschenberg, Larry Rivers, and William Wiley (64th American Exhibition, 1961). Beyond these, Paschke recalls the impact of three major touring exhibitions: "Picasso: 75th Anniversary Exhibition" (1957), "Seurat: Paintings and Drawings" (1958), and "Gauguin" (1959).

The impact of the Seurat exhibition was particularly strong. Rather than the obvious and continuing presence in the museum of the artist's masterwork, *Sunday Afternoon on the Island of the Grande Jatte* (1884–86), it was apparently Seurat's Conté-crayon drawings, a number of which were included in the exhibition, that most influenced Paschke. Soon after the artist graduated, in 1961, he received the first of twenty-eight commissions to illustrate stories for the Chicago-produced *Playboy* magazine. The first of these projects, published in May 1962, clearly illustrates Paschke's debt to the French Post-Impressionist. Executed in Seurat's technique of rubbing Conté crayon on rough-textured paper to produce a chiaroscuro effect, this drawing of a seated woman seen from behind is also imbued with the quietude that characterizes Seurat's figures (see figs. 8, 9).[12]

Paschke worked as a commercial artist as a means of support on a number of occasions until he reentered the School of the Art Institute as a graduate student in 1968. At various times he was employed by a graphic-arts firm, rendering geological maps to be used in the training of astronauts, and, most auspiciously, designing and then actually supervising the production of a block-long temporary façade at the entry level as part of a promotional campaign

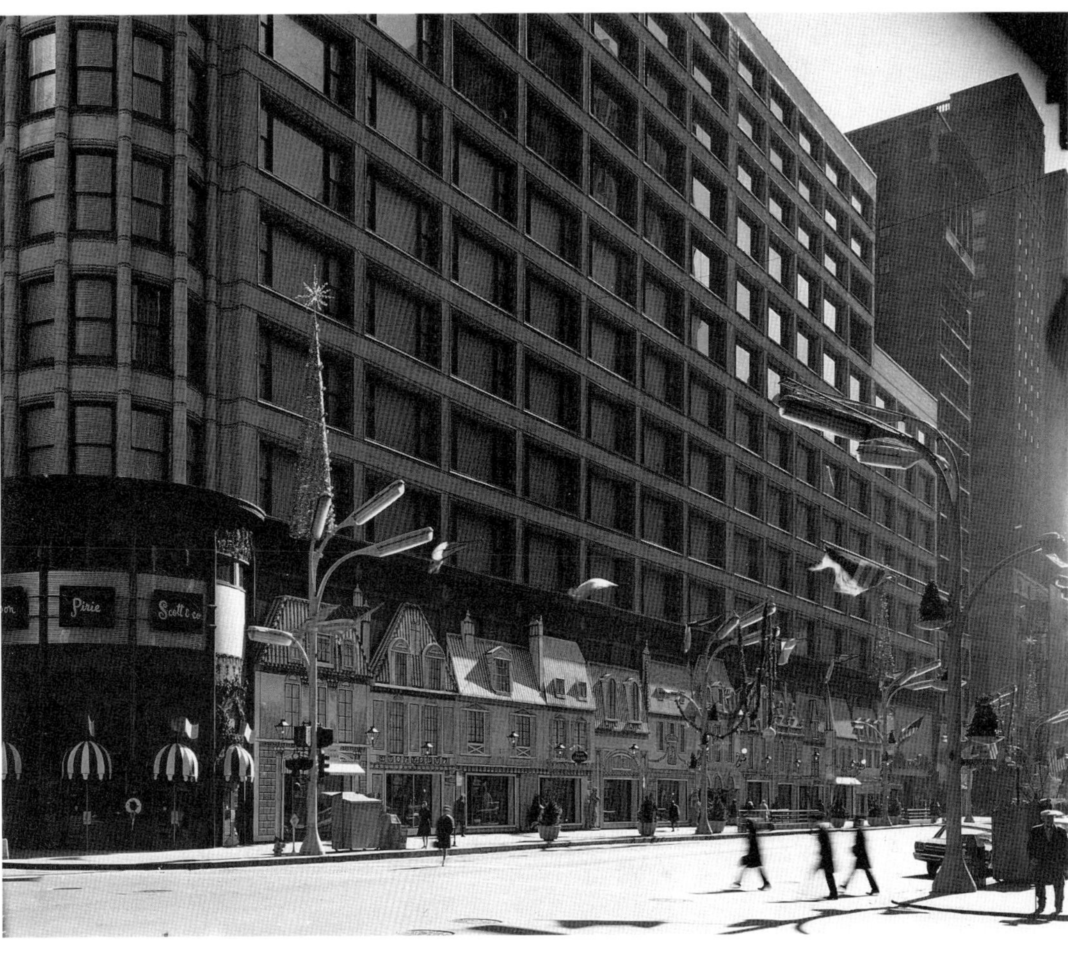

for Carson, Pirie, Scott and Company's State Street department store in Chicago (fig. 10).[13]

If Paschke was attentive to the work of the modern masters, and supported himself as a commercial artist, his heart nonetheless remained with the observation of urban life and culture. He consistently sought living and working situations that would place him in direct, daily contact with Chicago's diverse ethnic communities. While a student, for example, he worked for several summers in a factory that employed primarily Latinos, a setting that sparked his interest in nonmainstream patterns of dress and speech. After having been awarded an Art Institute travel fellowship upon graduation, Paschke spent the summer of 1961 traveling in Mexico with classmates Bert Phillips and Karl Wirsum. The following spring, in May 1962, he visited New York for the first time, and his abiding interest in outsider culture grew. Equipped with his portfolio, which included his recent work for *Playboy*, Paschke hoped to gain employment as a commercial artist. Although his stay was brief and unsuccessful from an employment standpoint, Paschke visited the re-

nowned jazz club Birdland and observed the street life in Times Square. On his return to Chicago, he obtained a civil-service position as a psychiatric-aide trainee at the Dunning Psychiatric Center.

I knew I was going to be drafted into the military and I always harbored a fascination for human abnormality. So I proceeded to get a job in a mental institution as a psychiatric aide. I just wanted to find out what happens inside the confines of those walls. It was a very potent experience for me. I didn't do it all that long but I think that the energies that I absorbed during that time have left a great mark on my soul and consciousness and subconsciousness.[14]

During the three summer months that Paschke spent working at Dunning, he received classroom training as well as practical experience in the wards. The latter involved tending to the needs of the patients—bathing and clothing them and observing behavior. Although Paschke's interest in the mentally ill was empathetic, it also proved to be intellectual and artistic, and the exaggerated poses and facial expressions that his subjects would later assume certainly owe something to this important formative experience.

Paschke's fascination with the human psyche first took preliminary form not in his paintings, but on film. With the impending prospect of military service, Paschke hurriedly returned to New York in September 1962. Rather than seeking employment as he had earlier that year, the artist now experimented with filmmaking for the first time. Setting out from his small rented room on the Upper West Side, Paschke worked the bus stations and subways, drifting "around with my camera and shooting what I felt was interesting or bizarre."[15] He frequented bars in Harlem and the Lower East Side, buying drinks for his subjects in exchange for a few moments of mugging, laughing, or screaming on camera.

The receipt of a draft notice in November 1962 concluded a period of intense activity for Paschke. Although he had completed relatively few paintings since graduating from the Art Institute in June 1961, the range of experience he had accumulated was vast. He had immersed himself in the subcultures that fascinated him, working with Latinos in a factory job, serving as a psychiatric aide, and venturing into sleazy bars in New York and Chicago. In the process, Paschke had gathered a storehouse of visual images of compelling psychological intensity that set the stage for his future work.

Still, these experiences might well have been stillborn and ultimately lost to his art had Paschke encountered less perceptive superiors while in basic training at Fort Leonard Wood, Missouri, and later while stationed at Fort Polk, Louisiana. His abilities as a draftsman were noticed immediately, and he was soon involved in rendering maps, charts, and detailed drawings of weapons to be used in the training of new troops. Rather than lying dormant, then, his drawing skills continued to develop. Moreover, Paschke's talent with a .45-caliber revolver on the firing range led him to be assigned to pursuing AWOL soldiers through the back country of Louisiana, Texas, and Mississippi. While on weekend leaves, Paschke found much to observe in the back-country towns and seedy bars of rural Louisiana. In short, his quest for artistic and life experience was not altogether frustrated during these years. Instead, as he himself noted, his period in the military served to discipline him, for it "made me appreciate time and how to use it [and] focused my thinking a great deal."[16]

Notably, it was precisely at this time that Pop Art exploded onto the American scene in numerous articles published in *Time* and *Newsweek* in 1963–64.[17] Although Paschke as a student in Chicago had seen the work of Robert Rauschenberg and Larry Rivers, it was not until this time that Pop made an "indelible impression" on him, giving him license to borrow directly from all manner of published sources and to treat "recognizable subject matter and forms, things that had narrative possibility" in fine art.[18] Warhol's images of public life—whether portraits of movie stars or images of commercial products—were particularly influential. That such material could constitute legitimate subject matter for paintings served as profound and lasting encouragement for Paschke. Predisposed as he was to life on the fringes of society, when he left the military in 1964 Paschke quickly adopted the printed media of popular culture and subculture as his exclusive source of visual imagery.

The first extant examples were made in the spring of 1965 in New York, where Paschke spent two months after traveling in Europe. Paschke worked on the Lower East Side, salvaging all manner of published material from the city streets. He began to make collages, typically pasting newspaper and magazine fragments to large sheets of illustration board. These would often be colored with translucent paint and then cut up and reassembled, the artist paying more attention to juxtaposition than to compositional unity. The most important of these, a small untitled work of 1965 (fig. 11), draws on an unidentified lingerie advertisement. In it, Paschke transformed a nondescript model into a woman of considerable confrontational presence. The monochrome tones of the published newsprint original were turned to orange and purple, and the central image was balanced by paired views of a different but also sun-glazed woman above. Back in Chicago, Paschke carefully enlarged the collage and transferred it to canvas. *Large Round Open* (1965) (fig. 12) alters the format by placing the lingerie model in the center of a simulated currency note. Although images of currency proliferated in the early 1960s—Warhol was among the first to employ the format—in placing such an openly sexual image in the position formerly reserved for statesmen, Paschke subverted the dignity of the form while proposing alternative

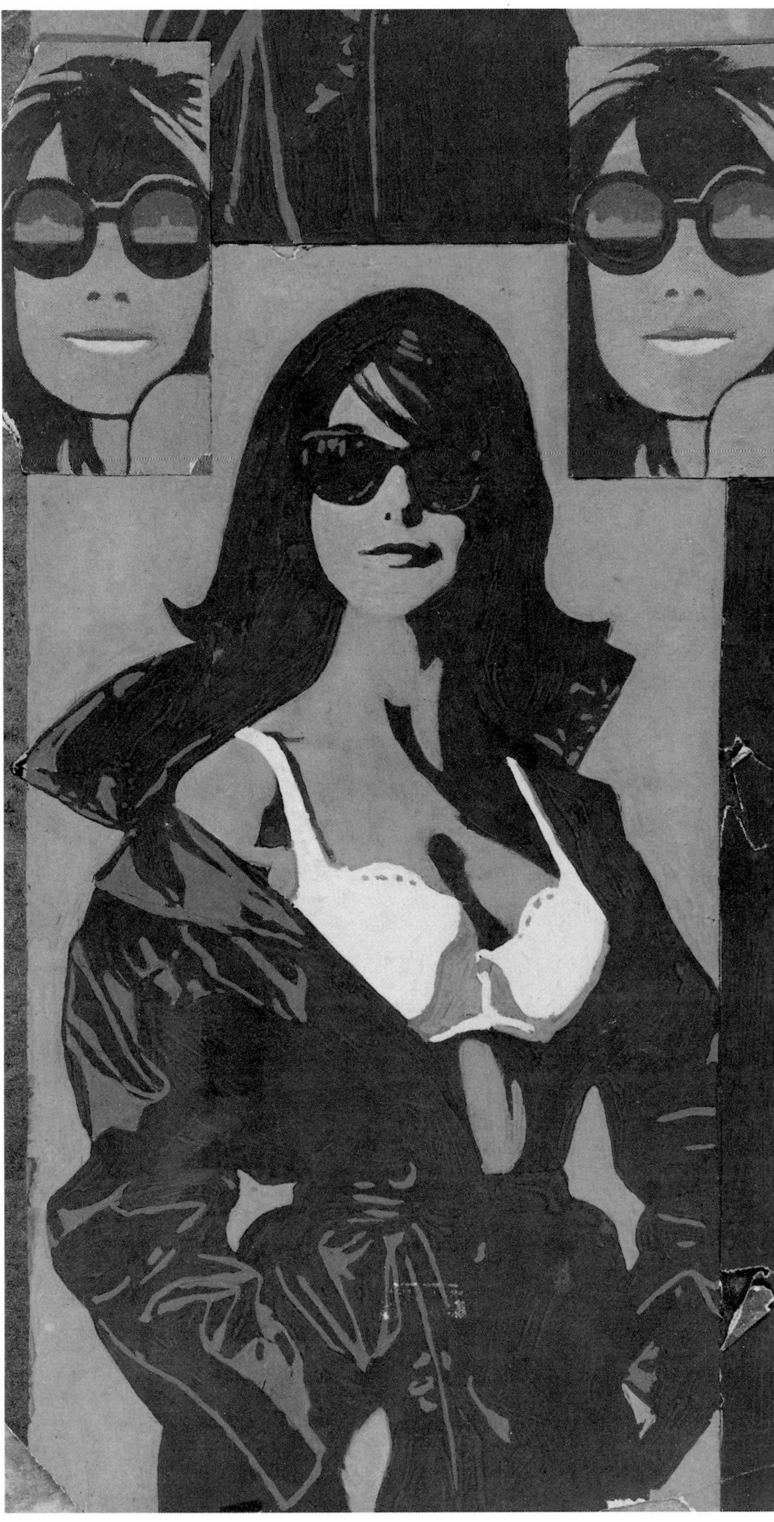

iconic themes: the American fascination with sex and money.

Large Round Open proved to be a breakthrough for Paschke. Increasingly interested in looking at reproductions as source material, the artist sought to expand the scale of several of his New York collages and to use additional images drawn directly from published sources. He was stymied, however, both by the slow pace of enlargement by hand and by a strong desire to editorialize as he worked. The painstaking process of translation—from original to collage to canvas—proved debilitating, and Paschke began, tentatively at first, to employ a small opaque projector in order to work directly on the canvas. Although he initially felt himself to be cheapening the painting process, with the example of Warhol's silkscreen paintings fresh in mind, he came to conceive of the paintbrush and opaque projector as simply tools in painting. It was at this time, as well, that Paschke began to paint on a black ground, rendering form from the darkness. Paschke found the black ground easier to draw on, both psychologically and practically, and it had the added advantage of intensifying whatever color he chose to work with. Typically, he would project an image onto one area of the canvas and then, editorializing all the while, he would alter color and form at will.[19]

As Paschke continued to develop and perfect this working method over the next two years, he simultaneously returned to filmmaking. Still dependent on commercial art for a living, Paschke was employed for several months in 1965–66 by Wilding Studio, an important film studio in Chicago where several Charlie Chaplin films had been made. He worked during this time making training films for astronauts, a process that involved painting and then filming topographical maps in order to simulate the appearance of the earth from space. His interest in film piqued, Paschke attended free screenings of avant-garde films at The Arts Club of Chicago and the Chicago Public Library. Not surprisingly, the influence of Warhol's films equaled that of the artist's paintings at this time, and Paschke was also aware of the work of the San Francisco sculptor and filmmaker Bruce Conner, who was then making fast-paced, black-and-white films.[20]

For the next two years Paschke would work on film as well as on canvas. In addition to the fragmentary footage he

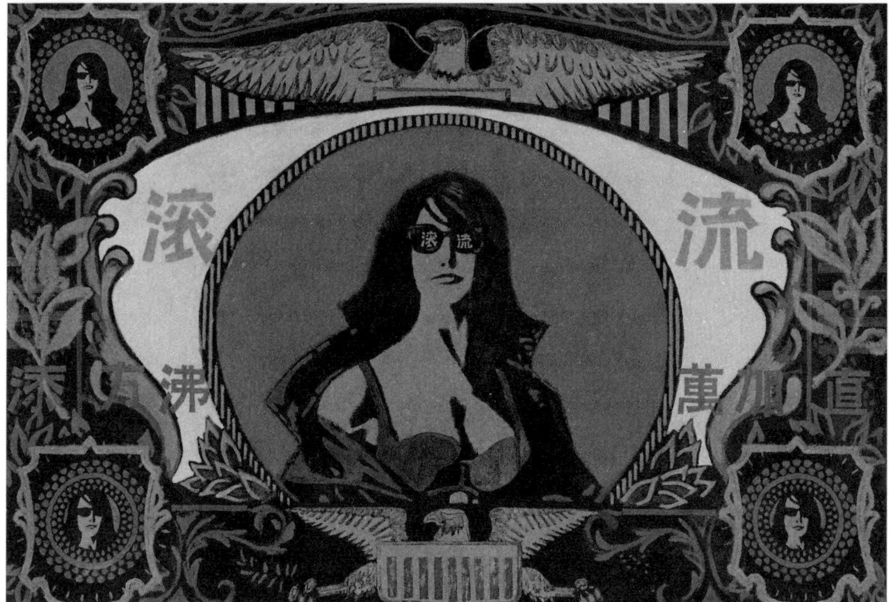

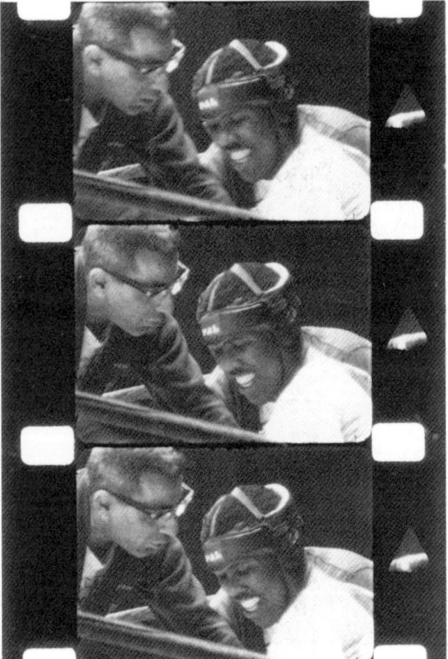

13

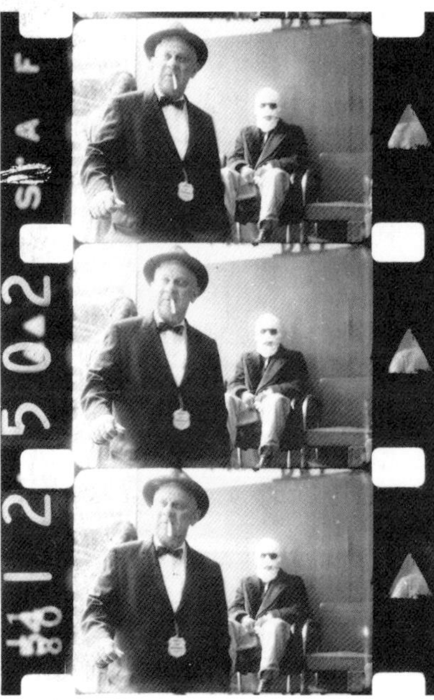

14

shot in New York in 1962, he obtained from his parents old cartoons he had seen as a child—the Three Stooges, Mickey Mouse, Donald Duck, and Little Black Sambo—as well as National Socialist military-training footage that his father had obtained when he served in the Allied occupation force after World War II. To these, Paschke added old newsreels and demonstration film clips that he purchased cheaply in Chicago. Working with a primitive hand splicer, Paschke then collaged these clips together into films of five-to-ten-minute duration (see fig. 13). These fast-paced films demonstrate a strong sense for ironic and biting juxtaposition of form and content. For example, a segment featuring a poor black man laughing with drunken abandon might be followed by an image of Little Black Sambo in a related pose. Conversely, the Three Stooges marching in mock military fashion would precede images of German troops marching in perfect goose step. Although there are occasional moments of loosely structured narrative—one memorable sequence features a masked Karl Wirsum as "The Invisible Man" (fig. 14)—a collage of contrasting, ironically composed images featuring exaggerated facial and physical expression is much more common.

In sum, the years 1965–67 were a period of experimentation for Paschke, a time in which work in one medium induced growth in another. The additive approach he had developed in creating the early collages proved applicable as a compositional device for painting. Ultimately, however, filmmaking was too demanding both technically and financially, and Paschke abandoned the medium to devote himself completely to painting. Toward this end, he enrolled in

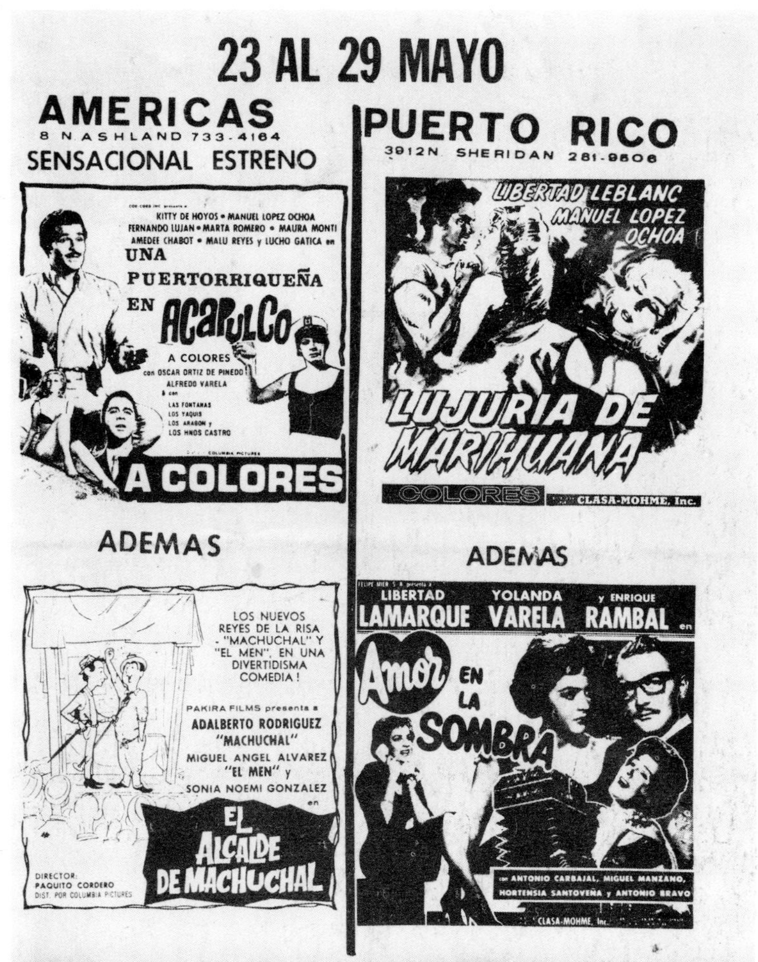

the graduate program in painting at the School of the Art Institute in 1968.

Several small, but very significant, paintings were completed that year. Among these, two are of special interest. One, *Amor* (cat. no. 2), is—like *Large Round Open*—a collage of fragments. Here Paschke worked from a handbill for a Spanish-language film, *Amor en la Sombra* (Love in the Shadows) (fig. 15). In the painting, the poster image is reproduced several times in different sizes and colors and is combined with a series of images of a showgirl. The focus of the painting, however, is a pair of circus performers in the center. Separated by an enlarged fragment of the title "Amor" drawn from the handbill, one peers upward while the other averts his glance. Garish in form, color, and content, *Amor* introduced into contemporary art images of Latino media, circus performers, showgirls, and, by implication, homosexuals—all subjects that were generally outside the purview of contemporary art. Indeed, although it displays the methods and attitudes of Pop Art—popular imagery, commercial painting methods, etc.—in its dark implications, *Amor* calls into question the optimism that we tend to identify with the art and culture of the 1960s.

Although *Amor* was not exhibited in 1968, a painting of the previous year, *Purple Ritual* (cat. no. 1), was. In November of that year, Chicago's Museum of Contemporary Art opened an exhibition titled "Violence in Recent American Art." Prompted in part by the widespread protest activity at the time of the Democratic National Convention held that summer in Chicago, the exhibition focused on themes of violence in the art of the 1960s. The survey included such well-known images as Warhol's *Race Riot* (1963) and Robert Indiana's *Alabama* (1965), among a number of other incendiary works. Although Paschke was only a graduate student at the Art Institute at this time, *Purple Ritual* was one of the works selected for the exhibition. Despite its small scale, the painting is potent in implication; it is based on a photograph of Lee Harvey Oswald (fig. 16) made by his wife in the spring of 1963, only months before the assassination of John F. Kennedy. The image was reproduced in newspapers and magazines around the world following the murder.[21] In translating the image to the painting, Paschke added a pale blue sky and replaced the Oswalds' backyard setting with framing patriotic bunting.

sky and replaced the Oswalds' backyard setting with framing patriotic bunting.

Artists devoted a great many images to John Kennedy during the 1960s, and in most the slain president is seen as personifying the expansiveness of the early years of the decade. Perhaps the finest examples are Rauschenberg's "Retroactive" paintings (see fig. 17), which bear photomechanical transfers and include images of heroic astronauts conquering space alongside the charismatic president. Kennedy's death is seldom, if ever, alluded to; the closest we come to an image of death are Warhol's many canvases depicting Jacqueline Kennedy either immediately prior to or soon after the assassination (see fig. 18). In contrast, Paschke is among the few artists to devote a painting to Lee Harvey Oswald and to discuss its implications. "I intended it to be a symbol of the American way of life," he noted in comments published in the catalogue of the exhibition.

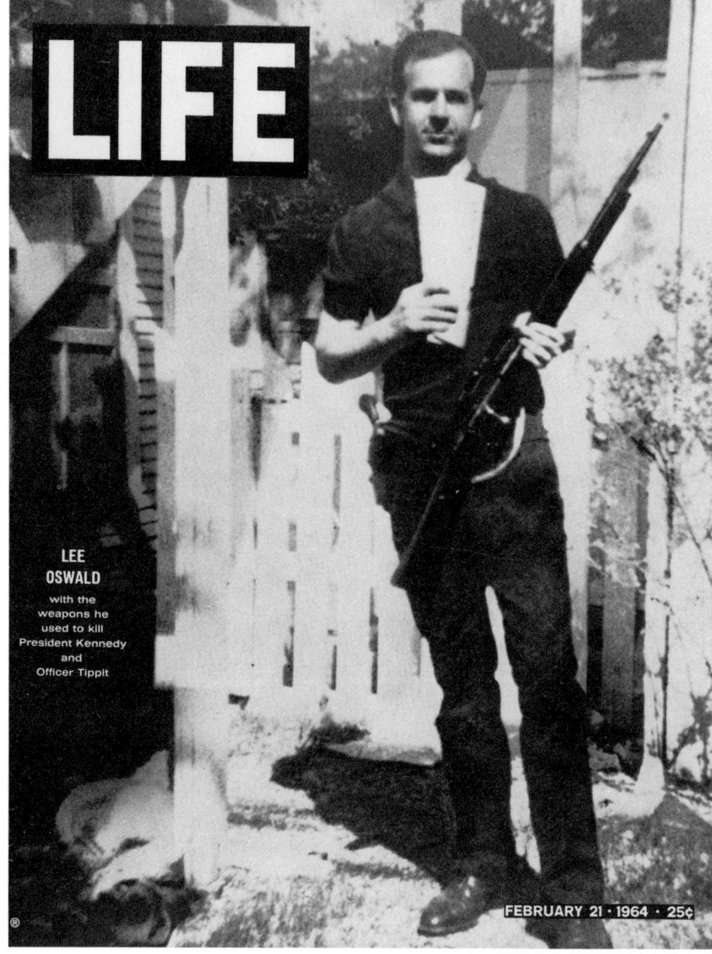

That is why I set Oswald down against the flag and seals. The only literal thing I did in the painting was to color him purple—the color associated with death and official mourning. But whose death? Oswald's or Kennedy's? Both, in a sense. My main concern was not the death of either man but rather the relationship between both incidents and their place in the fabric of our heritage.[22]

Beyond the social implications of the painting, it is noteworthy that Paschke possessed the reproduction of Oswald for a full four years between the time of its original publication in 1963 and the creation of the painting. The artist's fascination with Oswald as a social misfit was in part personal, as ironic biographical similarities exist between the two men: both Oswald and Paschke were born in 1939, both moved frequently as children, both attended an Arlington Heights High School (Oswald in Texas, Paschke in Illinois), both served in the military and demonstrated expertise with firearms, and, in fact, Paschke was married five years to the day after Kennedy's assassination. These are obviously coincidental associations, yet they offered Paschke, who has consistently identified himself with society's "outsiders," a type of personal link to an underworld of social misfits and criminals.[23]

In keeping with the thrust of *Purple Ritual*, throughout the late 1960s Paschke's work was characterized by a series of themes of aggression. The artist continued to collect all manner of visual material, but he now began to focus on more provocative sorts of imagery: "I loaded my studio walls with all kinds of visuals that I would find and [I would] look at them as a kind of psychic resource. In the beginning there was a specific concern for things that had a degree of aggressiveness, sensationalism, oddity, that provoked confrontation."[24]

Among the subjects that most interested Paschke at this time were images of boxers and wrestlers, whose "posing and narcissistic display of the body" fascinated him, as did "the costuming involved—the robes, the adornments, which they wear are very interesting visually, [particularly] the shiny colors."[25] The most important painting of this type is *Ramrod* (1969) (cat. no. 6). In this work the artist created an extraor-

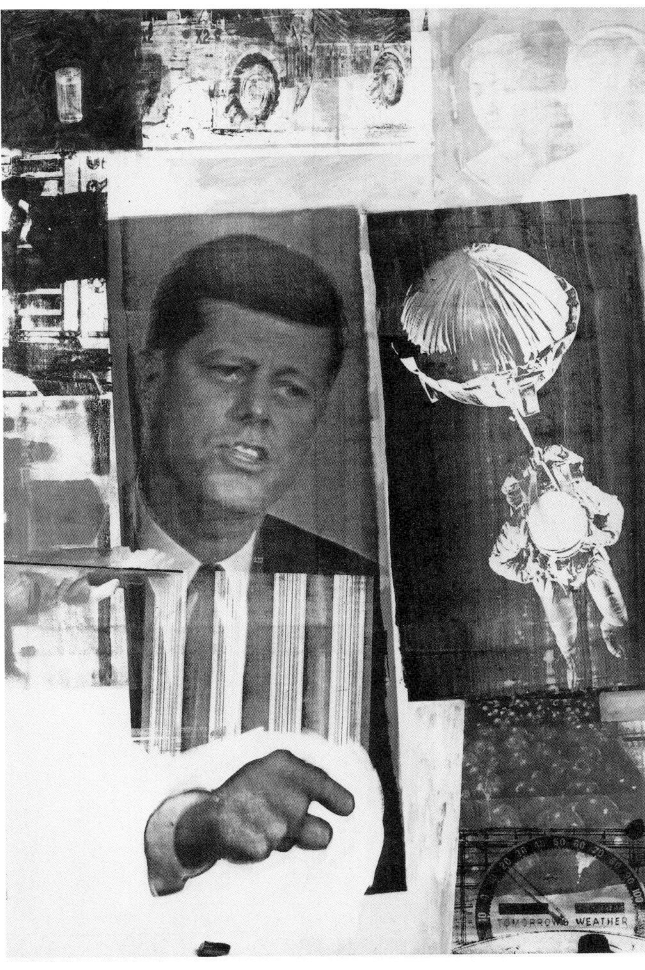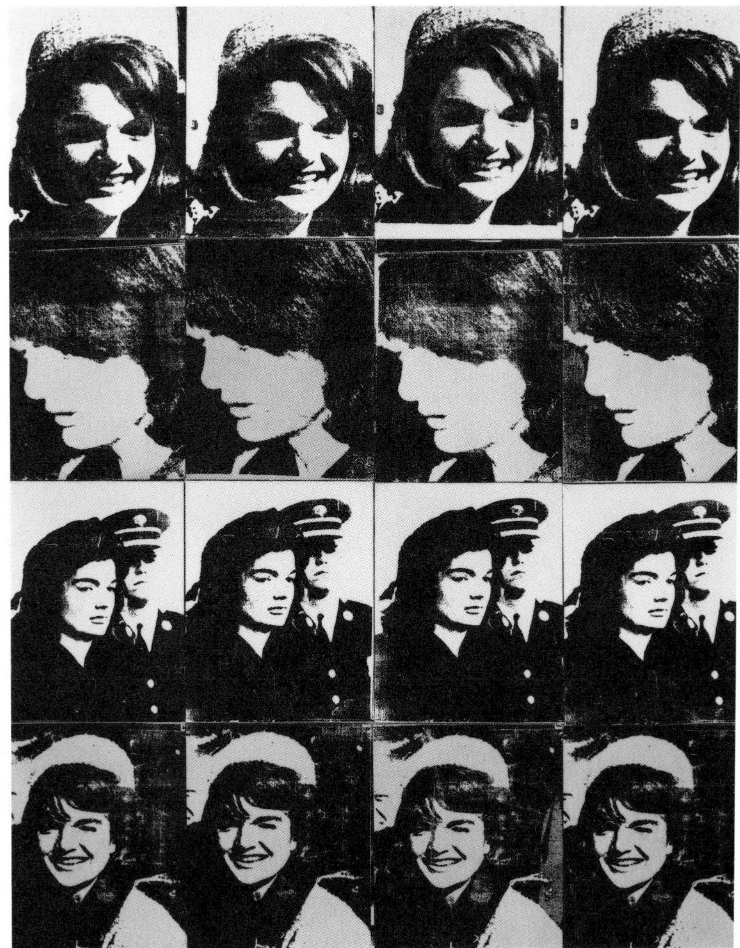

dinarily strong image of physical and psychological incongruity. Confronting us is a nearly full-length figure of a wrestler; set in a posterlike format complete with flanking titles, he displays his body with considerable pride from beneath a warm-up robe. Although tattooed and muscle-bound as befits his trade, the figure is otherwise subverted by the artist's flight of fantasy. Images of Mighty Mouse spring from the sides of his head, directly satirizing his athletic pretensions. Far more subversive, however, is the wrestler's appearance from the waist down, for he is unequivocally female in both anatomy and apparel. Indeed, Paschke admits to being captivated by "incongruous things that would have shock value —removing genitals or [putting] articles of female clothing [on a male body], or reversed genitals, and the idea of juxtaposition, taking things from two different places and putting them together."[26] In short, the artist presses the Surrealist device of juxtaposition to its furthest extremes. Rather than contrasting dissimilar images in the witty manner of Belgian Surrealist René Magritte, Paschke instead brutalizes the

human figure in order to call into question established social conventions of gender, dress, and behavior. It is also noteworthy that, in *Ramrod*, Paschke employed a new device for the first time in his painting: the mask. In his will to confront and shock, the mask served in a fundamental way, for it not only camouflages anatomy, it also serves to introduce additional levels of psychological ambiguity into a painting. Through time, the mask would become a prominent weapon in Paschke's arsenal, one that would have potent applications in his later painting.[27]

Paschke's fascination extended to criminals as well as athletes, and he actually made regular visits to several sites of Chicago's notorious underworld activity. Some of his finest works on the subject are, in fact, prints.[28] Among these, perhaps the most important is *Budget Floors* (1968–69) (fig. 19), a depiction of the infamous Chicago mass-murderer Richard Speck. In 1966 Speck committed one of the most shocking crimes in American history, brutally killing eight young student nurses in their dormitory on the city's South

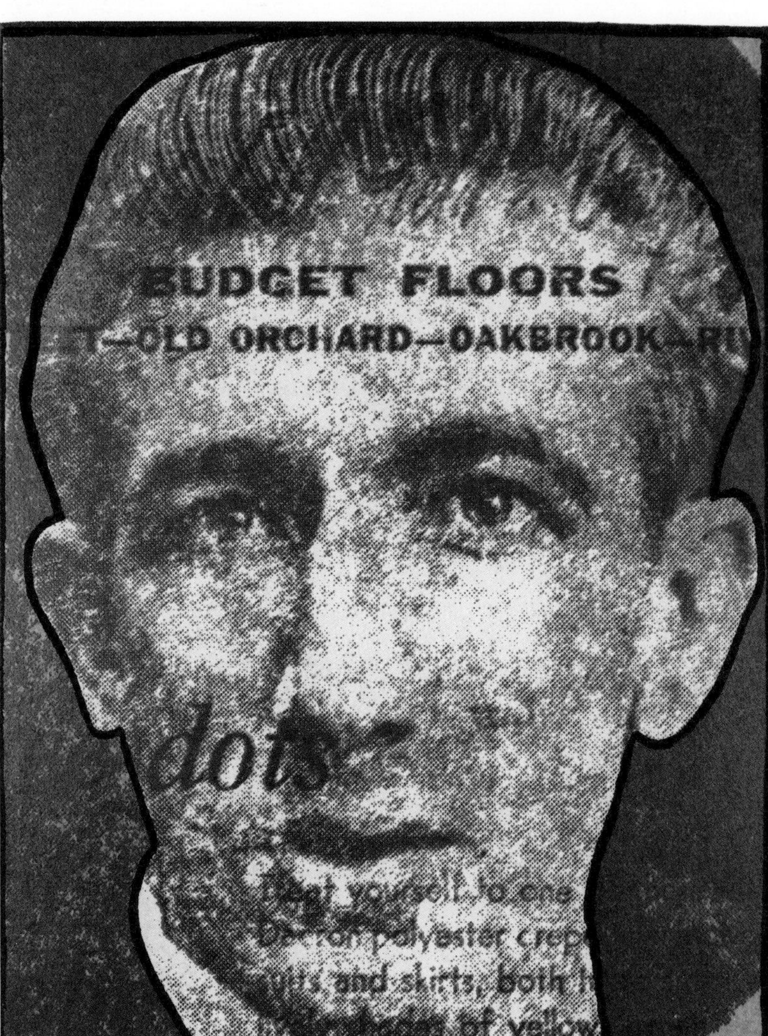

FIG. 19
ED PASCHKE
BUDGET FLOORS, 1968–69

Side. Interestingly, the murder also became a subject for the German artist Gerhard Richter, who chronicled the event in *Eight Student Nurses* (1971) (fig. 20), a series of eight dispassionate portraits of the nurses based on news-wire photographs. If anything, Paschke's print is even less sensational, as Speck himself is seen in a media-derived bust portrait. Superimposed over his face is an advertisement featuring several lines of type, a fragment of which serves as the work's title. If his representation of Speck appears curiously neutral, it should be considered similar to his depiction of Marilyn Monroe in *Pink Lady*; both images are intended to level and neutralize public figures by placing them in the most mundane possible context. Thus, while an anonymous wrestler might provide a vehicle for a shocking representation and social commentary, well-known public figures were, in turn, subject to leveling by Paschke's hand.

It should be stressed that, although Paschke was in his late twenties when he painted *Amor*, *Purple Ritual*, and *Ramrod* and made prints such as *Budget Floors*—some of his most arresting, yet troubling, images—he was still but a graduate student at the Art Institute. Because of his period of service in the military and his various other experiences following graduation in 1961, Paschke was four to five years older than many of his graduate-school colleagues. In addition, in 1968 Paschke married a former Art Institute student named Nancy Cohn and adopted her young son, Marc. With these new family responsibilities, Paschke began to question the pace of his professional development, and a desire to exhibit more extensively became increasingly strong.

This feeling corresponded chronologically to and was, in fact, exacerbated by three important exhibitions held in 1966–68 at the Hyde Park Art Center on Chicago's South Side. These were the "Hairy Who" exhibitions organized by Don Baum, an artist, curator, and professor of art in the city. Although the term "Hairy Who" subsequently came to characterize a larger group of Imagist artists emerging in Chicago in the late 1960s and early 1970s, it initially referred only to the six artists included in these three exhibitions: James Falconer, Art Green, Gladys Nilsson, Jim Nutt, Suellen Rocca, and Karl Wirsum.[29]

These artists were all in their mid to late twenties, and all had matriculated at the School of the Art Institute. The three exhibitions generated a good deal of excitement in Chicago, and gradually the artists attracted the attention of art dealers and collectors. Feeling the need to advance himself professionally, Paschke joined with a similar group of young artists and approached Baum with the idea of an exhibition.

Like the "Hairy Who" before them, the "Nonplussed Some" (Paschke, Sarah Canright, Edward C. Flood, Robert Guinan, and Richard Wetzel) selected a distinctive, tongue-in-cheek name for their group. Their exhibition ran from February 16 through March 22, 1968, and included some ten to twelve, mostly small works by each artist. Paschke would exhibit with these artists, although with some changes in participants, on three additional occasions: "Nonplussed Some Some More" (1969), "Marriage Chicago Style" (1970), and "Chicago Antigua" (1971). These exhibitions shared with all the other

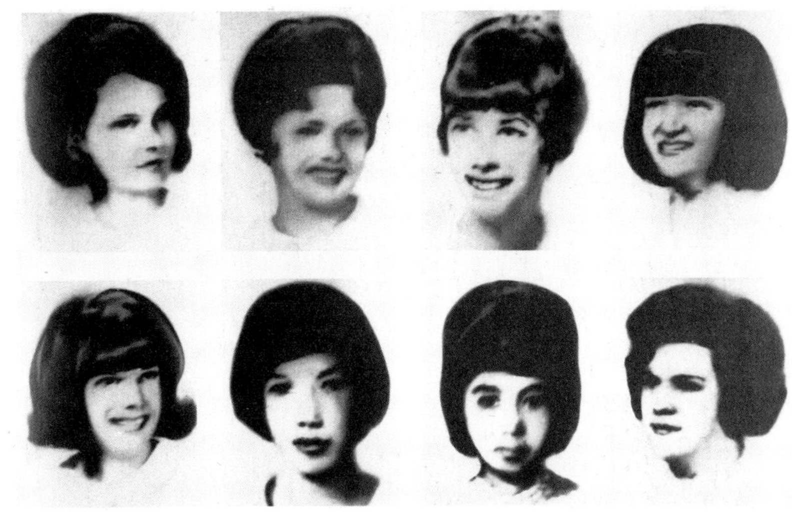

Imagist shows a self-conscious, even fanciful, informality, with casual installations and lively openings complete with costumes (see fig. 21). Strikingly original, the exhibitions generated considerable notice in the local and, eventually, the national press. Most often, the leading artists—Nutt, Nilsson, Wirsum, Roger Brown, and Paschke—were characterized as the "Hairy Who," or simply as "Imagists." Critics describing their work noted certain shared characteristics: the influence of folk, non-Western, and Surrealist art; a reliance on generally debased forms of popular imagery; and a widespread interest in busy, carefully worked surfaces, asymmetrical composition, and brilliant color. Virtually all of these commentaries were backhandedly negative. One of the first analysts of late-1960s Imagism, the Chicago-based art historian and critic Franz Schulze, for example, writing in *Art in America* in 1966, noted:

This Chicago group seeks out an exceptionally base and regressive kind of popular imagery.... The styles are mostly brutish and closely akin to the spastic drawing of illiterates and junior-high-school students.... This is not pop art, then, so much as sub-pop, the conscious reinterpretation of the unconscious and unregenerate iconography of the lower classes and early adolescent cultures.[30]

Writing further on the subject, this time in *Art News* in 1971, Schulze again contrasted Imagism with Pop:

But it has none of the bigness, the supermarket efficiency, and the fresh, impersonal cheer of New York Pop. It is smaller in format, more secretive, even solipsistic in mood, more subjectively comical, runny-nosed, raunchier and cruder.... They [the Imagists] cluster in small groups and—rather like the secret kids' clubs that flourished in the days of radio serials and the Sunday funnies—they even assume corporate names, like The Hairy Who... The Non-Plussed Some... The False Image.... They exhibit under these names, too, most of the time in the Hyde Park Art Center, an amiably dowdy rinkydink storefront on the South Side.[31]

For Paschke, a description such as this seemed misleading and limiting, if not altogether dangerous. Although the Hyde Park Art Center shows offered important exposure for his work—in 1969 he joined the Deson-Zaks Gallery in Chicago and held his first one-person show there the following year—the danger of being perceived as simply a regional artist was troubling. While he shared with his colleagues a background at the School of the Art Institute,

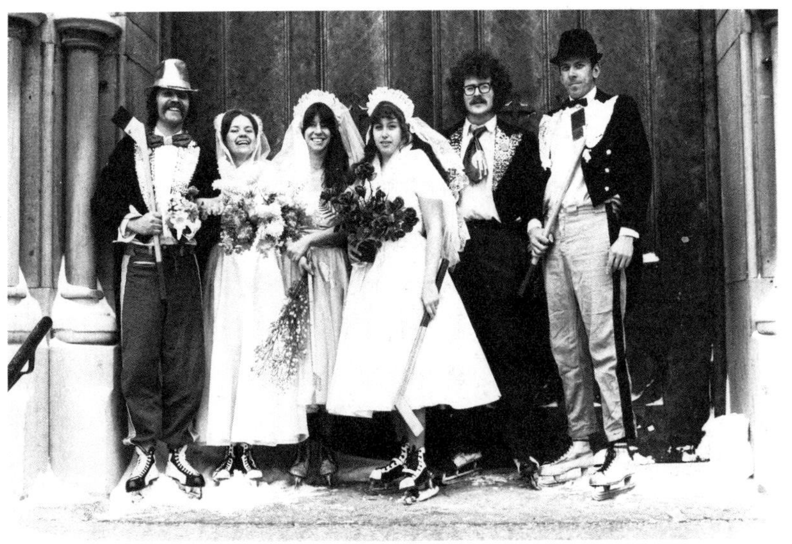

FIG. 21
OPENING OF THE EXHIBITION "MARRIAGE CHICAGO STYLE," HYDE PARK ART CENTER, 1970
FROM LEFT: KARL WIRSUM, BARBARA ANNE ROSSI, SARAH ANNE CANRIGHT, SUELLEN ROCCA, EDWARD FLOOD, AND ED PASCHKE

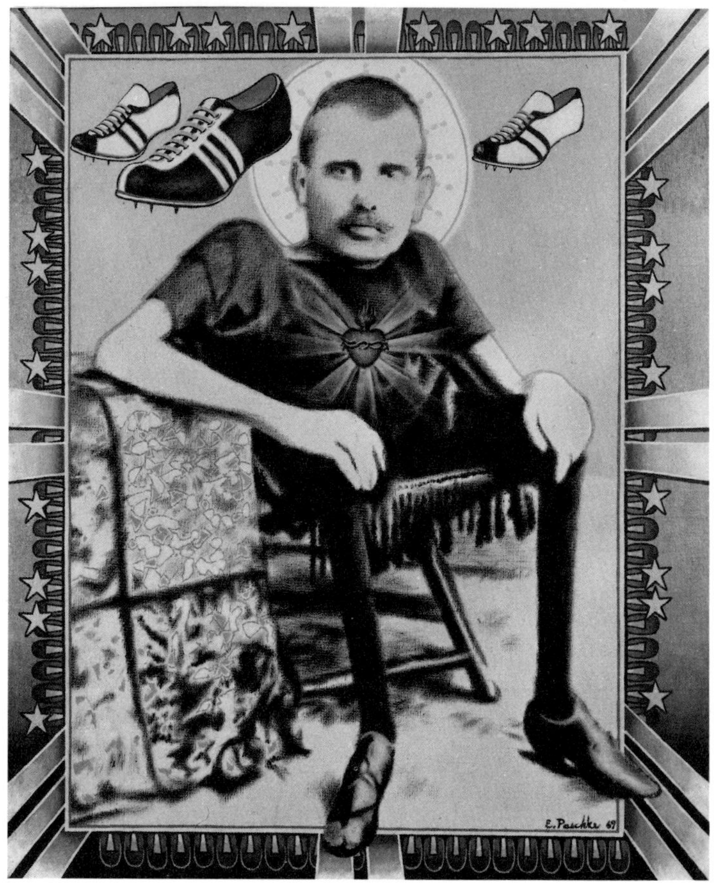

Paschke actually felt a stronger kinship with Pop Art than with Imagism. Unlike Roger Brown, who possessed an abiding interest in folk art, and Jim Nutt, who painted in an intricate way, often at minute scale, Paschke appropriated his images from the media and worked on an increasingly large scale. Perhaps most importantly, Paschke maintained only casual friendships with the other artists, and finding himself likened by Schulze and others to a juvenile compelled him gradually to sever his ties with the Imagists and pursue his own course.

I always felt like an orphan in the sense that everyone else seemed to share an enthusiasm [for *art brut*, folk, and non-Western art] and I wasn't really interested in these things. I think it was necessary to break away and establish a sense of individuality at a certain point. There was a time when [Imagism] had a degree of validity but people have gone on their own separate paths. Loosely you could still group them together, but I think that as a group idea it has served its purpose. To some degree the stigma or association still lingers.[32]

In the meantime, Paschke had received his Master of Fine Arts degree in June 1970. That fall he obtained a one-year teaching position at Meramec Community College, near St. Louis, which provided a salary, at least temporarily, as well as some distance from the Chicago art scene. He even considered a move to New York—as had many promising Chicago-based artists before him. He was dissuaded, however, both by the current predominance of Minimalism and abstraction in New York and by the response to his first one-person show in New York, held in April 1971 at the Hundred Acres Gallery. Writing in *The New York Times*, critic David L. Shirey described Paschke as "obsessed with the peripheral society of circus freaks, muscle men and transvestites. . . . All of Mr. Paschke's characters look as if their photos have been lifted from pulp literature and trash magazines. Mr. Paschke has not done his sources justice, for they at least have kitsch."[33]

The first major shift in the content of Paschke's work occurred at this time. Somewhat frustrated by the direction of his work and its reception in New York, Paschke decided to alter his approach. Always seeking to surprise himself with his art, Paschke had come to feel "a certain disenchantment" with his painting. Believing himself to be "both audience and performer," the artist felt himself becoming "bored, lackadaisical about what I [was] doing. I think that lack of energy, enthusiasm, and commitment is transmitted in the work." Seeking "to get away from the figure for awhile,"[34] the artist began to focus intensively on a surprising subject: shoes.

This subject first appeared in 1969 in a work titled *Holy Stick Man* (fig. 22). While the first shoe paintings were somewhat literal representations based on purely visual concerns, in the better works, such as *Bag Boots* (1972) (cat. no. 10), these inanimate objects bear humorous implications concerning their owner. Lest the shoe paintings be dismissed too lightly, however, consider the implications they came to assume for the artist:

When I began painting shoes I was initially making no structural changes. Then I decided that I wanted to get more personally involved. . . . I considered that leather, at one point, was living flesh for some animal. This could have been related [in my mind] to the atrocities of the Second World War, when the flesh of people was used in a barbaric, sadistic way.[35]

This realization led Paschke to reintroduce tattoos into his work—they had been used previously in *Ramrod*—and to treat the shoe leather as human flesh. For example, in *Hairy Shoes* (1971) (cat. no. 9), a trio of nondescript shoes floats in midair and bears both tattoos and bearded soles. As Paschke noted: "I began using tattoos, implying that this was living tissue of some organism; it was a conscious idea of the interchangeability between leather and flesh. People were becoming like objects in that they were tattooed, and shoes were reasserting their living qualities in superficial ways."[36]

It is noteworthy that shoes and feet have a particular resonance in contemporary art, especially in the impassioned early paintings of Georg Baselitz and the late works of Philip Guston.[37] Whereas shoes and feet assume a personal and perhaps even autobiographical relevance for these artists, Paschke's shoe paintings are of a different, even transitional order. First, given the consistent attention that he has generally devoted to his chosen subjects through the years, the relatively brief period around 1972 when he concentrated on shoes suggests their transitional meaning. As Paschke himself has noted, the shoe paintings allowed him to "divorce myself to some degree from certain constraints about dealing with the figure. . . . When I went back to working with the figure I was armed with the capacity, or the willingness, to make those same kinds of structural changes, distortions, changes of scale, etc., and apply these to the figure."[38]

If these generally small paintings allowed the artist a respite from the figure, they also provided him with a new level of interpretive freedom. This is implied in Paschke's comments associating shoe leather and human flesh, which, although not fully developed either in word or in deed, do nonetheless suggest a level of meaning beyond the desire merely to shock, which had previously been the primary goal. Beginning in the early 1970s, Paschke's paintings, while less literal and explicit, nonetheless become more allusive and bear broader cultural implications. This new ambition—to see his paintings as conveyers of broader ideas and cultural meanings—would evolve more fully, first in his paintings of women of the mid-1970s and later in the electronic images of recent years.

The first group of paintings devoted to women performers, particularly strippers, began in earnest in 1973. Paschke had returned to Chicago in the fall of 1971 to accept a teaching position at Barat College in Lake Forest, an affluent suburb north of the city. With Nancy, Marc, and newborn daughter, Sharon, Paschke rented an apartment in Rogers Park, an ethnically diverse neighborhood on Chicago's North Side. This allowed Paschke to reestablish contact with Chicago's night life and underclasses. As a student, he had explored such neighborhoods by day and by night, often changing clothes several times in a single evening according to the clientele he was likely to encounter in a given locale. He now returned to these same haunts, and they inspired the subsequent body of work.

I got interested in doing strippers—which goes back to a time in my life when I used to frequent a few places that had strip shows, and one in particular had a lot of blown-up photographs on the wall—2 x 3 feet—of typical PR shots of strippers. I had to make a certain kind of psychological breakthrough in my relationship with the photograph in that I was not quite as literal, and was in the position to make more structural changes with the figures.[39]

For Paschke, who has always been an admirer of poster art, these large-scale advertisements served as an important impetus. The paintings that he made in 1973 assume just such a format. Vertical and measuring five feet in height, each depicts a different scantily, even outrageously, clad performer at life-size. Most pose frontally, hands on hips or raised. All are unmistakably grotesque characterizations, with mouths agape, limbs tattooed, and coiffures impossibly exaggerated. Although each is titled with a woman's name—*Francine, Jeanine, Joella*, etc. (cat. nos. 11–13)—despite these direct references, each is far less reliant on photographic or real-life sources than any of his previous paintings. Paschke was not interested in painting particular people, but rather in achieving a series of imaginary theatrical portraits.

Perhaps the most riveting painting of this group is *Joella* (cat. no. 13), in which the stripper is seated with her legs at eye level, simulating her position on stage, above the viewer. Her brilliant, shimmering red dress serves as a horizon line, above which her ample body explodes. Her arms stretch to the uppermost corners of the painting, freezing her gesture on the surface of the canvas and her expression in our mind. Just how much Paschke's work had changed can be seen if *Joella* is compared with a slightly earlier work, *Painted Lady*

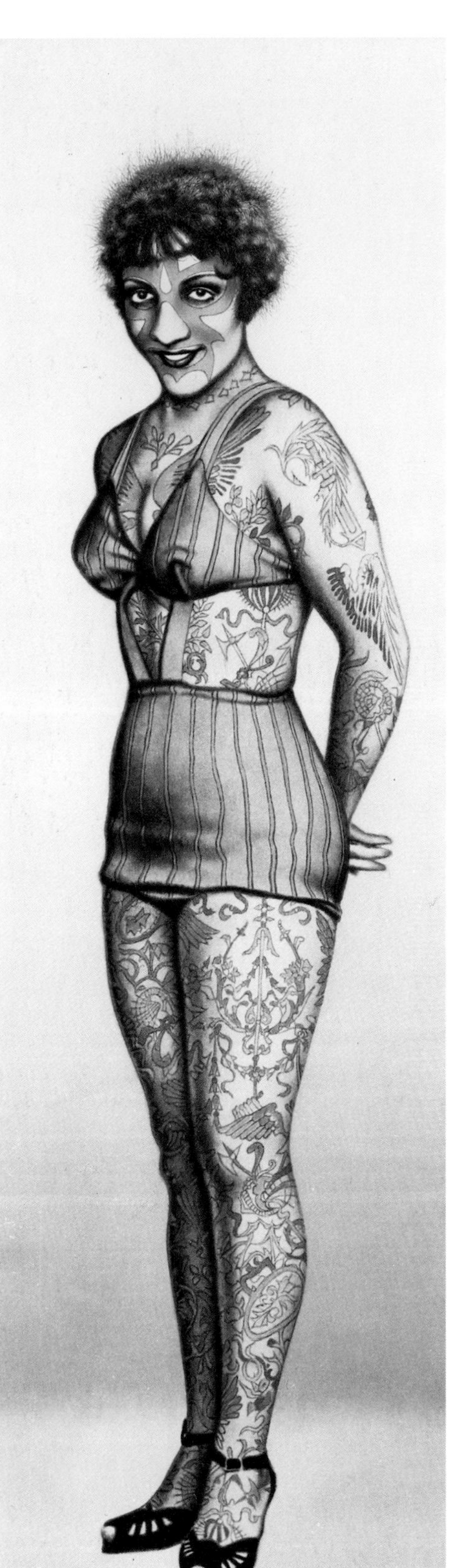

(fig. 23) of 1971. A full-length figure study of the actress Claudette Colbert, the earlier painting is obviously based on a photograph, despite the artist's fanciful addition of tattoos. The actress's demure expression and comportment are at odds with Paschke's articulation of her body, suggesting once again the same concern for surprising incongruities—albeit in somewhat more subtle form—that motivated earlier works such as *Ramrod*. In contrast, the 1973 paintings all display a gritty frankness and a generalization of facial expression that rule out any direct dependence on photographic sources. In these paintings Paschke also took startling liberties with the figure that simply were not possible before. The women Paschke created are femmes fatales, not so much in their sexual bearing as in their staggering, even threatening, physical presence. The expressive coolness that often accompanies the translation of images from photographic original to canvas is now transcended, and thus Paschke's immediate debt to Pop Art is no more. The stridency and direct power of these women no longer recall Warhol, but rather the more emphatically imagined and compulsive work of Lindner and Francis Bacon.

Another element of Paschke's break with the earlier work exists in the artist's new-found ability to trigger a type of voyeuristic response in his viewers. Although a painting such as *Ramrod* possesses all the brutal directness that is contained in the work of 1973, because of its dependence on photographic sources as well as words, the painting still admits a distance between subject and viewer. By contrast, the new paintings produce a response that is simultaneously sympathetic and vicariously thrilling. That is, Paschke has involved and even inculcated his audience to a much greater degree than was previously the case. In effect, in these paintings he presented elements of society that most people are curious about but would never dare experience. This approach served as his working method through 1976, as he continued to paint single figures, all carefully conceived and imagined. In 1974–75, for example, he completed a number of drawings and paintings of pimps and prostitutes, many of them black. These works differ from the stripper paintings in important ways. Each individual is now carefully attired in complex layers

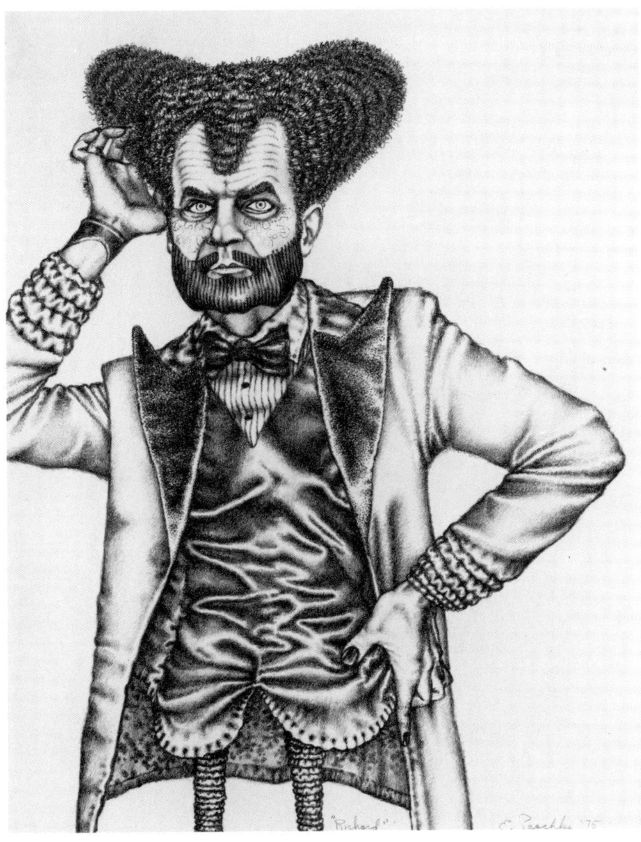

FIG. 24
ED PASCHKE
RICHARD (AFTER NIXON), 1975

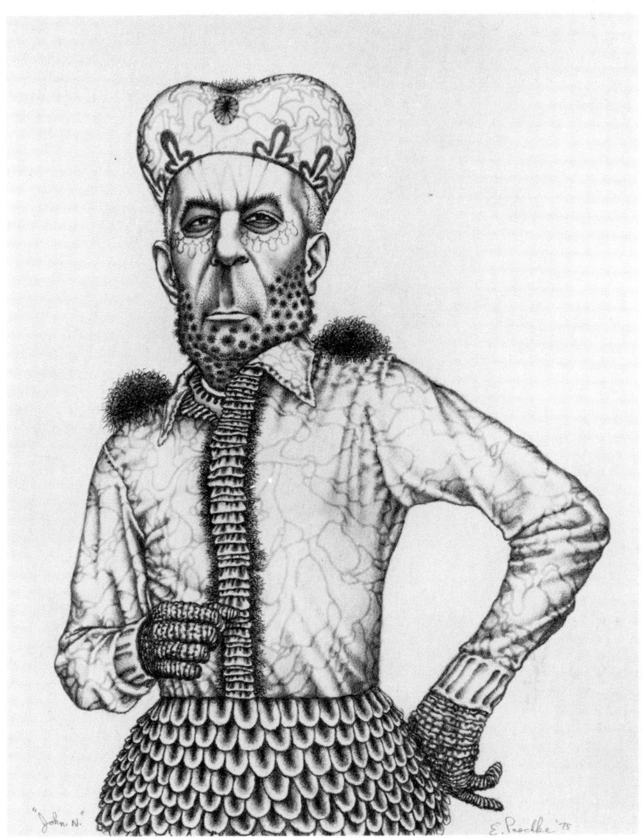

FIG. 25
ED PASCHKE
JOHN N. (AFTER MITCHELL), 1975

of brilliantly colored clothes. In addition, each is set against a shimmering background surface, as though standing on stage before a curtain. Formally, then, these figures are bound to the picture plane, both compositionally and coloristically, in contrast with the prior paintings in which each figure is set in space. Beyond this, however, are the composure and pride that each figure exhibits. Despite the radical alteration and even amputation of limbs in the case of *Red Sweeney* (1975) (cat. no. 17), or the facial masking of *Rufus* (1974) and *Armondo* (1975) (cat. nos. 15, 16), all of these characters possess a self-conscious dignity that extends beyond the willful display of the earlier strippers.

One senses in these paintings, in particular, Paschke's respect for his subjects:

The underbelly of society doesn't often get the chance to be given a degree of credibility on more legitimate levels. And this was a way of maybe giving them their due. . . . I think there is also something about energy that usually filters up from the lower levels, and winds up near the top. Very rarely are the people at the bottom influenced by the people at the top. It usually works the other way around.[40]

A statement such as this is unusual, for Paschke generally avoids political commentary, either in his work or his words. On occasion, however, national events have spurred him to a response; certainly this occurred with *Purple Ritual* in the context of the events of 1968, and the Watergate crisis proved another such occasion. In 1975 Paschke produced a series of graphite drawings of the leading figures in the investigation: Richard M. Nixon, H. R. Haldeman, and John Mitchell among numerous others (see figs. 24, 25). Like his contemporary drawings of pimps and prostitutes, each is a grotesque likeness, with extraordinary liberties taken with anatomy and dress. Although Paschke would later conclude that the drawings are aesthetically too literal and politically too obvious, they nevertheless reveal the artist's consummate handling of line, a dimension of his work that is often unrecognized.

Meanwhile, the figure paintings culminated in 1976 with a group of large works, two of which are uncommissioned portraits: *Adria* (fig. 26), a depiction of the Chicago-based critic and art historian Dennis Adrian, and *Machino* (cat. no. 18), a portrait of the theatrical producer Mac McGinnes, for whom Paschke had designed stage sets.[41] The others, however, are all imaginary, if rather specific, characterizations. As a group, these paintings bear similarities to the former work, particularly in the willfully exaggerated anatomy, clothed in sparkling if bizarre detail. In fact, paintings such as *Sabreena* (cat. no. 19) and *Machino* reveal considerable continuity with *Red Sweeney* and *Rufus* of the previous year or so, especially in the placement of the figure against a patterned background. This compression of figure and ground effectively stills the gestures and stabilizes the composition. Beyond this the faces are now more masklike and betray little of the subject's psyche.

Because of the singular nature of his figurative work, Paschke had long been active as a portrait painter. Yet he began to refuse such commissions at this time, feeling that too many compromises were required in order to satisfy a particular patron.[42] In part a response to the Watergate drawings, this feeling now extended to all his work, and Paschke sought to move away from literal references and toward overt masking of identities.

I felt that the degree of obviousness was something that could be edited out to some degree. I began to remove, initially, some of the facial characteristics.... There were a lot of hijackings during this time ... and I used to see a lot of people in pictures, in the news media, people with ski masks, pillow cases, there was something about that that appealed to me quite a bit.[43]

This change in Paschke's painting becomes evident in three paintings of 1977: *Dominant Nurse, Mandrix,* and *Melon-Lamé* (cat. nos. 20–22). Significantly, these were the first figurative paintings in several years not to bear given names as titles, and appropriately, each figure is now quite literally masked beyond recognition. References to subclasses of society or the entertainment world are less obvious here, as the figures inhabiting *Melon-Lamé* and *Mandrix* are more traditionally and respectably attired. *Dominant Nurse*, a figure characterized by eerily elongated fingers, seems a reference to the artist's experience as a psychiatric aide in the early 1960s. In fact, it is the more overt postures of these figures that distinguish these paintings, particularly the excessively mannered hand gestures found in *Dominant Nurse* and *Melon-Lamé*.

Perhaps a more obvious change in these paintings exists in the addition of a few searing, electrified lines. In the case of *Dominant Nurse*, these orange and gold beams of unnatural light delineate the face, effectively replacing the anatomy. The effect is different in *Melon-Lamé*, in which a piercing yellow line shrieks across the top of the canvas, echoing the contour of the hands and thus introducing another type of link between figure and ground.

The impact of electronic imagery in Paschke's painting—the formal and conceptual element that has characterized his work since 1977—appears as early as 1973, in a painting titled *Lucy* (cat. no. 14). In this work, which is otherwise a characteristic, single-figure image of a stripper, horizontal bars appear through the field, elongating the figure's limbs and neutralizing her gestures and facial expression. Indeed, the image appears out of focus and thereby a bit distant.

If this was the first manifestation of such imagery, Paschke's intellectual interest in electronic imagery originated even earlier. While teaching in Missouri in 1970–71, Paschke became interested in the writings of Marshall McLuhan, which were of great currency at that time.[44] Like Paschke, McLuhan was a student of the media and was captivated by the way in which changes in the technology of media affect human perception of the environment. With McLuhan, terms such as "hot" and "cold" media entered our vocabulary, as did a generalized perception that electronic media was beginning to supersede the written word. In fact, in describing his paintings in several statements published since 1977, Paschke has often employed a vocabulary strongly reminiscent of McLuhan's: "Perception, or what we experience through our sensory apparatus, is being affected by the rapid acceleration of media-related technology. Our view of the world is changing as the global environment expands through media accessibility and the information reservoir gets deeper."[45]

Compare this with McLuhan's introduction to *Understanding Media: The Extensions of Man* (1964): "In the electric age, when our central nervous system is technologically extended

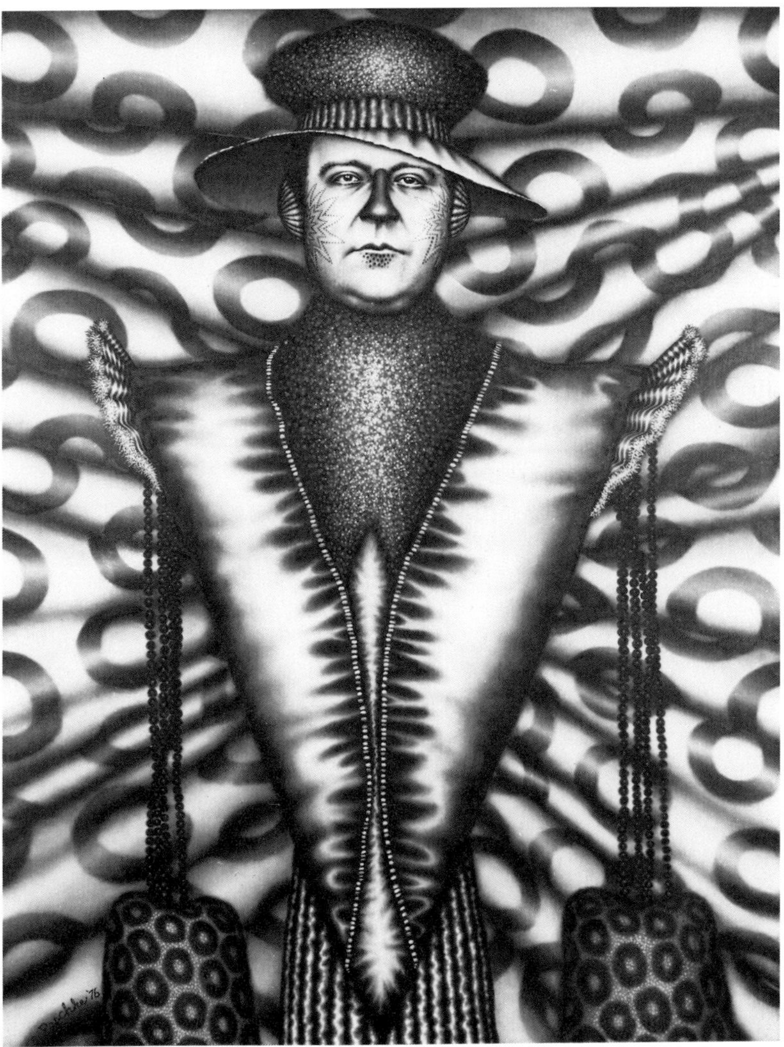

to involve us in the whole of mankind and to incorporate the whole of mankind in us, . . . the globe is no more than a village."[46]

In addition, in his teaching Paschke often screened the film *This Is Marshall McLuhan: The Medium Is the Message.*[47] A documentary that presents McLuhan discussing his ideas on the historical development and implications of media, the film is impressive in its use of experimental color effects, as McLuhan is typically bathed in color, and the spoken word is brilliantly joined with the visual image.

The influence of McLuhan encouraged a shift in Paschke's work, and the electronic media of the middle and upper classes came to replace the printed media of the lower classes as his most important resource. Initially, the artist was particularly fascinated by television and its impact on consciousness: "My belief is that these elements [such as television], for better or worse, have woven their way into the collective fabric of our lives. For me, the distinction between direct experiences and those which are modified through mass media is becoming smaller and smaller."[48] Paschke began to consider his subjects as anonymous actors in television-style dramas. They became "ambiguous and . . . less specific. They are like frozen moments in a theatrical sense . . . more involved with the idea of gesture and the implications involved with those things."[49]

These words suggest a growing interest in implied narrative, and thus an alternative format for the paintings; in addition to the single-figure, predominantly vertical format, Paschke now began to devise multifigured, horizontal, and often quite complex compositions. This began with paintings like *Melon-Lamé* of 1977 and evolved quickly and impressively in two paintings of the following year: *Cho Chan* and *Duro-Verde* (cat. nos. 25, 26). By replacing facial likenesses with masks, and personalized, identifying titles with seemingly arbitrary ones, Paschke here foreclosed any single interpretation of these works. All expression is communicated through a stylized mode of dress and gesture, and each figure becomes a performer in a superficial drama. This is particularly evident in *Cho Chan*, in which two couples embrace in mock-romantic fashion. The combination of outmoded style, gesture, expression, and dress creates the media-derived

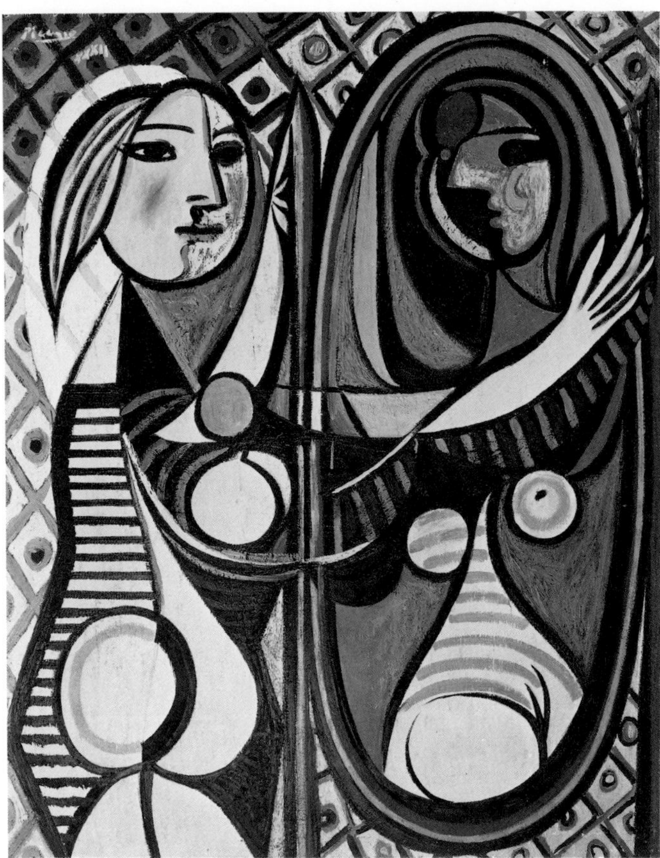

superficiality that Paschke desired. Just as the composition is frozen in a two-dimensional relationship near the surface plane, the interaction depicted is locked in the shallow reality of televised experience.

Over the course of the last decade, Paschke has expanded his formal vocabulary, and this growth has encouraged the gradual development of a number of new themes. In his exploration of the electronic media as a working mechanism or structure for his painting, the ability continually to alter perception of the painted surface has been of primary importance for Paschke. His formalist training as a student has served him surprisingly well here, and since the late 1970s Paschke has created fascinating shifts between two- and three-dimensional space in order to render a shifting balance between naturalism and abstraction.

I was interested in the 2-dimensional and 3-dimensional fluctuations within a picture plane. . . . I used those to further the degree of abstraction and the disruption of the solidity of a particular image in the sense that some parts were developed in a fairly believable 3-dimensional sense and other parts were flat.[50]

This balancing of two and three dimensions, and abstraction with representation, has governed the appearance of

Paschke's work since the early 1980s. The most graphic example of how these formal advances could yield new expressive effects is *L'Impression* (1981) (cat. no. 32). Here the artist contrasted oblique, mirrored images of a single figure holding a beam of electronic light. The figures are cognizant of one another, yet they are separated both formally and psychologically by the range of colors that overlay their expression. That is, although the two figures are one and the same, because of their oblique placement and contrasting color schemes, as well as the masking of facial detail, they are, in fact, quite remote from one another.

The mirror is, of course, one of the most persistent motifs in the history of Western painting, with a brilliant heritage that can be traced to Velázquez, Titian, Rubens, and, in our own century, Picasso. The mirror has provided a vehicle for artists to display a model's front and back simultaneously, and in Picasso's *Girl before a Mirror* (1932) (fig. 27) this extends to the representation of an inner as well as an outer countenance. For Paschke, the mirror is a mechanism for indirect cultural commentary, signifying the loss of self in a technologically advanced environment. Although small, *L'Impression* is among Paschke's most effective paintings, one in which a compelling union is found between form and content.

A second device that Paschke has employed to great effect is the diptych format. This evolved for the first time around 1982, in works such as *Fernsehen* and *Mechanique* (cat. nos. 35, 36). Whereas artists such as David Salle have produced diptychs in which separate canvases are abutted in order to heighten extreme contrasts in content from one side to the other (see fig. 28), Paschke instead works on a single canvas, composing the diptych in paint alone and thus encouraging a dialogue between figures at the left and right. Sometimes, as in *Mechanique*, one figure journeys across this division, but on other occasions these separations are more emphatic, both coloristically and compositionally, and serve to divide two figures attempting to embrace. These paintings of 1982 are particularly impressive, because they both demonstrate Paschke's return to the cinematic vision that encouraged his youthful experiments with film, and expand upon the narrative possibilities inherent in his recent work.

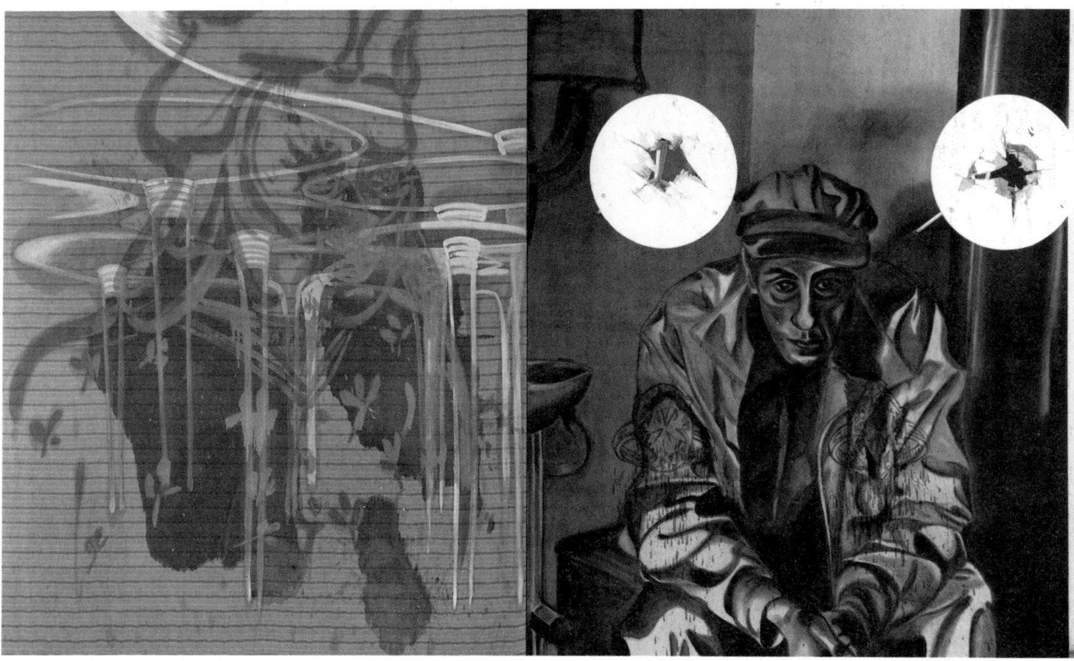

Another important mechanism has been Paschke's radical alteration of scale in many recent works. Perhaps the finest example is *Troika* (1985) (cat. no. 47), in which the artist, again working with the exaggerated horizontal format, contrasts three faces. One is seen in profile, one in three-quarter view, and the third frontally. While the first two share a depth of electronic color, an abstract persona, and a common scale, the figure to the right is fully frontal and dramatically enlarged. While the shift between abstraction and realism is well developed in Paschke's work by 1985, this surprising shift in scale is new and offers remarkable interpretive possibilities, particularly in suggesting themes of domination and subordination that run through many of the artist's recent works. Altering scale for expressive effect has thus become yet another important weapon in Paschke's increasingly impressive arsenal.

Finally, a clear distinction can be drawn in Paschke's recent work between the single-figure canvases and the compositionally more complex, multifigured paintings. No move toward either compositional complexity or simplicity is discernible in the last decade, as Paschke works simultaneously in both formats and moves between them with relative ease. Rather, these contrasting approaches provide means toward different expressive ends, and within each format the artist is able to achieve an impressive range of expression. Although it is risky to generalize too broadly, the multifigured paintings are usually the richest in narrative possibilities and tend to follow certain thematic directions, while the single-figure paintings are often less direct and more speculative and thoughtful.

Perhaps the dominant theme explored in the multifigure canvases is that of violence and terror. These works appeared initially around 1980–81, with paintings such as *Violencia* and *Televismo* (cat. nos. 31, 33), in which Paschke took great liberties with anatomical accuracy, as naturalistic fragments such as noses, mouths, or hands contrast with flattened, abstract bands of color. In *Violencia*, a male figure turns toward the viewer while gripping the throat of a female victim bearing two shrieking mouths. *Televismo* is even more haunting: two pairs of similar figures, one above the other, now virtually dematerialize as they are engulfed in a range of cool color.

Paschke pressed this theme to its furthest bounds in 1982–83, and *Der Tanz*, *Towanda*, and *Vosotros* (cat. nos. 37, 40, 41) are perhaps unrivaled in the artist's career as images of terror. In each, naturalism is reduced to an occasional trace: a hand in *Vosotros*, the men's ties in *Towanda*. While the repetition of shrieking faces recalls the art of Edvard Munch, the liberties that allow Paschke to join disfigured souls in *Vosotros* are the artist's own invention. The color scheme here—largely cool blues and grays, with an occasional burst of overheated red or yellow—enforces the brutality of expression, as these figures inhabit a world of nightmarish fantasy.

Finally, it is noteworthy that the haunting images found in both *Violencia* and *Vosotros* derive, in fact, from the social pages of magazines. Paschke's transformation of images of socialites at leisure into paintings of grotesque terror finds a parallel in his early work, in which social outcasts—pimps, prostitutes, and the poor—are accorded status in the rarefied world of the fine arts.[51]

If the multifigured paintings are directed toward particular themes such as violence or terror, the single-figure works offer a quieter form of expression. For example, in late 1979 and early 1980, Paschke created a group of paintings that are images of solitude and reflection. Slightly smaller than most of the paintings of the period, *Ambrosia, Fumar,* and *Nervosa* (cat. nos. 27, 28, 30) are character studies that, despite the anonymity of each sitter, are strikingly immediate and personal. In the manner of historical portraits, Paschke focused here on the hands and face, the traditional bearers of character and expression in the portrait genre. In each case, the head effectively dissolves into the surrounding field of color, joining figure with ground and placing the burden of expression on the naturalistically rendered hands. The eyes are particularly evocative as they act as one-way windows, not into the heart and soul of the mysterious and anonymous subject, but rather for the sitter out into the world. For Paschke, who had largely abandoned formal, commissioned portraiture by this time, these works serve as particularly evocative studies of individual emotional states without the specifics of identity or likeness—characteristics that Paschke now found to be debilitating.

Since 1980 Paschke has produced a number of paintings of single figures or individual heads, and these are of two distinct types. Spanning the period are images of anonymous faces, all depicted in shimmering color that overwhelms likeness. Among the first of these paintings is *Electalady* (1984) (cat. no. 43), in which the artist proved himself a colorist of the first order. While many of the recent paintings are dominated by either a hot or cold color scheme that produces a corresponding expression, in this work Paschke unified the two to extraordinary effect. As the title suggests, *Electalady* is an image in which electric light and color replace skin, which dissolves beneath the more prominent eyes, lips, and hair. Unique in Paschke's work is the clarity with which the bone structure of the head is handled, with tones reversed as if to suggest a color X ray.

Whereas in many of Paschke's recent works the titles bear only vague implications for the particular head depicted, in the case of a pair of paintings—*Caliente* and *Frio* (both 1985) (cat. nos. 45, 46)—color clearly induced the chosen appellation. The former, based on an image of the actor Laurence Olivier, is rendered in a range of hot hues, and the latter, derived from a photograph of Lillian Hellman, is far cooler in character, as determined by the dominating greens and blues.[52] In these works color serves a masking role, as fragmentary facial expressions return in full force, particularly in the area of the mouth and nose.

More recently, Paschke has made paintings of individual black men. *Blackstone* and *Negrette* (both 1988) (cat. nos. 56, 57) are both frontal images that approach portraiture in their specificity of likeness. *Blackstone* is, in fact, an image of Jeff Fort, the imprisoned leader of the El Rukns, a notorious Chicago gang formerly known as the Blackstone Rangers, hence the painting's title.[53] Both men betray little of themselves, as they appear before us with eyes and mouths closed. Each seems withdrawn from the outside world, offering instead the appearance of great inner strength and composure, an effect reminiscent of Paschke's paintings of blacks of the mid-1970s, which, although more flamboyant, nonetheless reveal a similar strength of character.

More direct forms of cultural expression reemerge in a second group of single-image paintings, all of which date to 1986–87: a series of works devoted explicitly to figures from history, both political and cultural. These include George Washington in *Prima Vere*, Adolf Hitler in *Cosmetica*, Abraham Lincoln in *Libredo*, and Elvis Presley in *Matinee* (cat. nos. 49, 51–53). In these paintings Paschke selected images of individuals that are well known and continually reproduced, images that define our awareness and knowledge of elements of history and culture. This is the Washington of the American Revolution and the Constitution and the presidency, this is the Lincoln of the Civil War and the freed slaves, this is the Hitler who has come to symbolize the tragic folly of modern times, and this is the Presley of film and gossip magazine who epitomizes the boisterous American spirit. In each case, Paschke distorted or veiled the image, as if to suggest metaphorically that our secondary, media-derived knowledge of our history, our culture, and ultimately, of ourselves, is perhaps equally distorted.

In a related work, *Yin and Yang* (1988) (cat. no. 59), Paschke manipulated perhaps the most sacred likeness in the history of art, the *Mona Lisa*. Superimposed beside this ultimate symbol of feminine beauty and Western culture is a head that, the artist suggests, resembles Paschke's own. This is Paschke's only self-portrait to date,[54] a surprisingly late appearance given the artist's devotion to the human figure throughout his career. It is fitting that Paschke views himself in the context of this painting; the most celebrated image in all of art history, the *Mona Lisa* is also the most reproduced and has long been an object of great popular fascination and speculation. In a sense, the combination of the unprecedented exposure of this face and the mystery that has accrued to it in the popular imagination is not at all dissimilar to the mechanisms at work in Paschke's own art. That is, the work of Ed Paschke demonstrates how exposure to the media has colored our perception of all aspects of both contemporary culture and our historical heritage as well.

Yin and Yang provides an apt stopping point, for it offers a résumé of the concerns that have characterized Ed Paschke's painting through the last twenty-five years. Paschke began with images derived from underground printed materials, and his early paintings were impressive in their ability to shock. As time passed, this approach seemed limiting to the artist, and he began to focus on the electronic media and its impact on broader, more universal themes. Believing that the media has become an omnipresent element in our lives, through his painting Paschke has demonstrated that "the distinction between direct experiences and those which are modified through mass media is becoming smaller and smaller."[55] In persistently questioning the relationship between humanity and technology, Paschke continues to alert us to the manner in which our most basic thoughts, memories, and even instincts are neutralized by contemporary culture.

NOTES

1 See Lawrence Alloway, "Marilyn as Subject Matter," *Arts Magazine* 42, 3 (Dec. 1967–Jan. 1968): 27–30; and New York, Sidney Janis Gallery, *Homage to Marilyn Monroe*, exh. cat. (New York, 1968).

2 That this is indeed an image of Marilyn Monroe was confirmed in conversation with the artist, June 23, 1988.

3 Perhaps the most important exception is the painter Ivan Albright, who lived and worked in Chicago until 1963.

4 The term "Imagism" is used here to apply generally to these artists, and it has also been applied to succeeding generations of Chicago artists who work in the subjective, Surrealist-influenced manner described below. The first generation of Imagists—Golub, Cohen, Campoli, etc.—have also been referred to as the "Monster Roster," and subsequent groups exhibited together under a variety of whimsical names as described below. For the first generation, see Franz Schulze, *Fantastic Images: Chicago Art since 1945* (Chicago, 1972); Schulze, "Chicago Letter," *Art News* 57, 10 (Feb. 1959): 49; and Patrick T. Malone and Peter Selz, "Is There a New Chicago School?" *Art News* 54, 6 (Oct. 1955): 36–39.

5 The text of Dubuffet's lecture, excerpted below, is published in New York, Richard L. Feigen and Co., *Dubuffet and the Anticulture*, exh. cat. (New York, 1969); and in *Arts Magazine* 53, 8 (Apr. 1979): 156–57. See also Dennis Adrian, "Jean Dubuffet in Chicago and the Midwest," *Jean Dubuffet: Forty Years of His Art*, exh. cat. (Chicago, 1984), pp. 27–30 (reprinted in Adrian, *Sight Out of Mind* [Ann Arbor, Michigan: UMI Research Press, 1985], pp. 183–88.

6 *Arts Magazine* (note 5).

7 Ibid.

8 In recalling Dubuffet's visit and his influence, Cohen has written: "Seeing Dubuffet's work was surprising and stimulating. Its source seemed to be the source we were seeking. . . . A Chicago collector, the late Maurice Culberg, had been collecting Dubuffet . . . and interest in Dubuffet had grown to the point of his being invited to lecture at The Arts Club of Chicago in 1951. I knew a member of the club, Bill Eisendrath, who took me and some of my friends, Leon Golub and Cosmo Campoli, to the lecture" (George Cohen to Richard L. Feigen, in New York, Richard L. Feigen and Co. [note 5]).

9 For general histories of The School of The Art Institute of Chicago, see Roger Gilmore, ed., *Over a Century* (Chicago, 1982); and Chicago, The Art Institute of Chicago, *100 Artists 100 Years*, exh. cat. (Chicago, 1979–80).

10 Paschke quoted during a videotape interview with Kate Horsefield and Lyn Blumenthal in 1983. The videotape is in the collection of the Video Data Bank of The School of The Art Institute of Chicago, and the transcript is published in *Profile* 3 (Sept. 1983): 2–36.

11 Paschke (note 10), p. 2.

12 I am grateful to Art Paul, former Art Director for *Playboy*, for his comments, and to Barbara Hoffman for her assistance in obtaining tear sheets of Paschke's work for the magazine.

13 Paschke in conversation with the author, June 23, 1988.

14 Paschke (note 10), p. 4.

15 Paschke, in Michele Vishny, "An Interview with Ed Paschke," *Arts Magazine* 55, 4 (Dec. 1980): 147.

16 Paschke (note 10), p. 5. The artist described his military experiences in conversation with the author, Aug. 18, 1988.

17 Among the articles chronicling the rise of Pop Art were "Pop Art—Cult of the Commonplace," *Time*, May 3, 1963, pp. 69–73; "Pop Pop," *Time*, Aug. 30, 1963, p. 40; and "Saint Andrew," *Newsweek*, Dec. 7, 1964, pp. 100, 103, which variously illustrate works by Hefferton, Lichtenstein, Ramos, Rauschenberg, Rosenquist, Warhol, and Wesselmann.

18 Paschke in conversation with the author, June 23, 1988.

19 Paschke (note 15), p. 148.

20 Paschke has described his work with film in Paschke (note 15), p. 147, and Paschke (note 10), p. 6, and with the author on several occasions during the past year. I am grateful to Barbara Scharres, Director of the Film Center of The School of The Art Institute of Chicago, for her comments on Paschke's films.

21 For example, this photograph was reproduced on the cover of *Life* 56, 8 (Feb. 21, 1964), and again on p. 80.

22 Paschke, in Chicago, Museum of Contemporary Art, *Violence in Recent American Art*, exh. cat. by Robert Glauber (Chicago, 1968), unpag. It is noteworthy that in a drawing titled *Oz Park* (1967), Paschke made use of the same image of Oswald.

23 These observations are noted in the master's thesis of Carol Schreiber, The School of The Art Institute of Chicago, "Ed Paschke: Beneath the Paint," 1988, p. 28.

24 Paschke (note 10), p. 7.

25 Paschke, in an unidentified interview, dating to approximately 1973. Transcript courtesy of the artist.

26 Ibid.

27 For an excellent discussion of *Ramrod*, see Dennis Adrian's untitled essay in Chicago, The Renaissance Society at the University of Chicago, *Ed Paschke: Selected Works 1967–1981*, exh. cat. (Chicago, 1982), pp. 8–9.

28 As a graduate student, Paschke studied printmaking with Sonia Sheridan. His prints are catalogued and illustrated in Chicago, The David and Alfred Smart Gallery, The University of Chicago, *The Chicago Imagist Print*, exh. cat. by Dennis Adrian and Richard A. Born (Chicago, 1987), pp. 108–25.

29 The principal sources concerning this period of Chicago art are Washington, D.C., National Collection of Fine Arts, Smithsonian Institution, *Made in Chicago*, 1974; Sunderland, England, Ceolfrith Gallery, Sunderland Arts Centre, *Who Chicago?* 1980; Dennis Adrian, "Aspects of Form among Some Chicago Artists," *Art Scene* 2, 7 (Apr. 1969): 10–15 (reprinted in Adrian [note 28], pp. 21–24); Franz Schulze, "Chicago Popcycle," *Art in America* 54, 6 (Nov.–Dec. 1966): 102–4; Schulze, "Chicago," *Art International* 11, 5 (May 1967): 41–44;

and Schulze, "Art News in Chicago," *Art News* 70, 7 (Nov. 1971): 48–55.

30 Schulze, "Chicago Popcycle" (note 29), p. 103.

31 Schulze, "Art News in Chicago" (note 29), p. 51.

32 Paschke (note 10), p. 6.

33 David L. Shirey, "Downtown Art Scene: Celebrities and Horses," *The New York Times*, Apr. 13, 1971, p. 24.

34 Paschke (note 10), p. 15.

35 Paschke (note 25), pp. 1–2.

36 Ibid., p. 4.

37 It is important to note that in the 1950s Andy Warhol devoted a large body of commercial art to renderings of shoes.

38 Paschke (note 10), p. 17.

39 Paschke (note 25), p. 2. Paschke referred here to a bar called The Backstage, then located on Chicago's North Side (see note 23, p. 55).

40 Paschke (note 10), p. 8.

41 In 1972 McGinnes, then manager of the Kingston Mines Theater in Chicago, invited Paschke to create sets for *Turds in Hell*, written by Charles Ludlum and Bill Vehr. For reviews, see Dennis Adrian, "And Now, Theater Sees His 'Hell,'" *Chicago Daily News*, July 29–30, 1972, Panorama sec., p. 5; and Terry Curtis Fox, "Murky Muddle in the Mines," *Chicago Daily News*, Aug. 20, 1972, p. 16. In this con-

text, it is noteworthy that in 1968 Paschke played the male lead in Red Grooms's film *Tappy Toes*.

42 Paschke in conversation with the author, Sept. 22, 1988.

43 Paschke (note 10), pp. 20, 22.

44 Paschke in conversation with the author, June 23, 1988. See also Paschke (note 23), p. 20.

45 Paschke (note 10), p. 29.

46 Marshall McLuhan, *Understanding Media: The Extensions of Man* (New York: McGraw-Hill Book Company, 1964), p. 20.

47 *This Is Marshall McLuhan: The Medium Is the Message*, 1967, produced by Iowa State University and the University of Illinois. I am grateful to Carol Schreiber for locating this film.

48 Paschke (note 10), p. 29.

49 Ibid., p. 23.

50 Ibid., p. 22.

51 For the sources of *Violencia* and *Vosotros*, see Schreiber (note 23), pp. 15–16, 53–54.

52 Ibid., p. 57.

53 Ibid., p. 62.

54 Paschke in conversation with the author, Nov. 17, 1988.

55 Paschke (note 10) p. 29.

PLATES

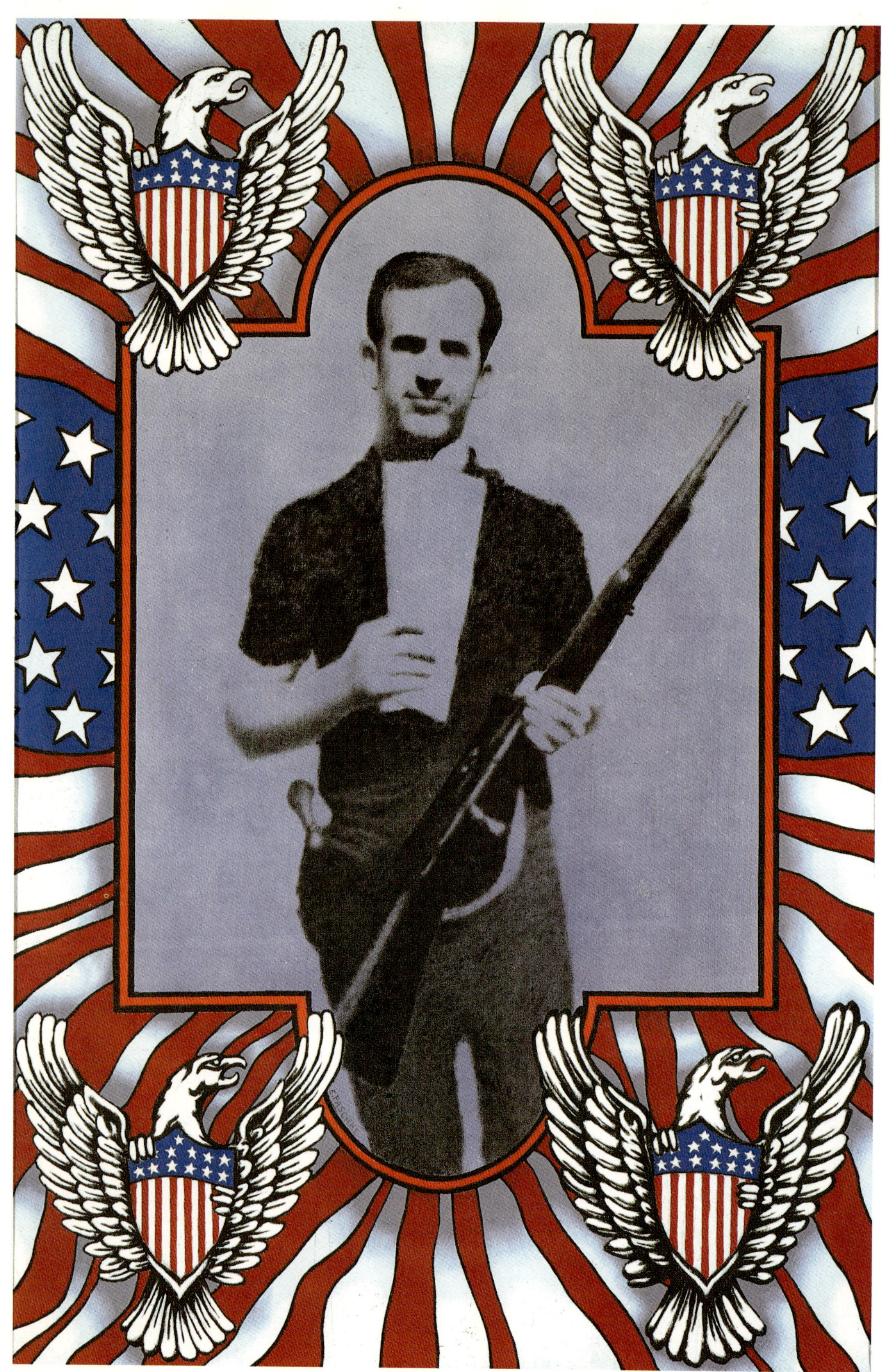

1

PURPLE RITUAL, 1967

A COLORES
COLOR
LAMARQUE VARELA RAMBAL
Amor EN LA SOMBRA
Amor
LAMARQUE VARELA RAMBAL
Amor EN LA SOMBRA
LAMARQUE VARELA
Amor EN LA SOMBRA
E. Paschke '68

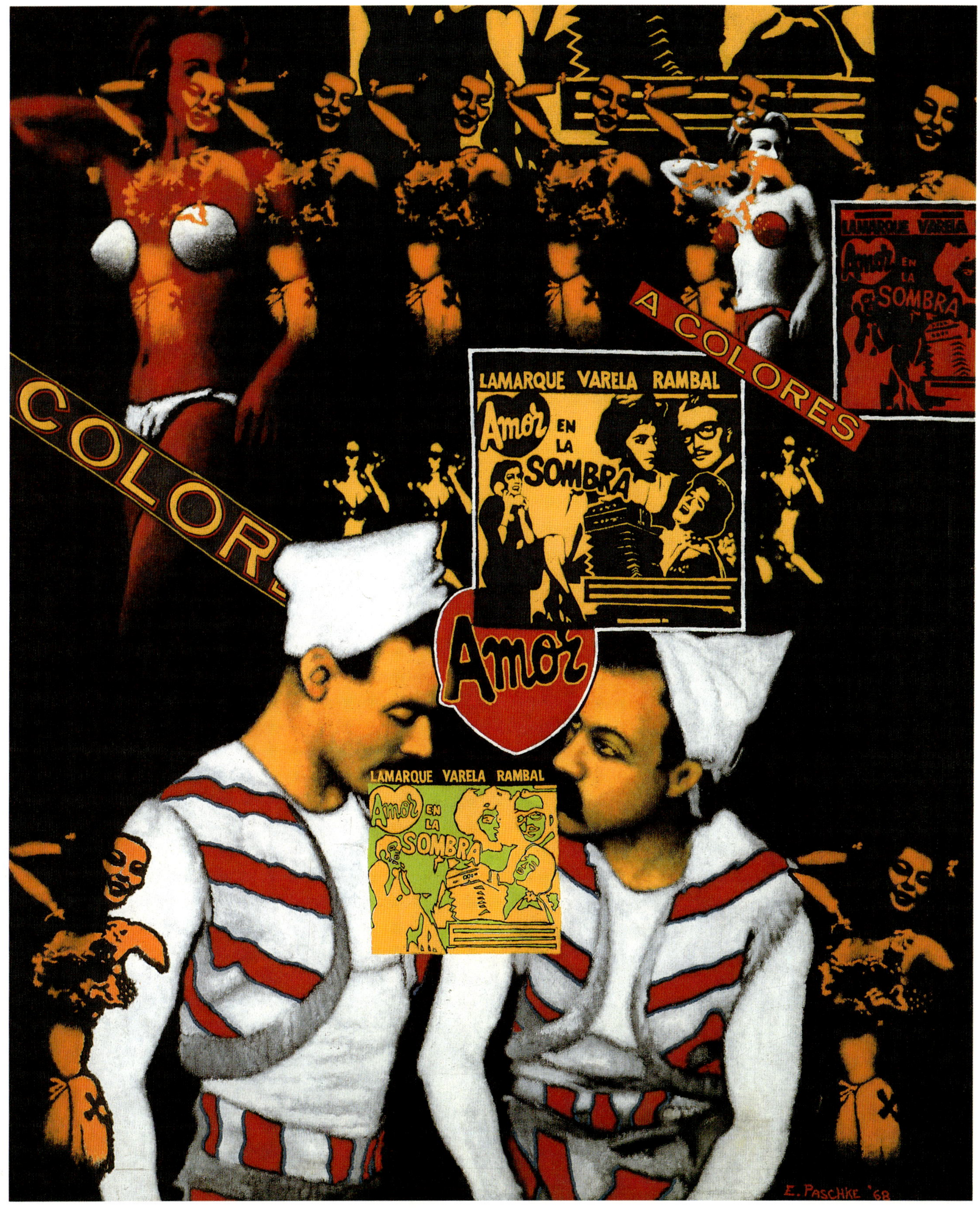

2

AMOR, 1968

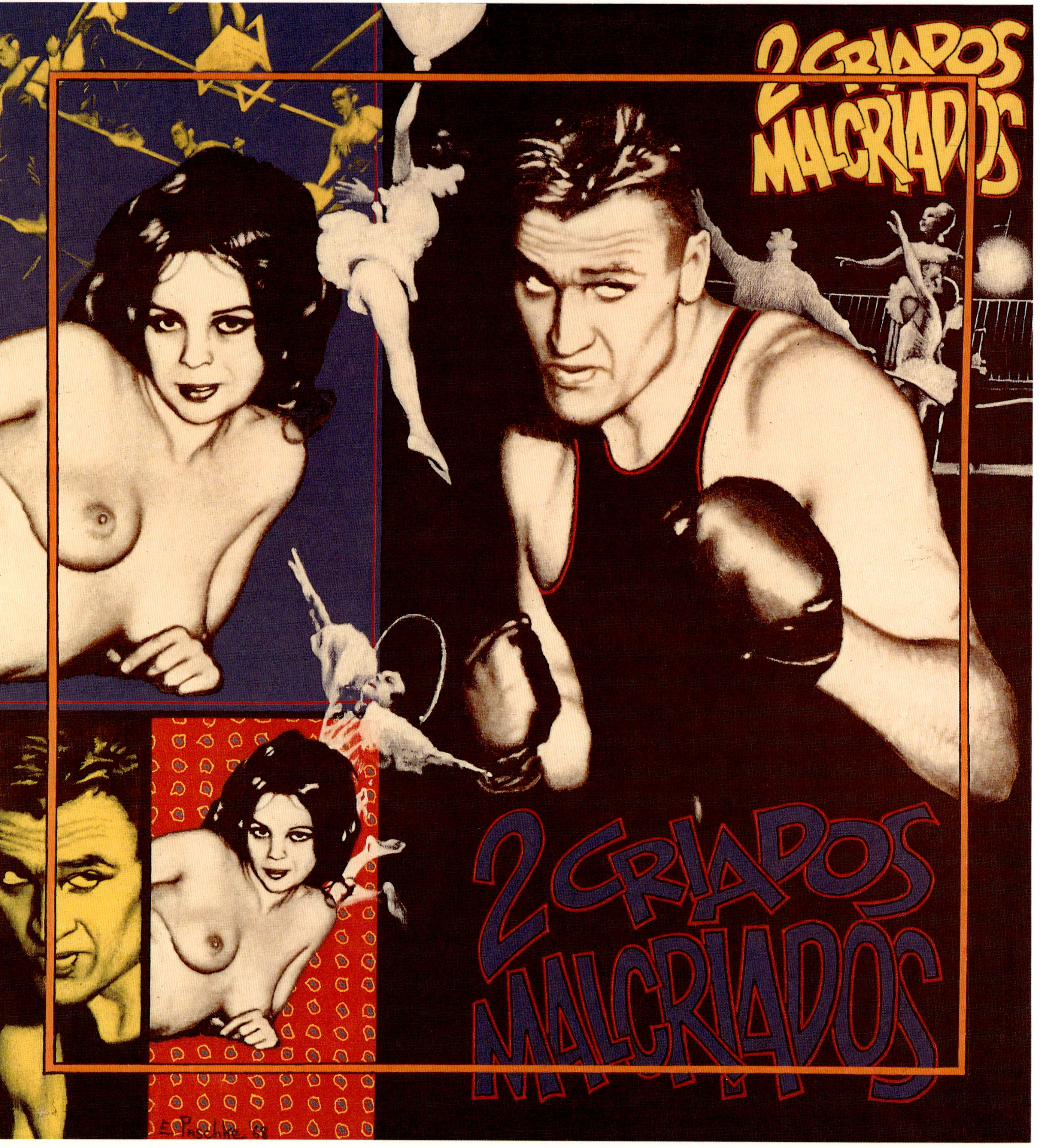
2 CRIADOS
MALCRIADOS
2 CRIADOS
MALCRIADOS

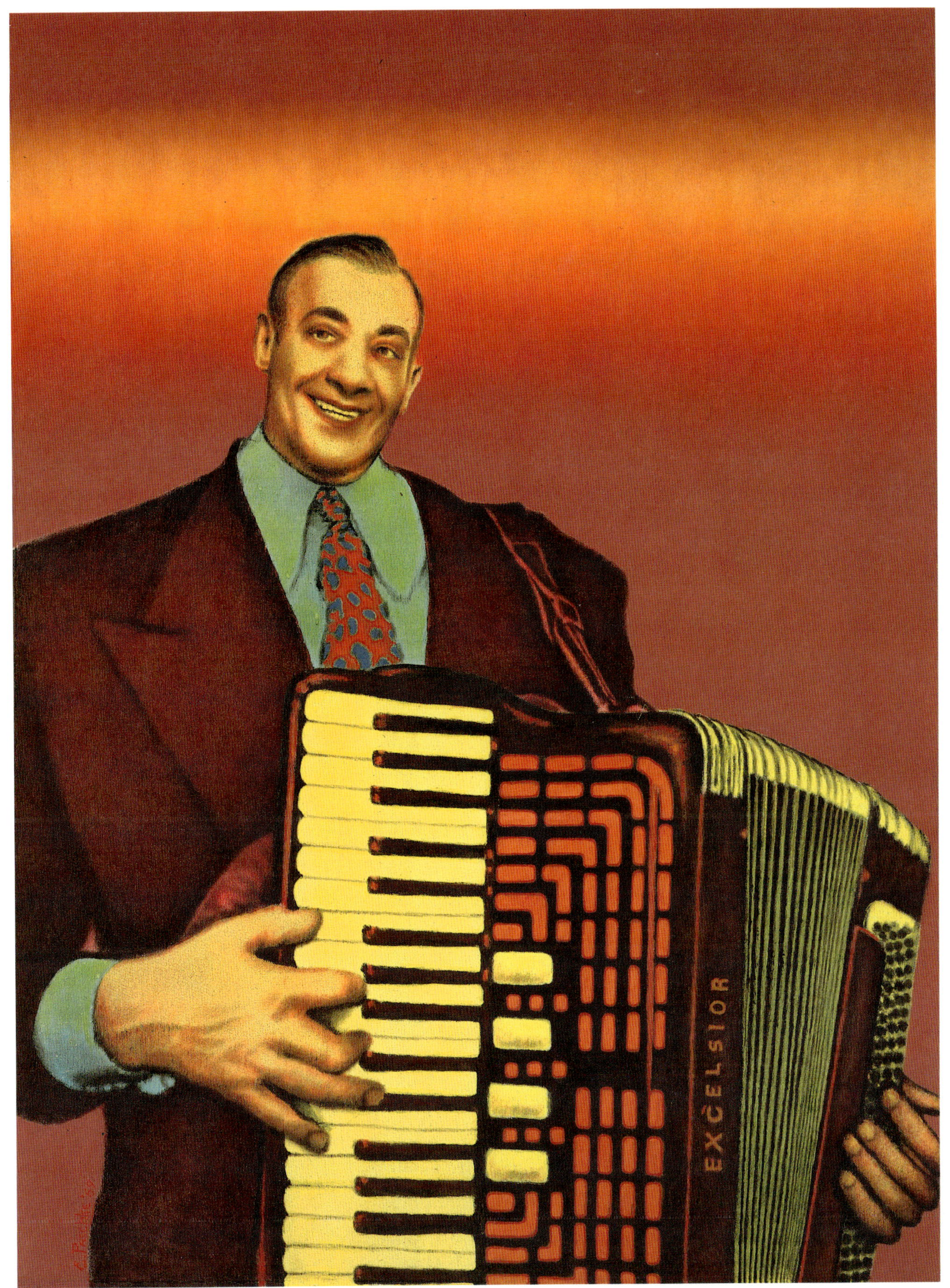

3
DOS CRIADOS, 1968

4
ACCORDION MAN, 1969

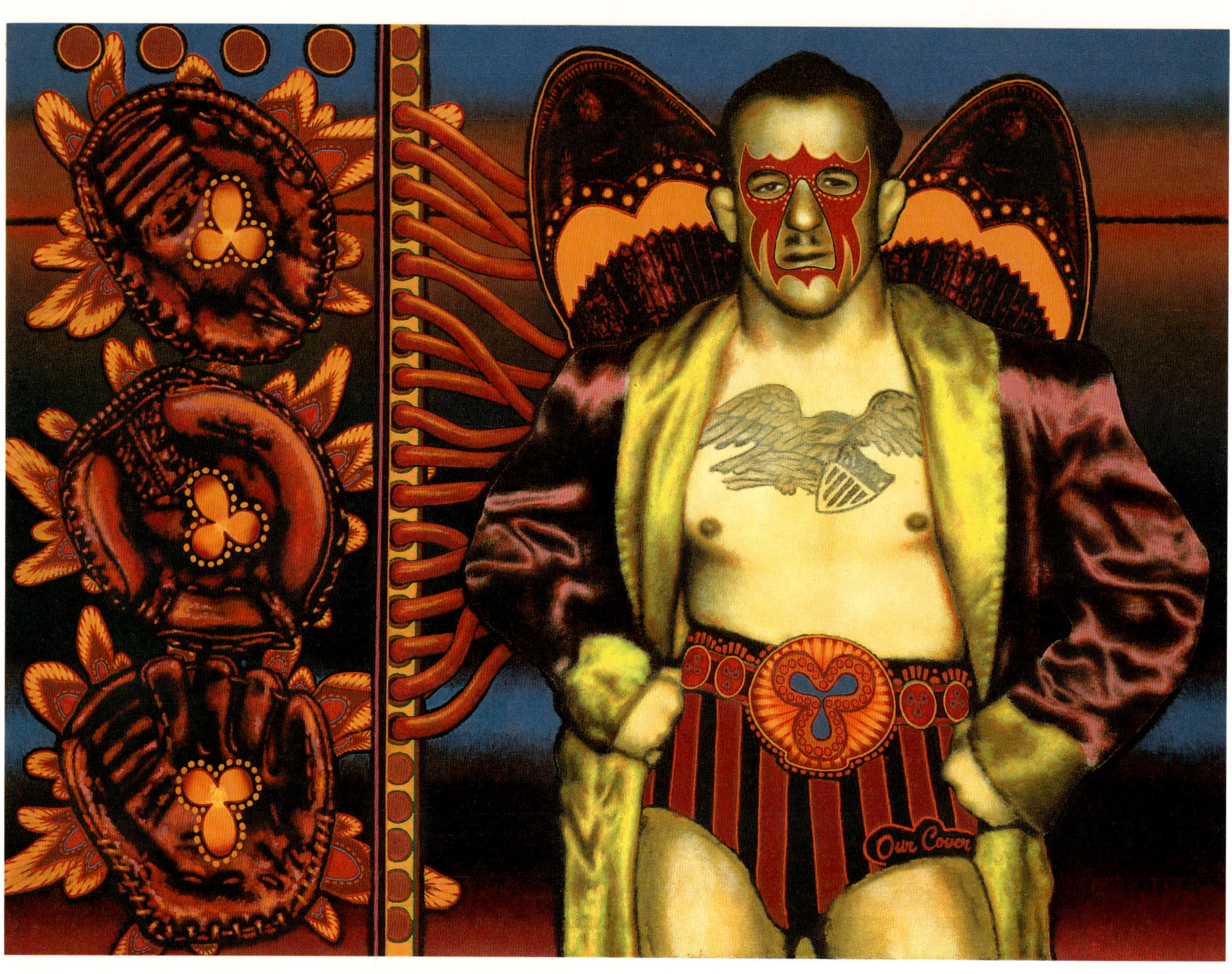

5
MID AMERICAN, 1969

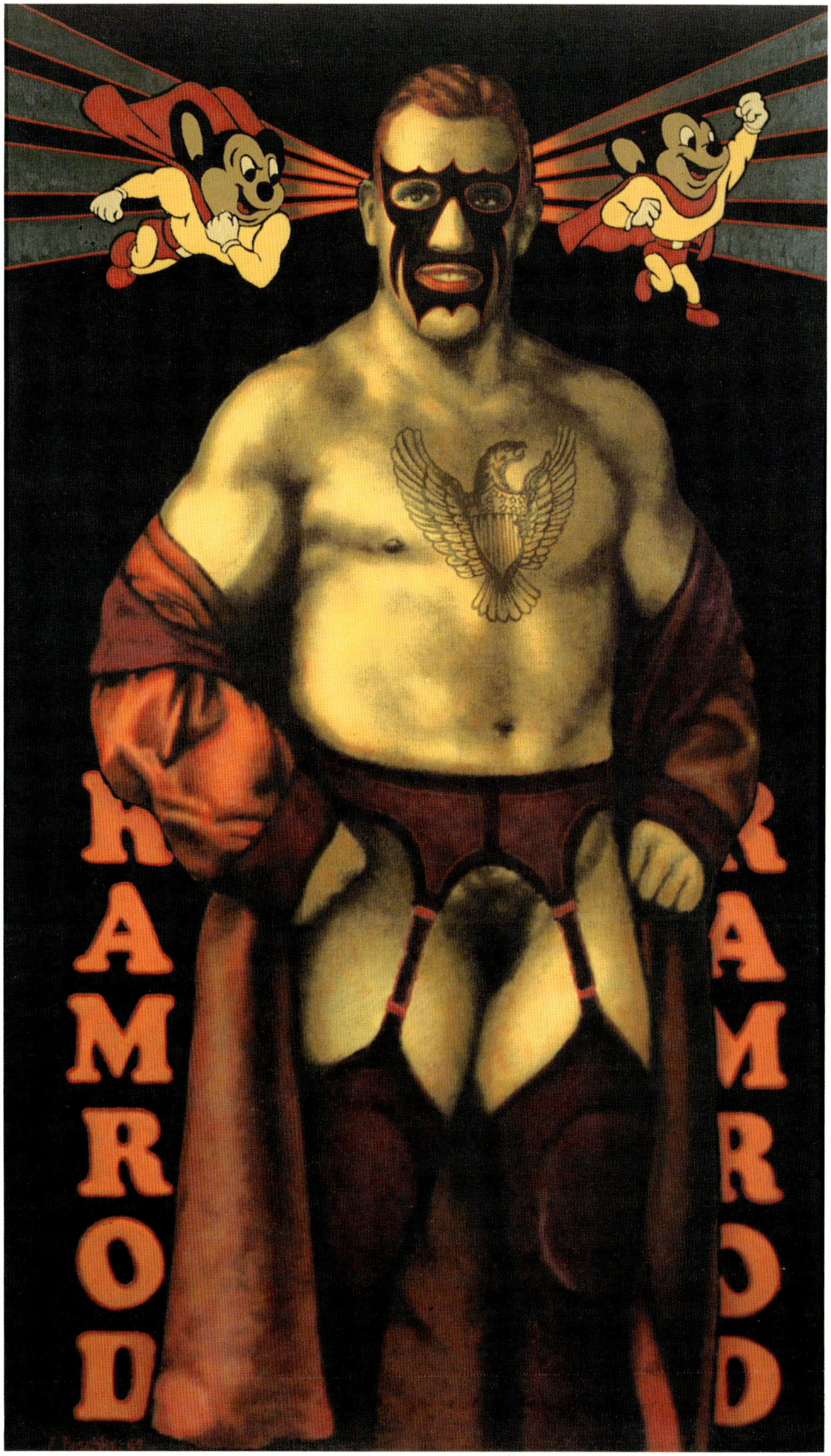

6
RAMROD, 1969

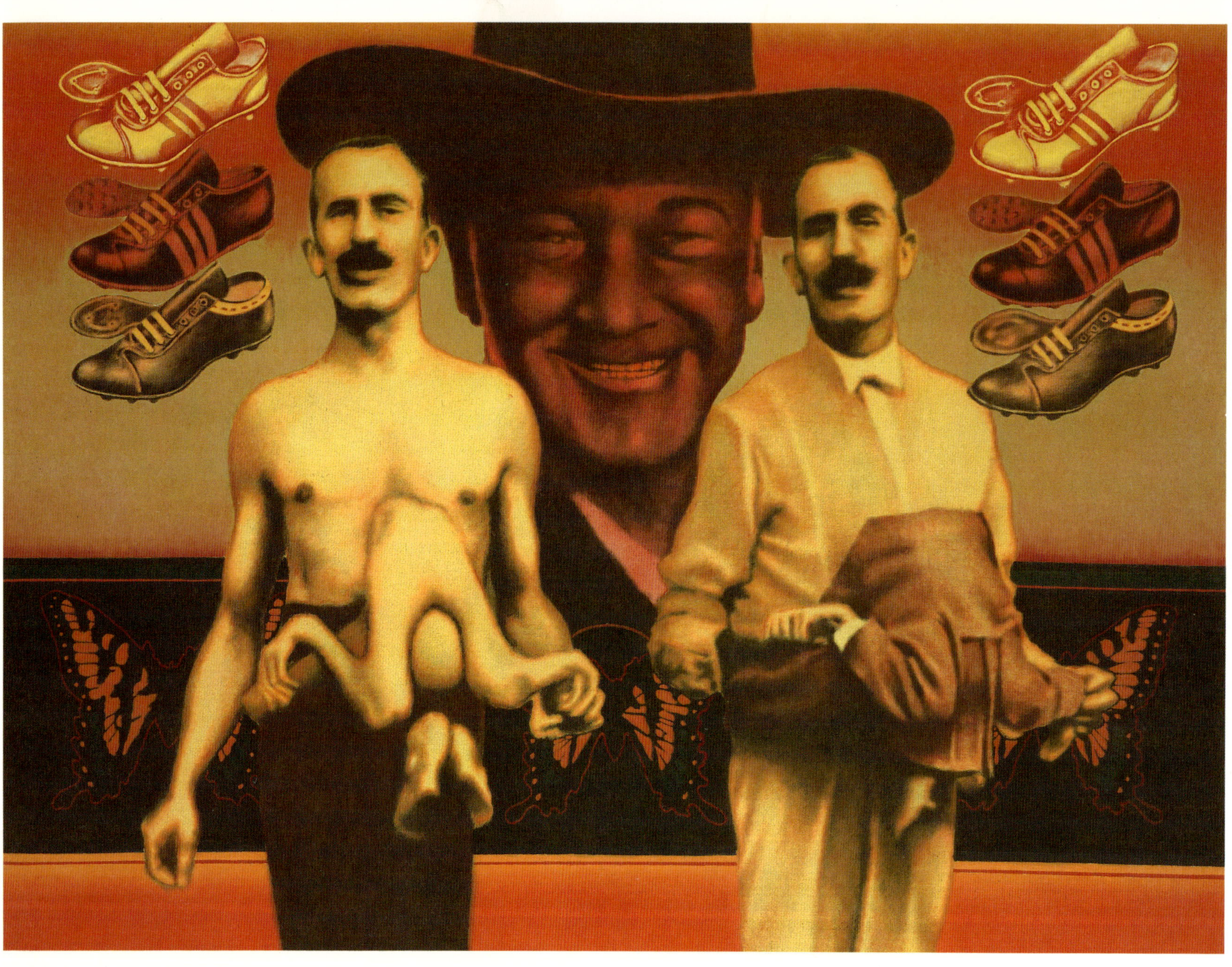

7

HOPHEAD, 1970

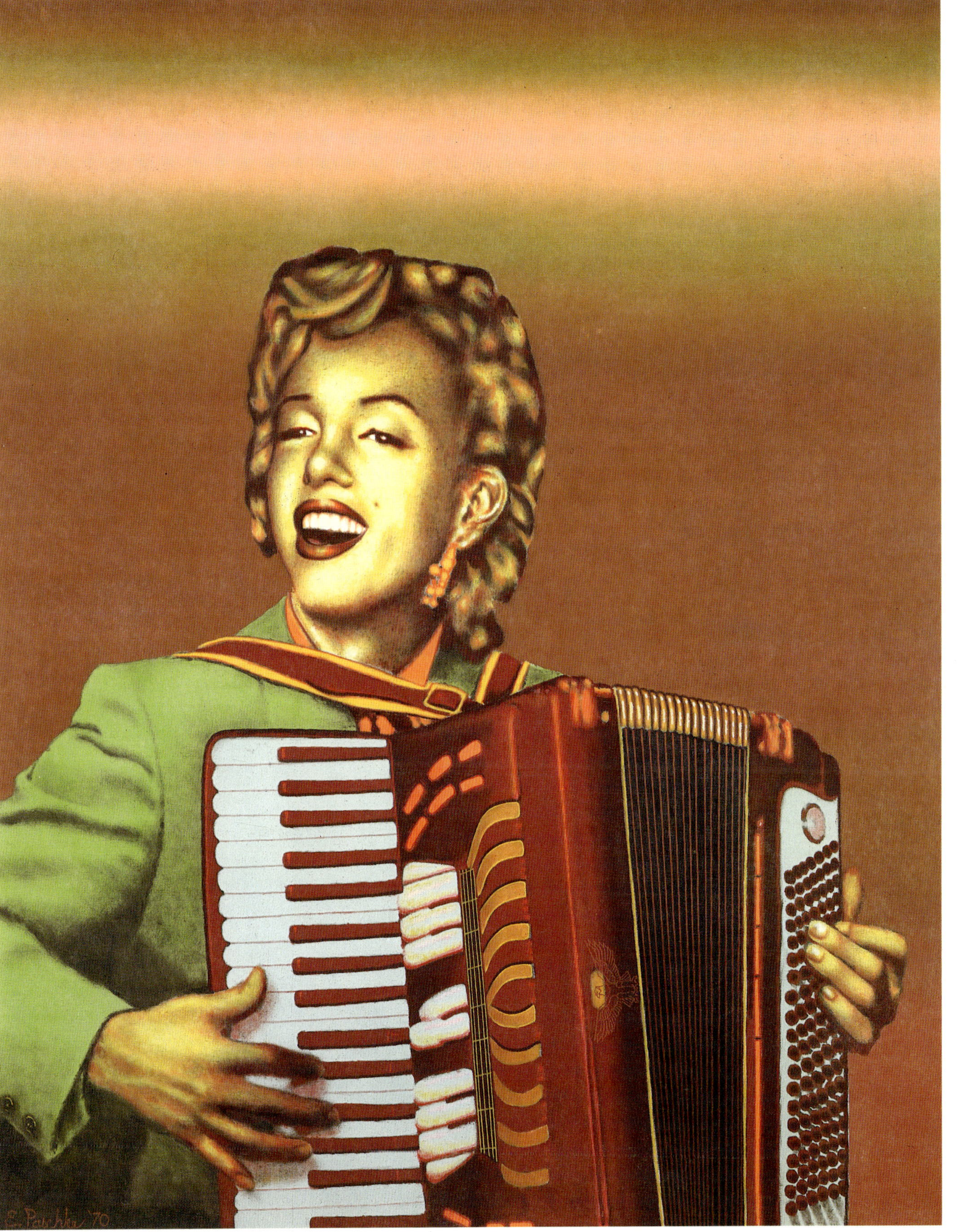

8
PINK LADY, 1970

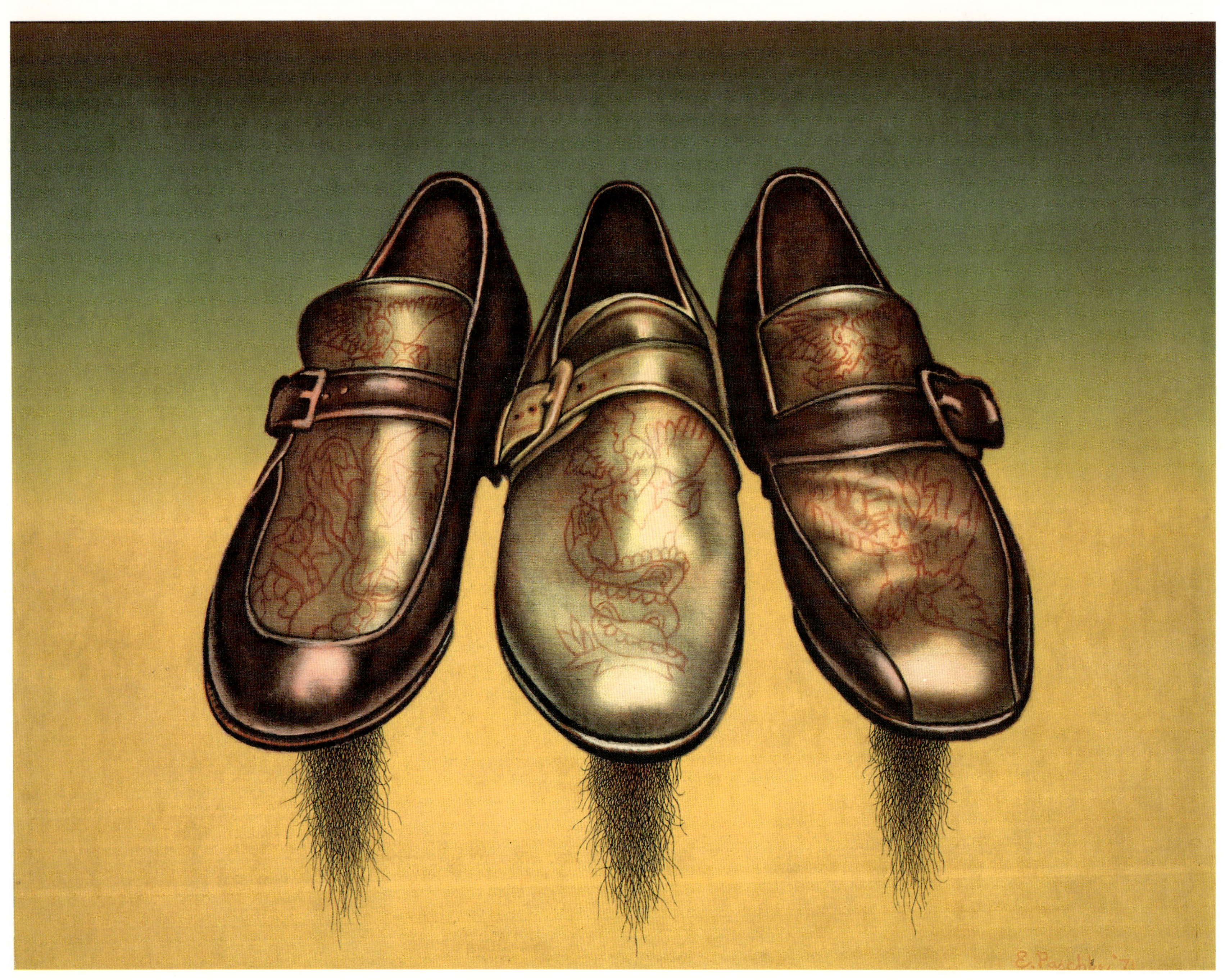

HAIRY SHOES, 1971

BAG BOOTS, 1972

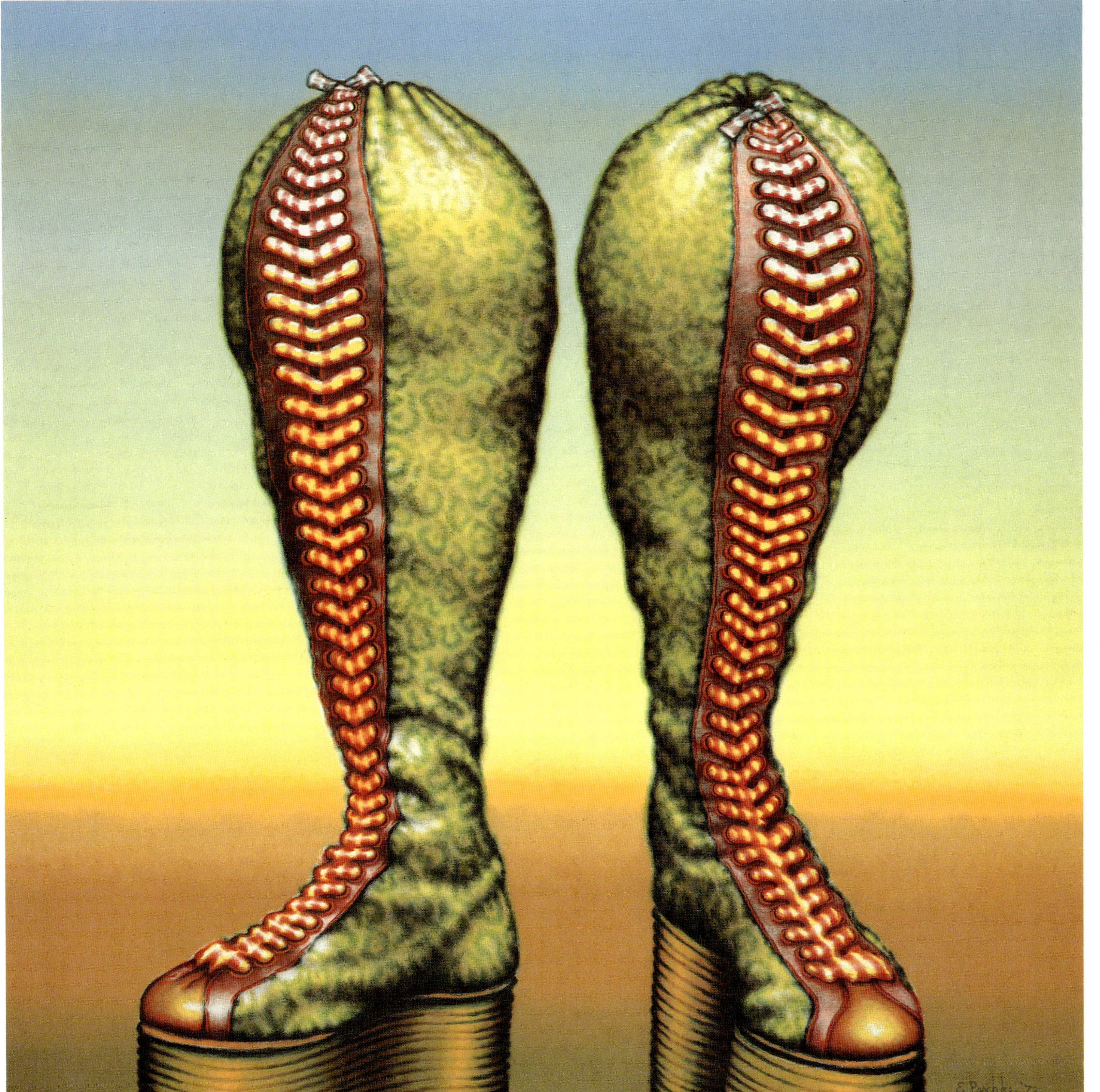
E. Paschke '72

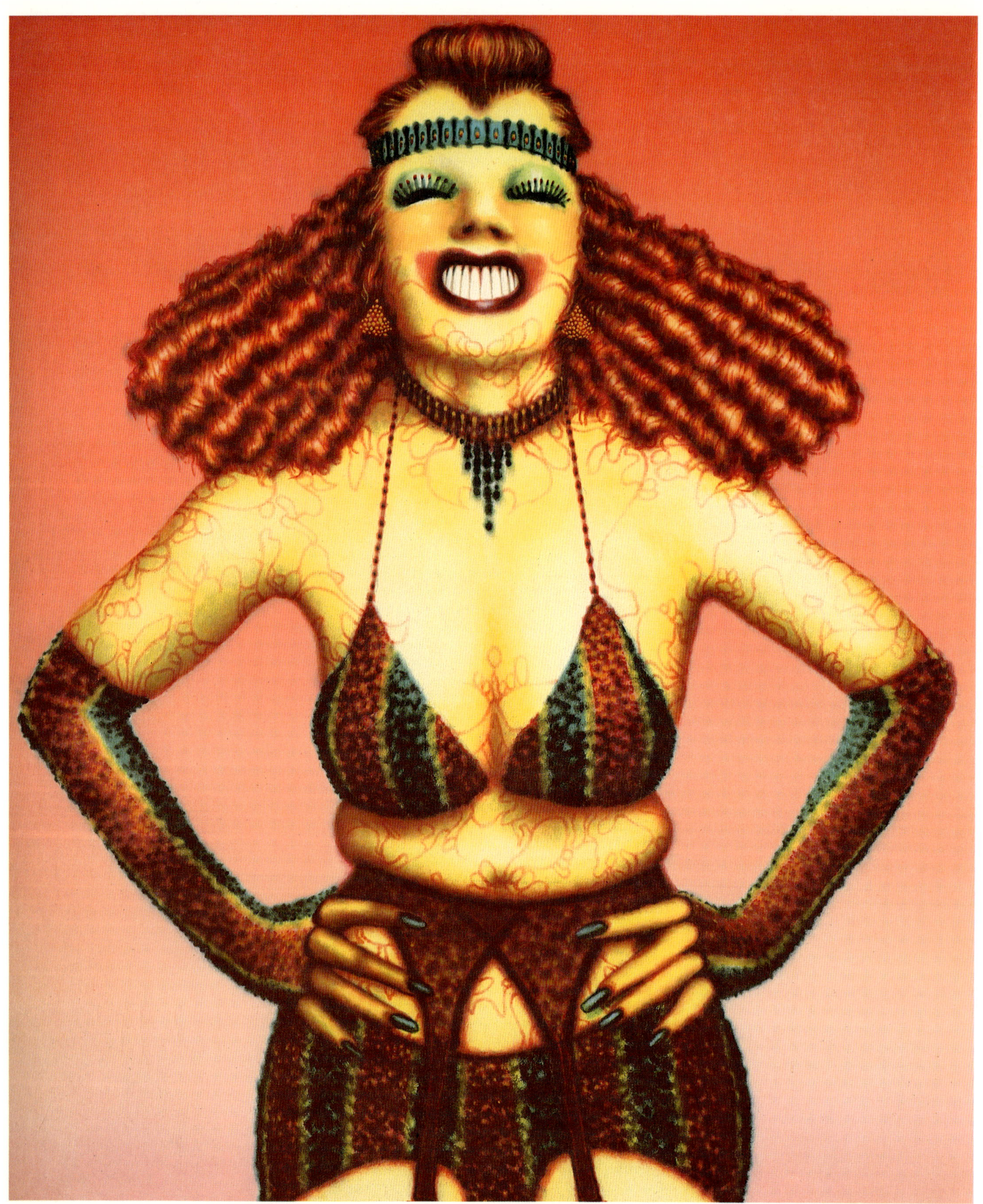

11
FRANCINE, 1973

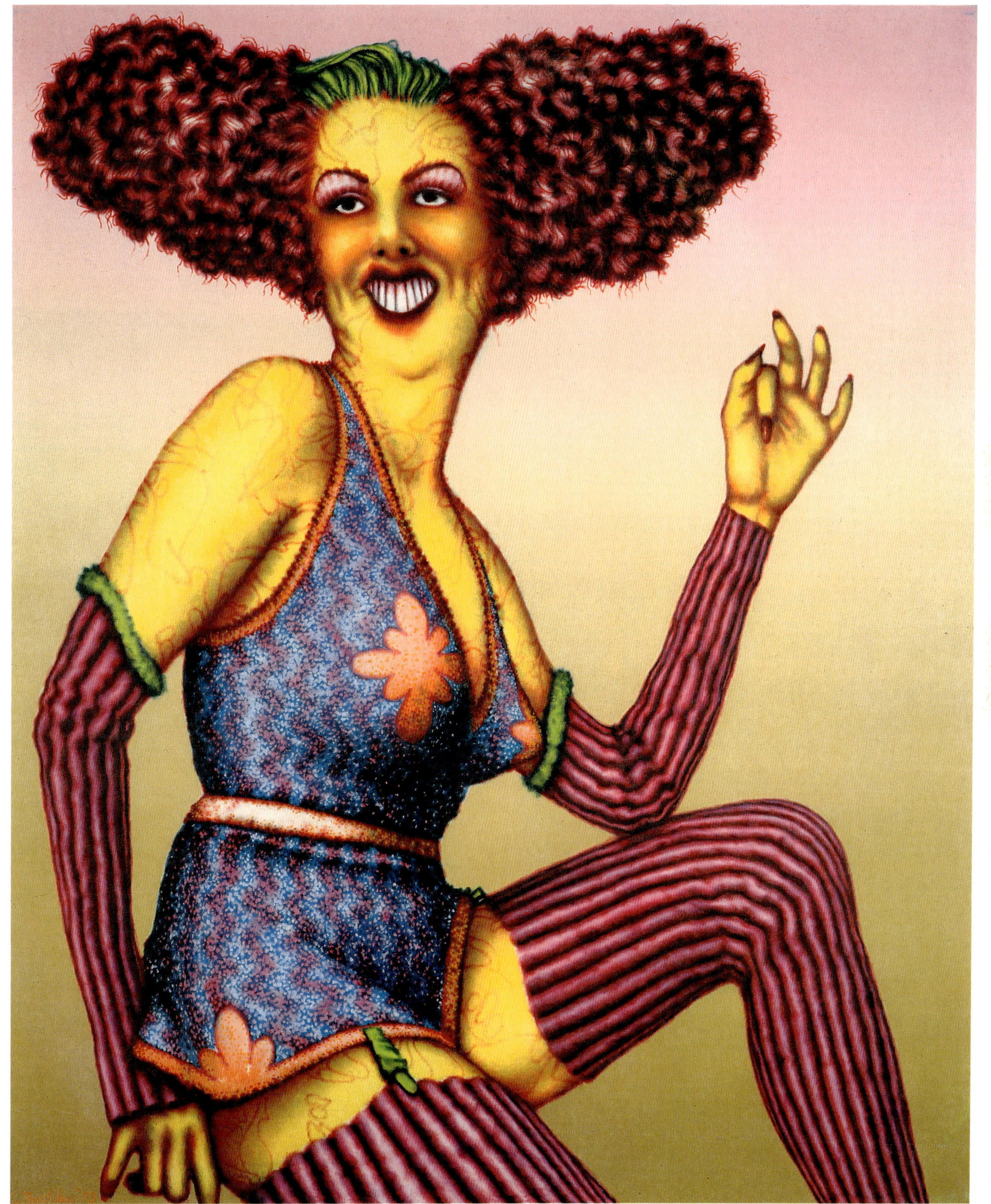

12
JEANINE, 1973

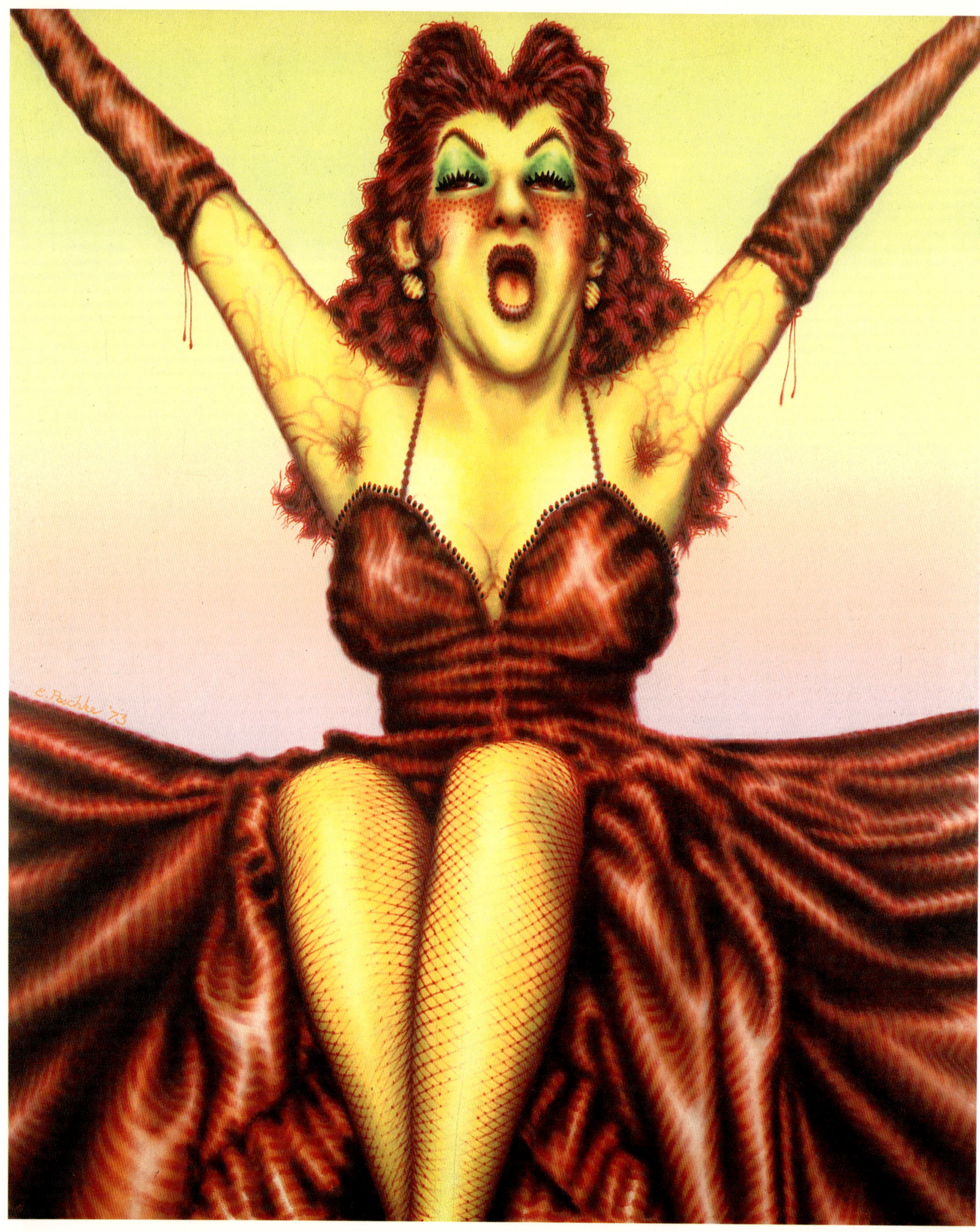

13
JOELLA, 1973

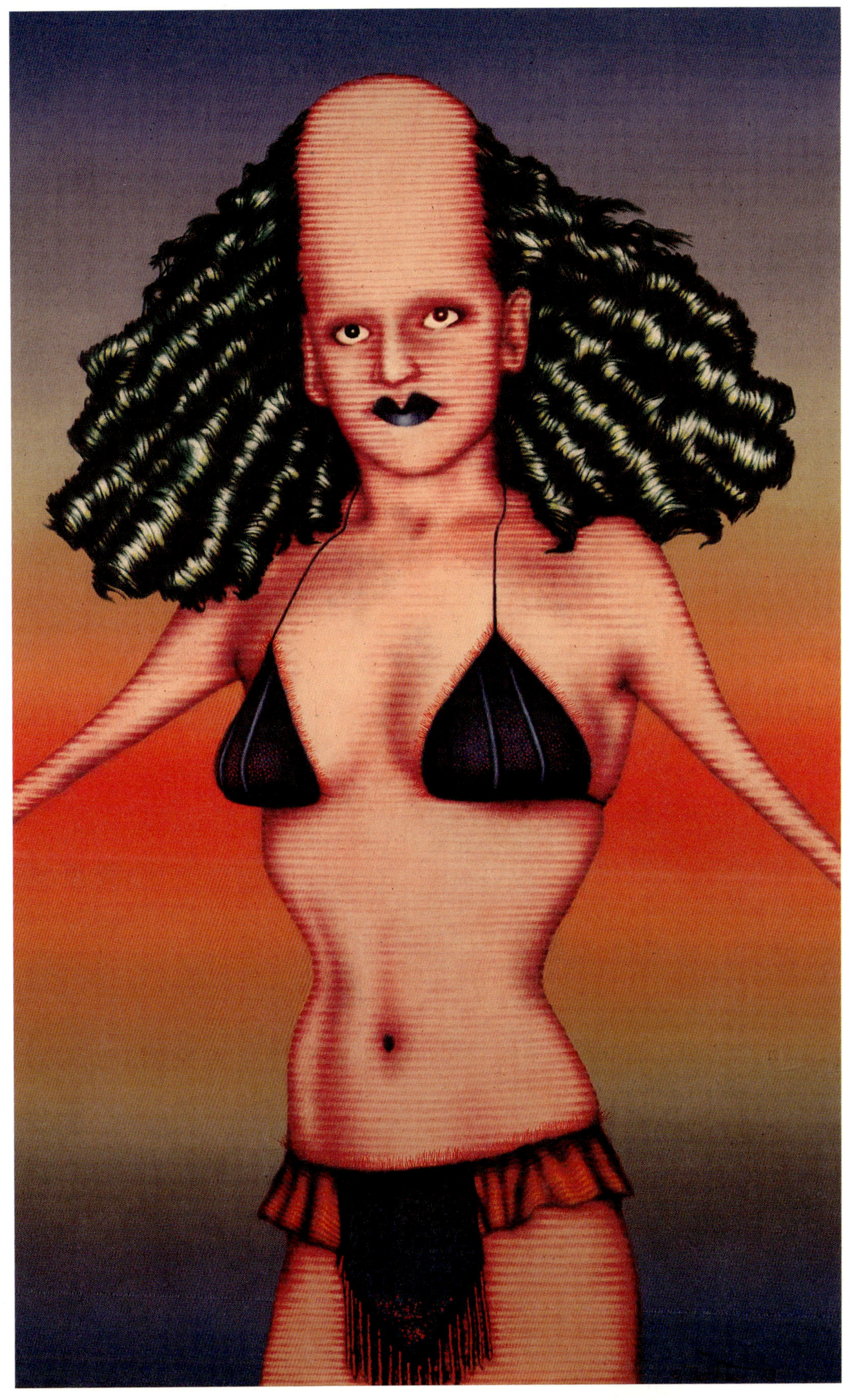

14
LUCY, 1973

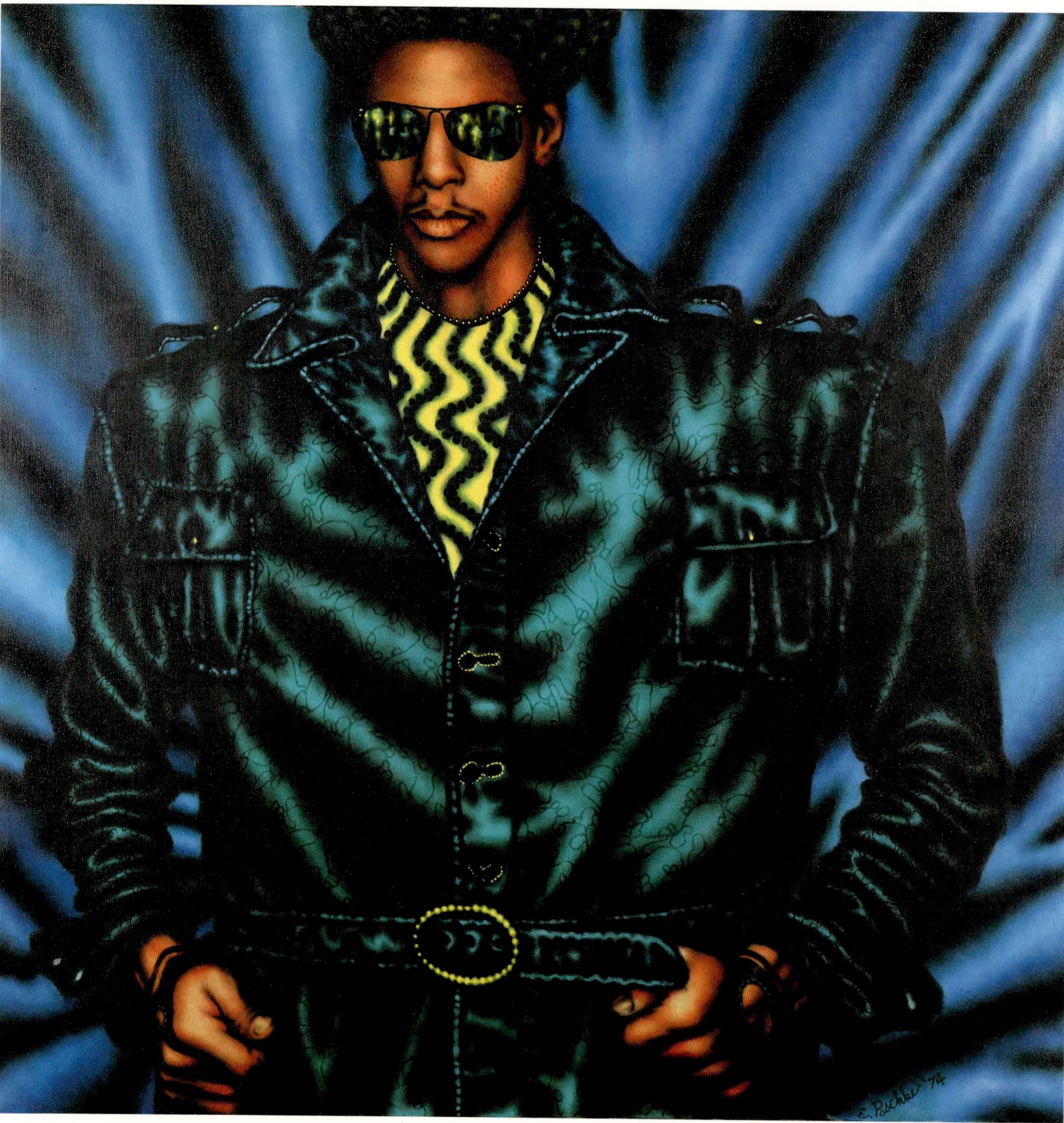

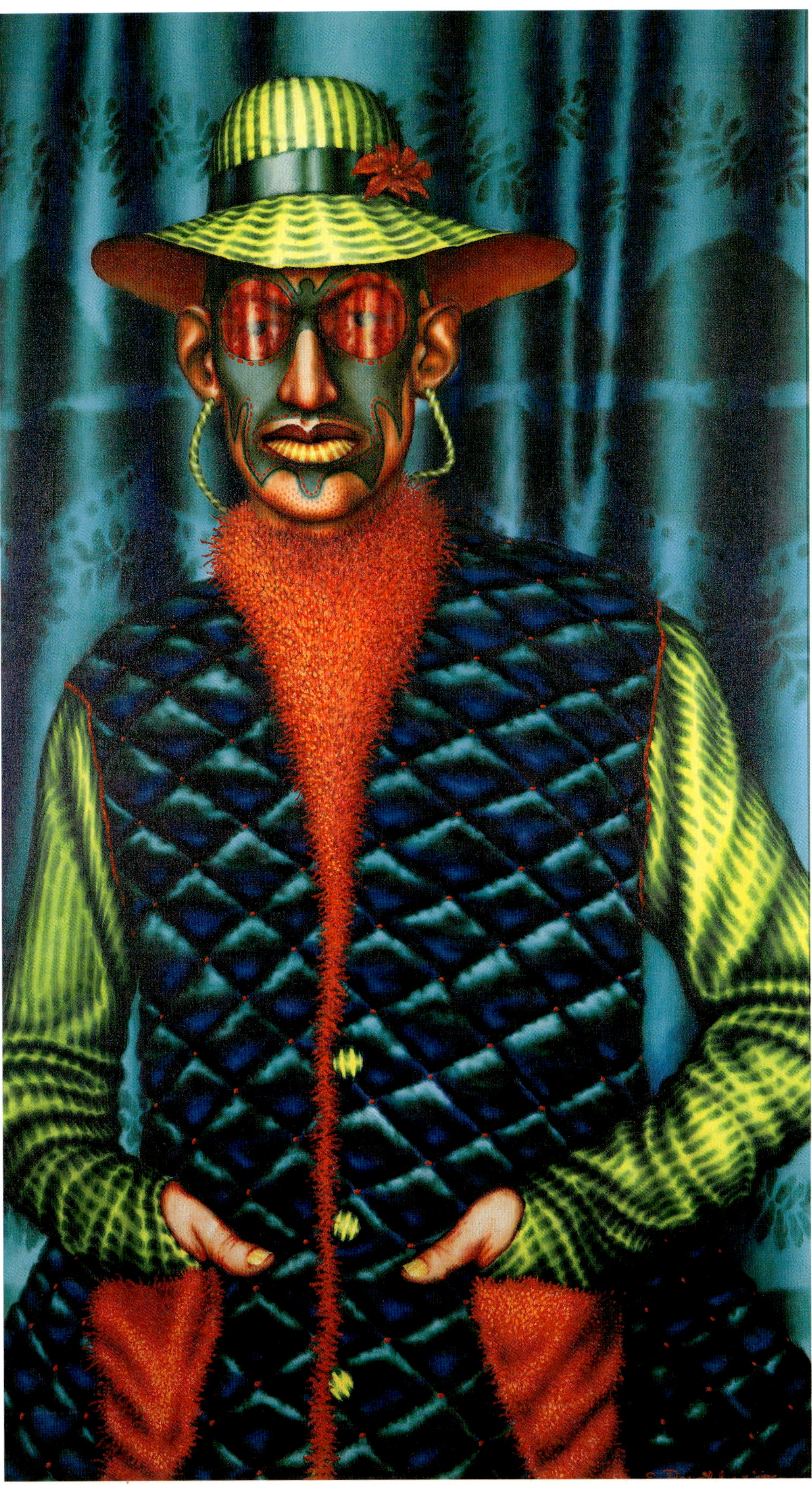

15

RUFUS, 1974

16

ARMONDO, 1975

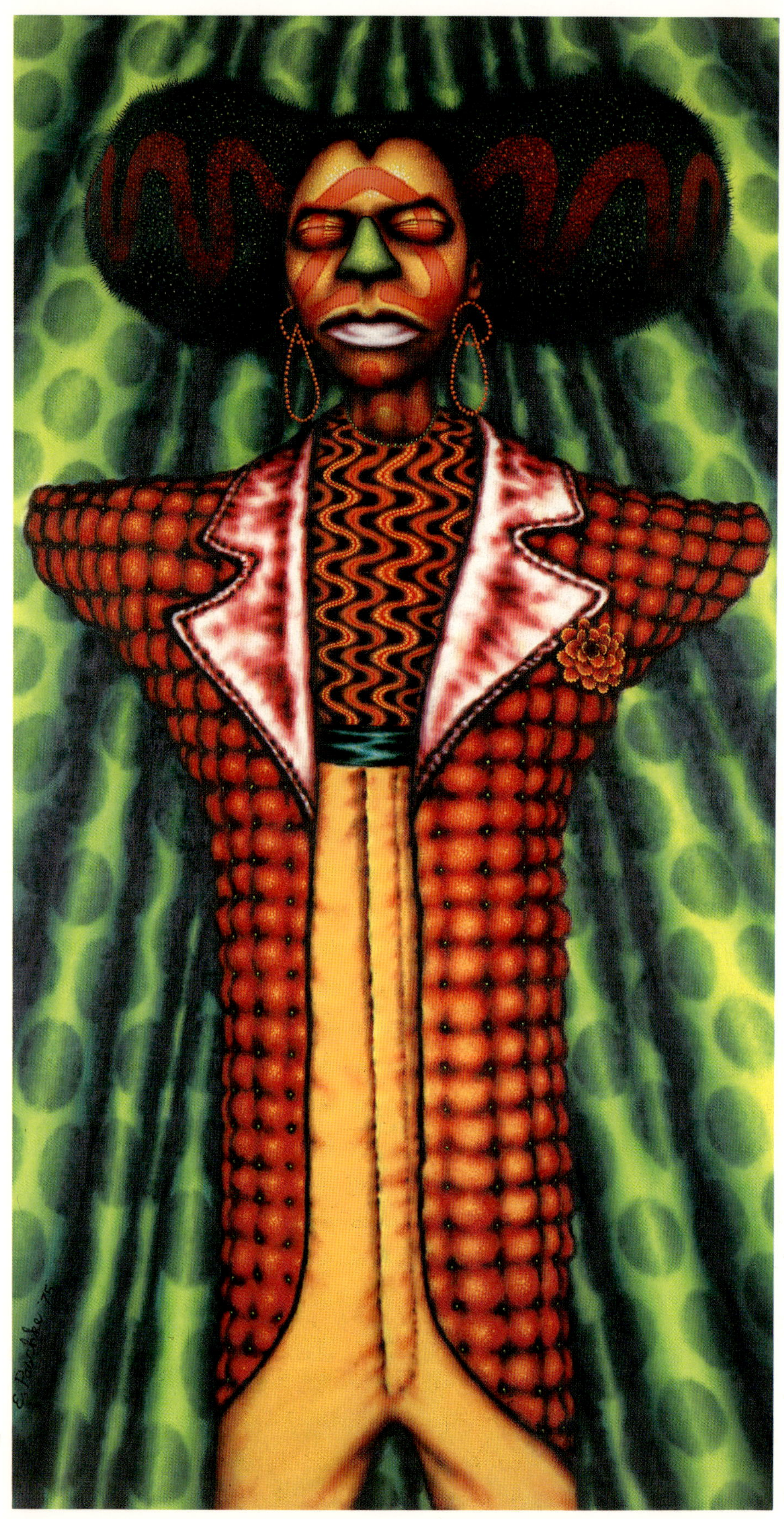

17
RED SWEENEY, 1975

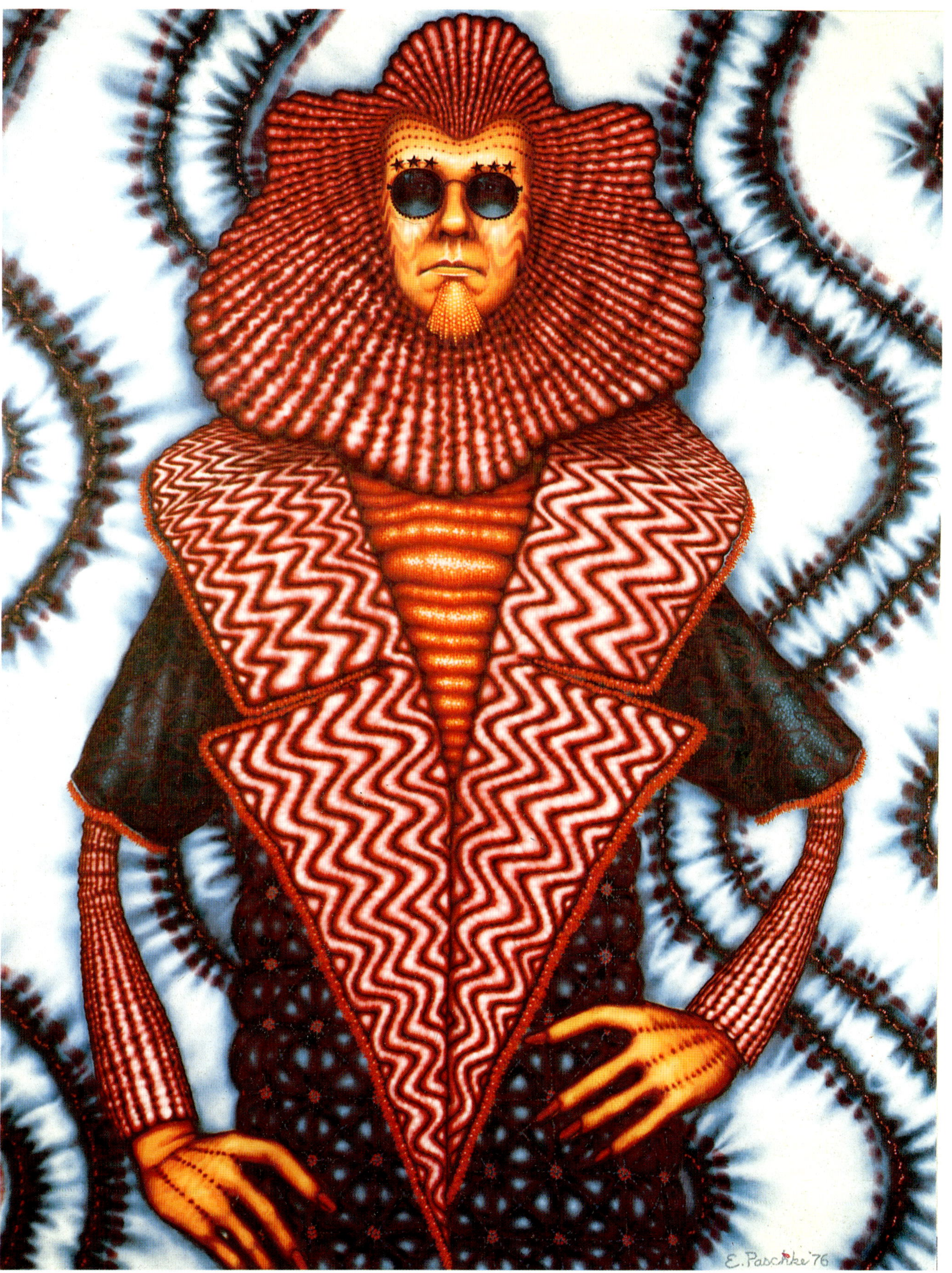

18
MACHINO, 1976

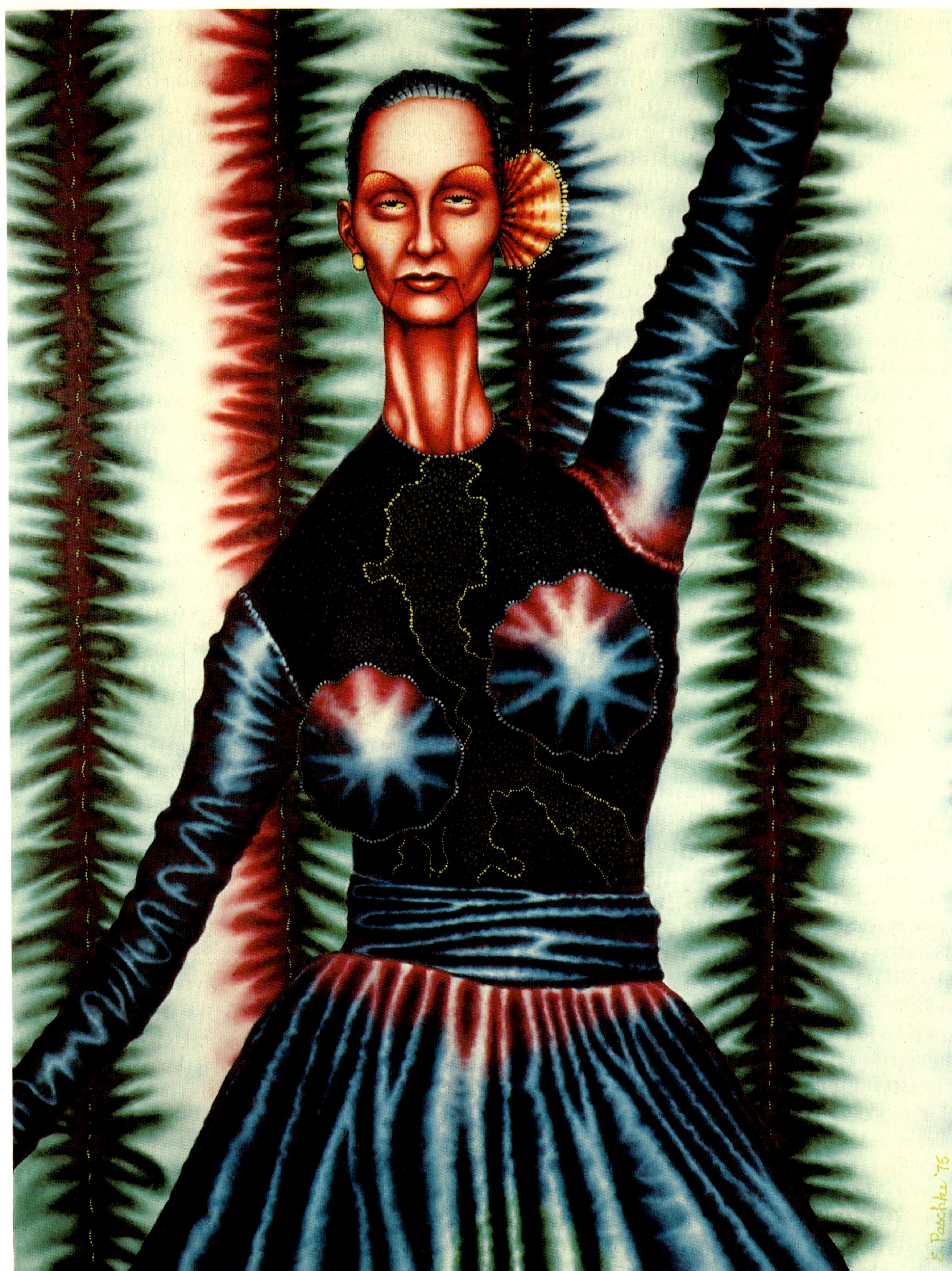

19
SABREENA, 1976

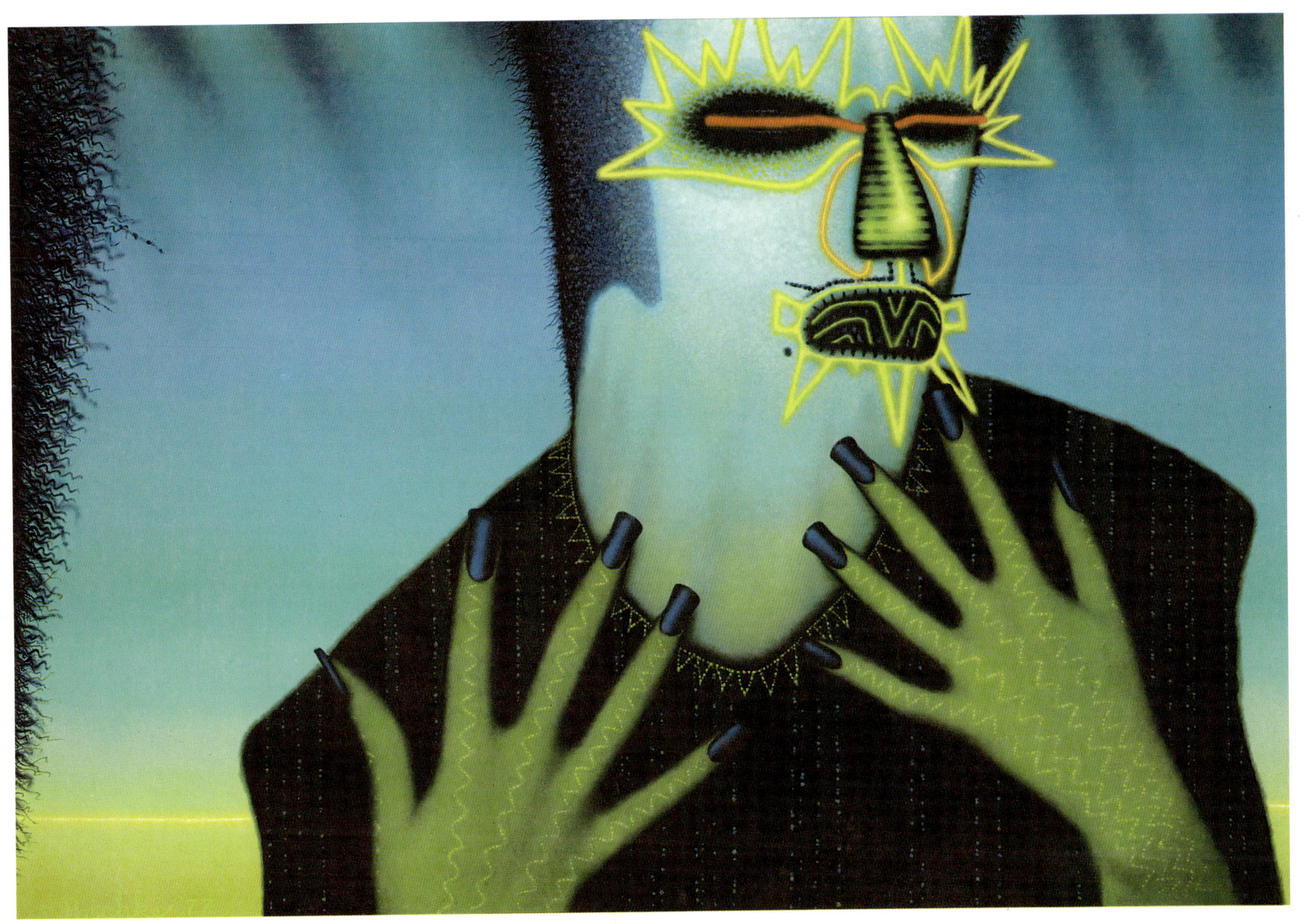

DOMINANT NURSE, 1977

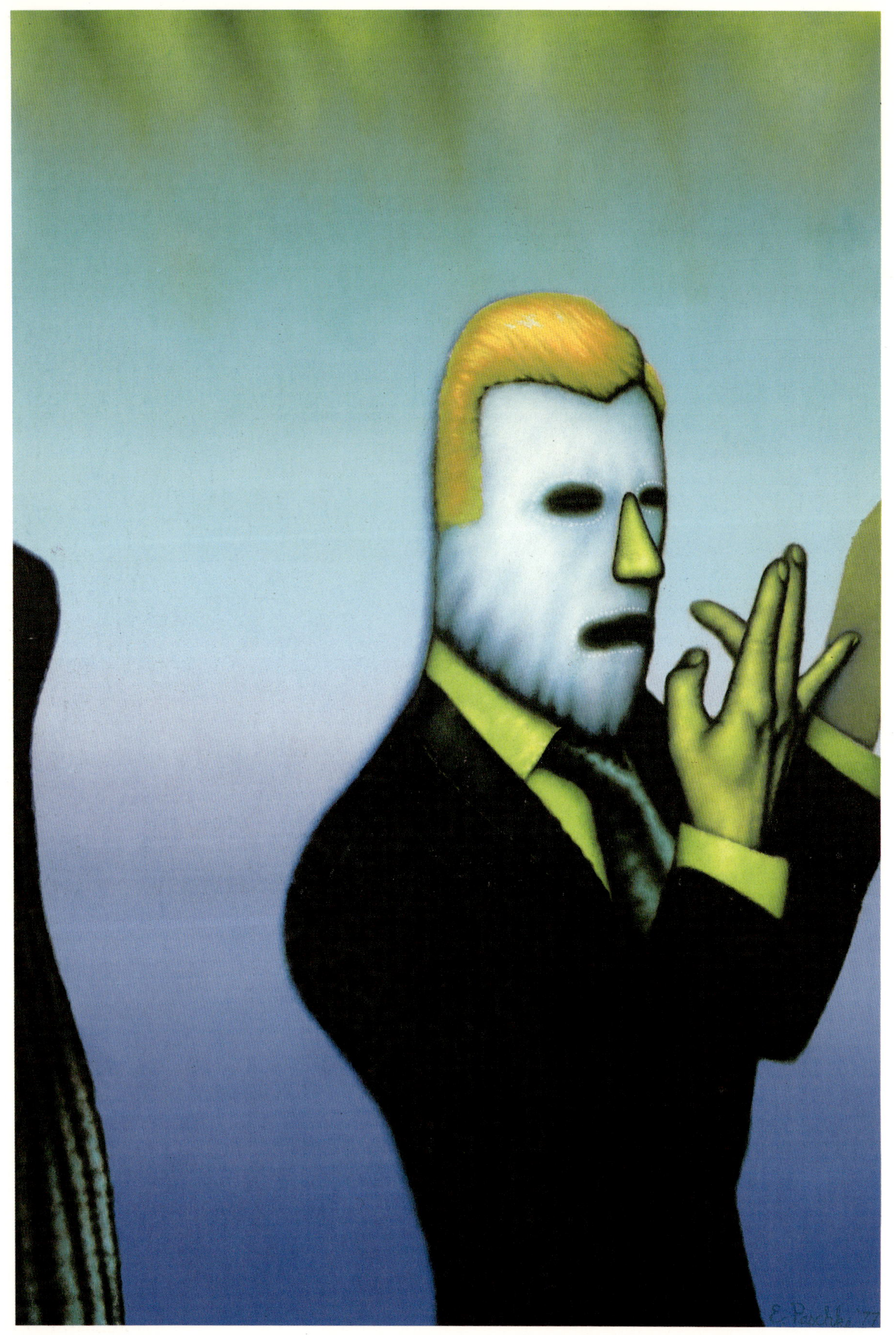

21
MANDRIX, 1977

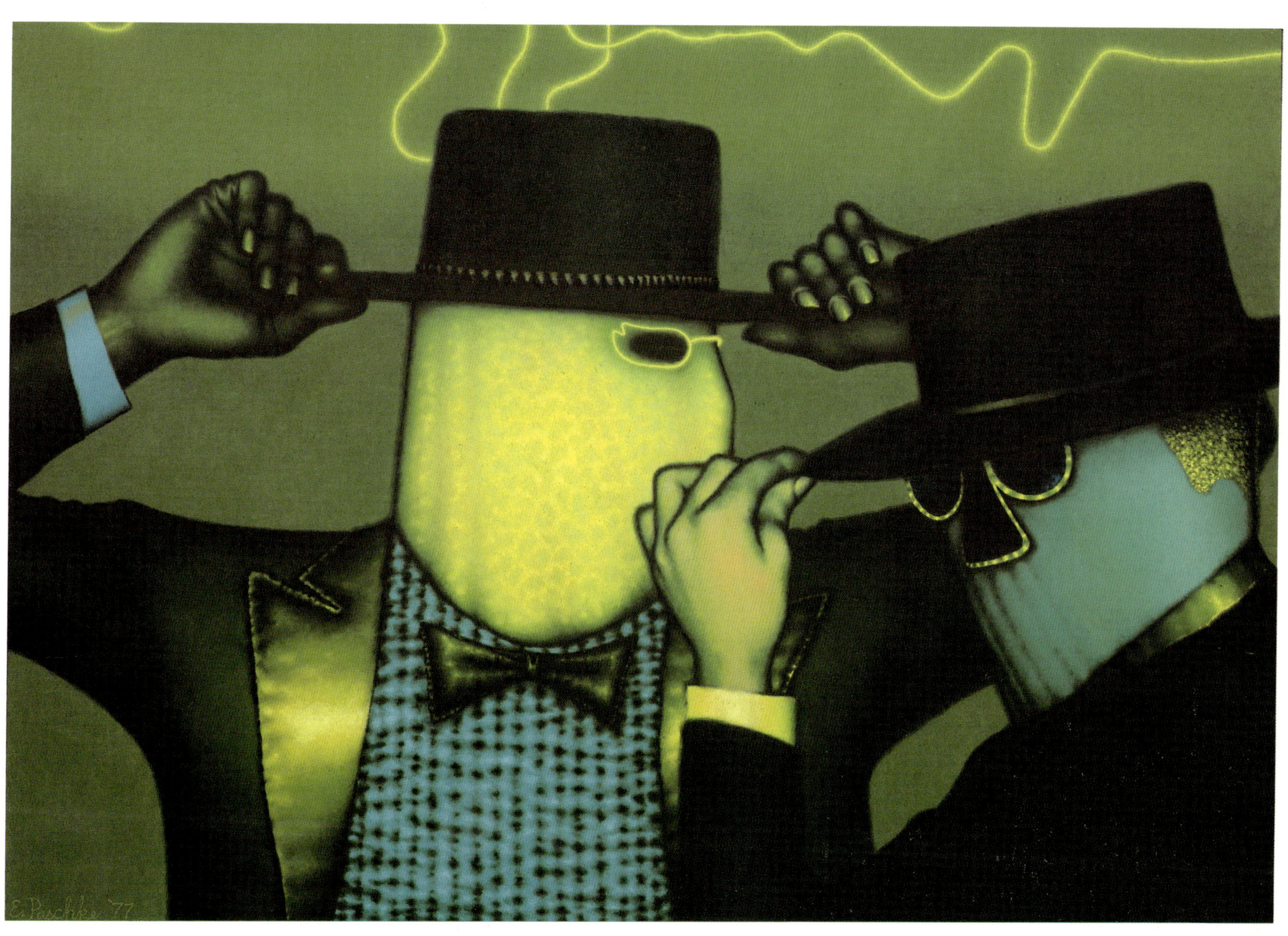

MELON-LAMÉ, 1977

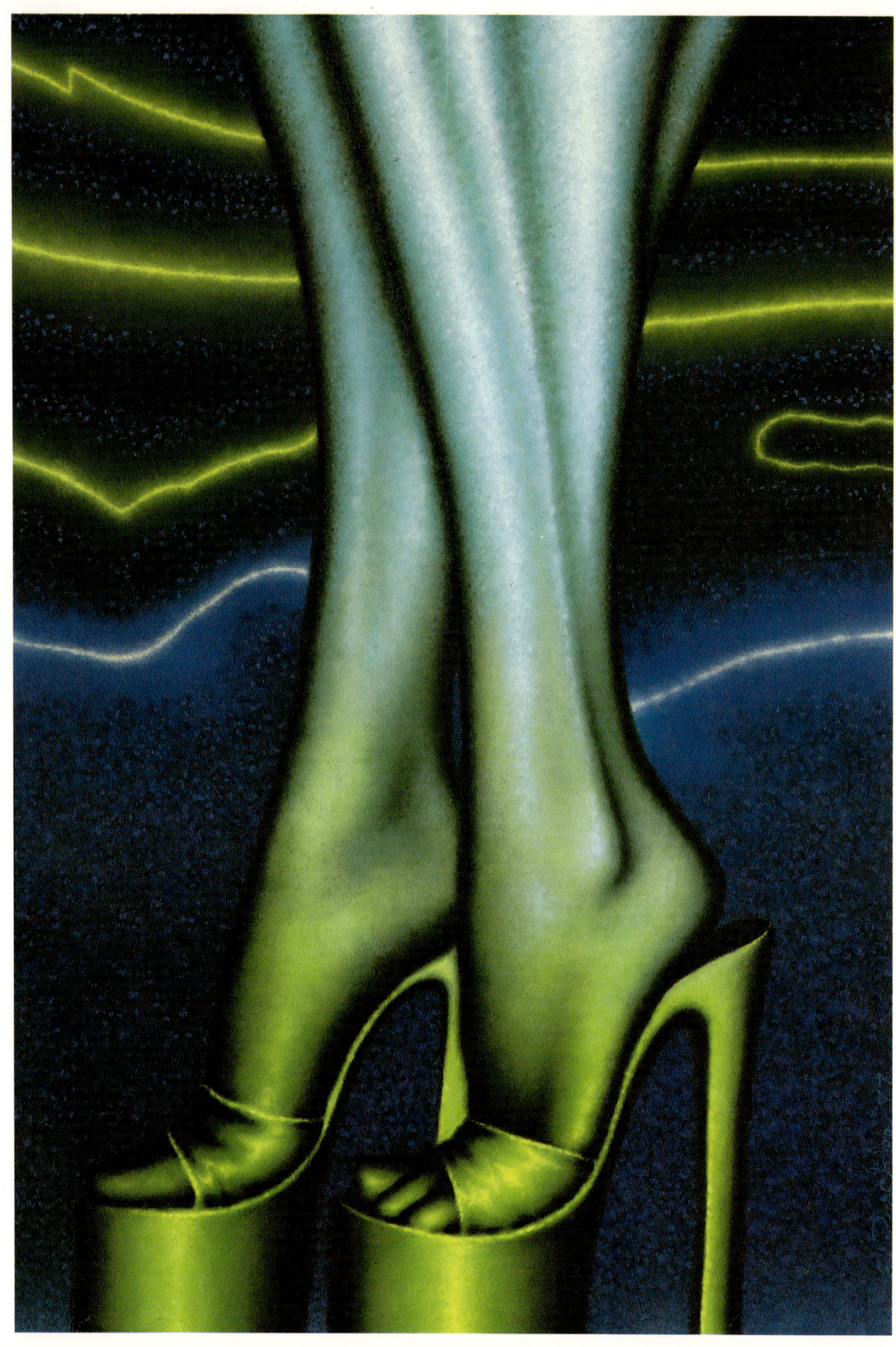

23
METAL DE BLEU, 1977

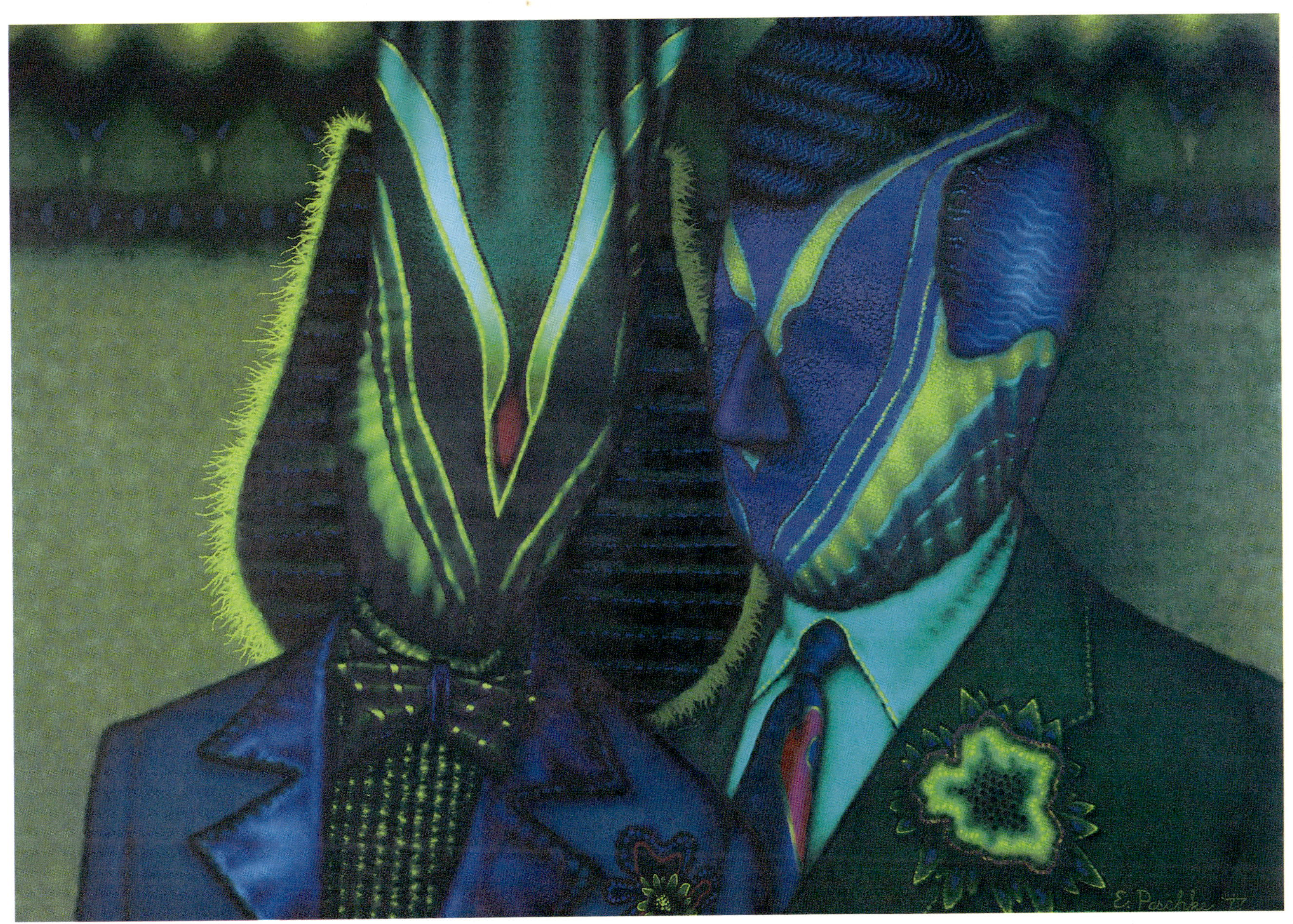

24
TERMINALE, 1977

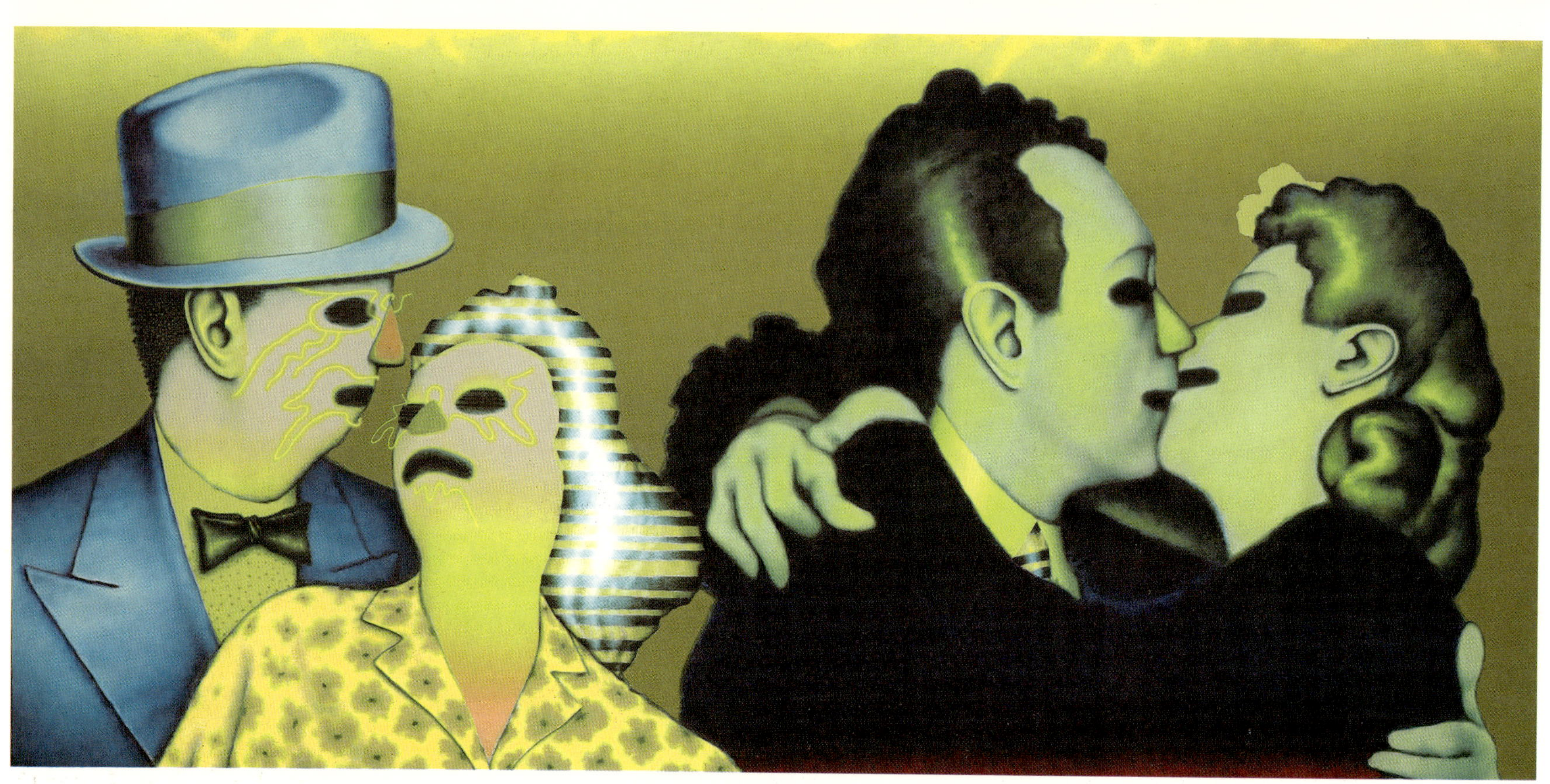

25
CHO CHAN, 1978

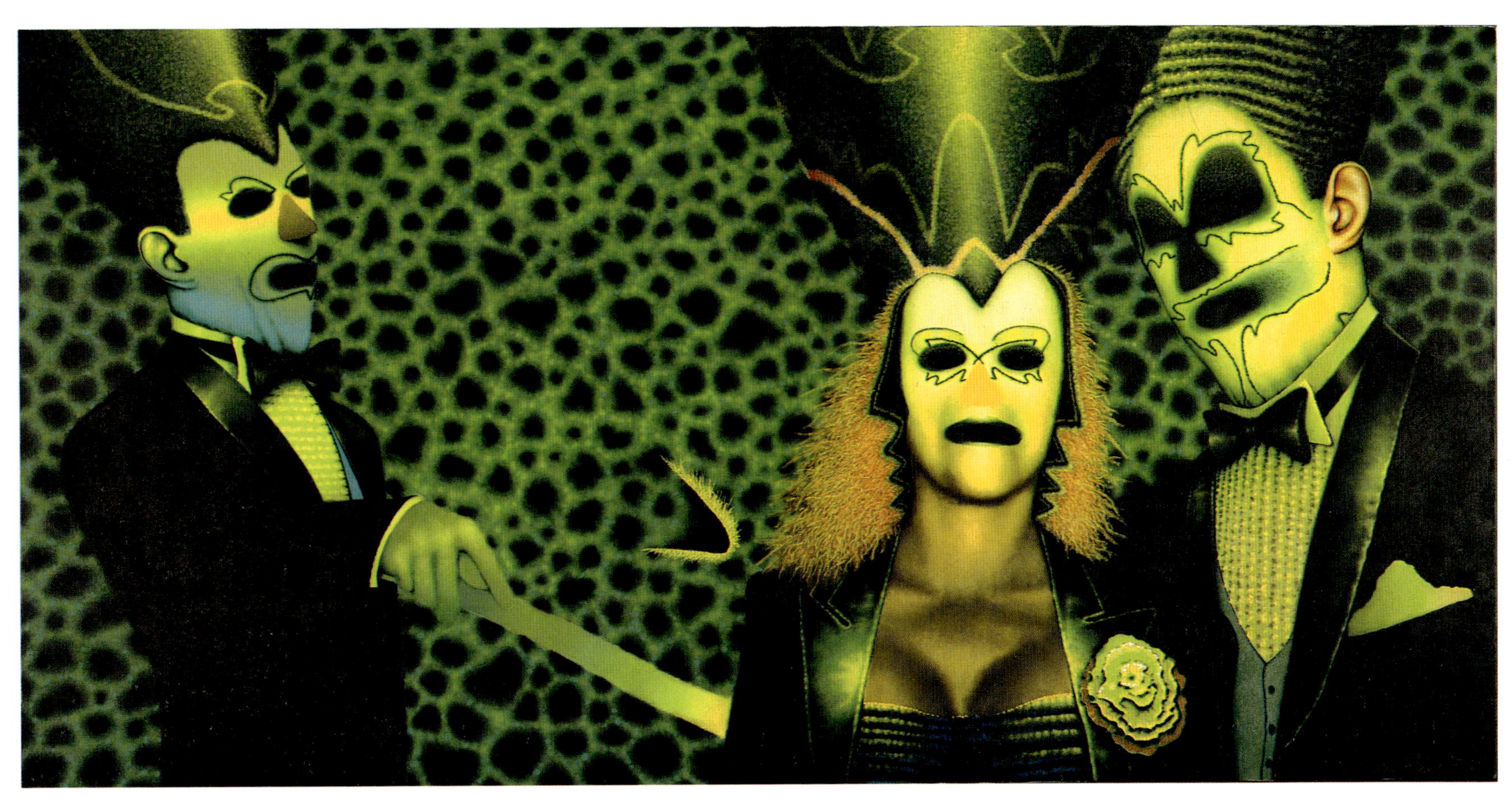

26
DURO-VERDE, 1978

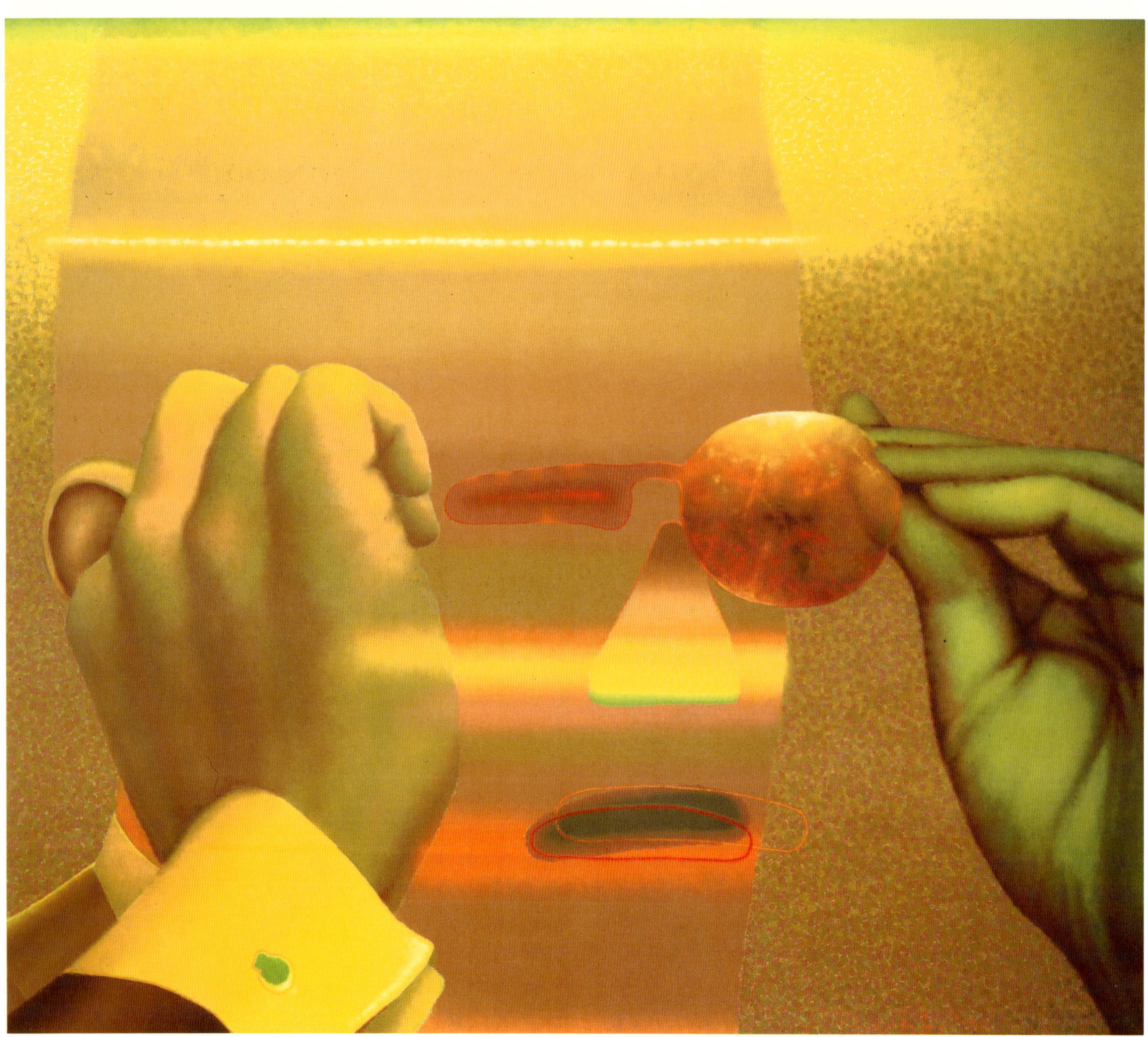

AMBROSIA, 1979

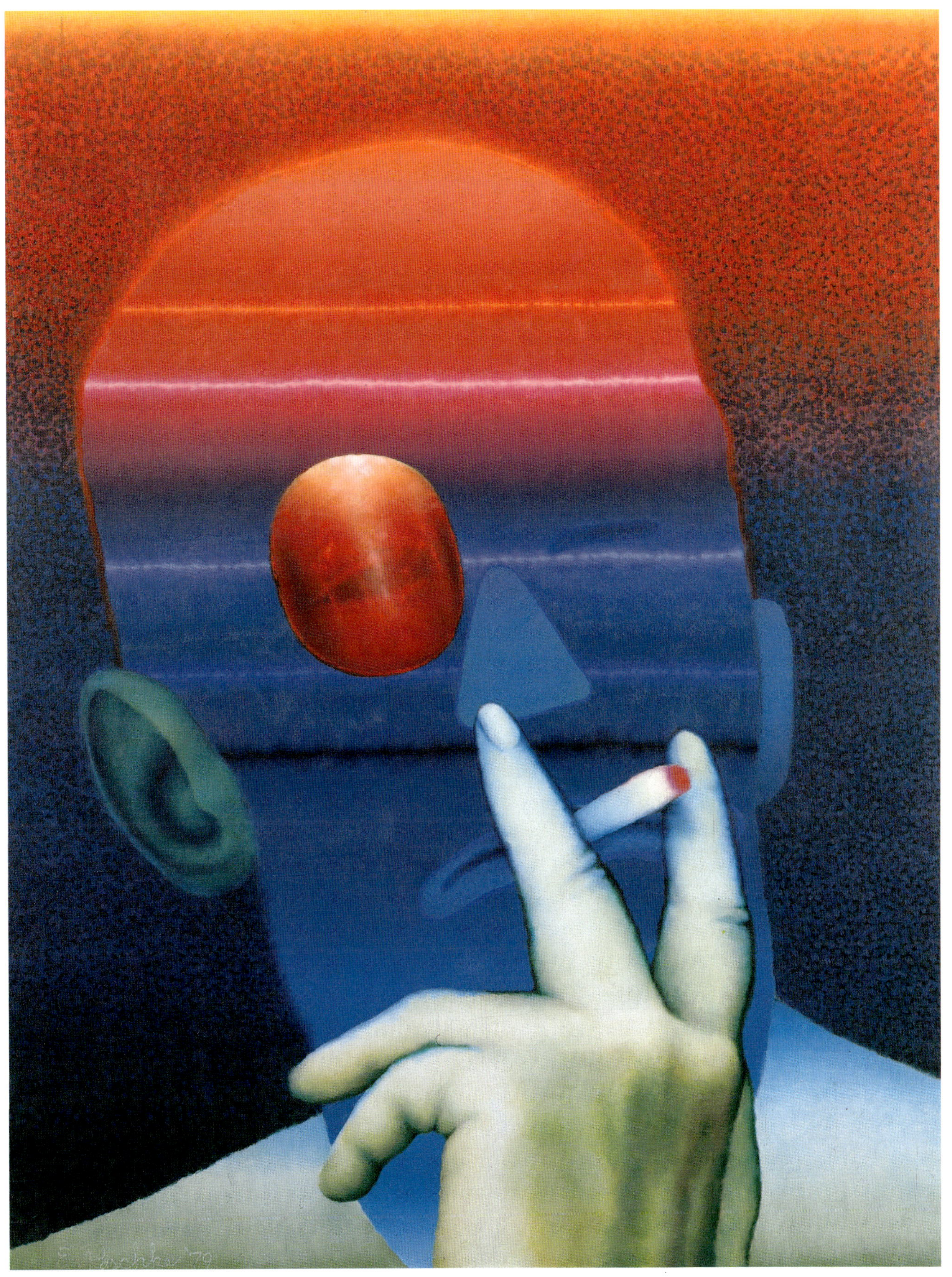

28
FUMAR, 1979

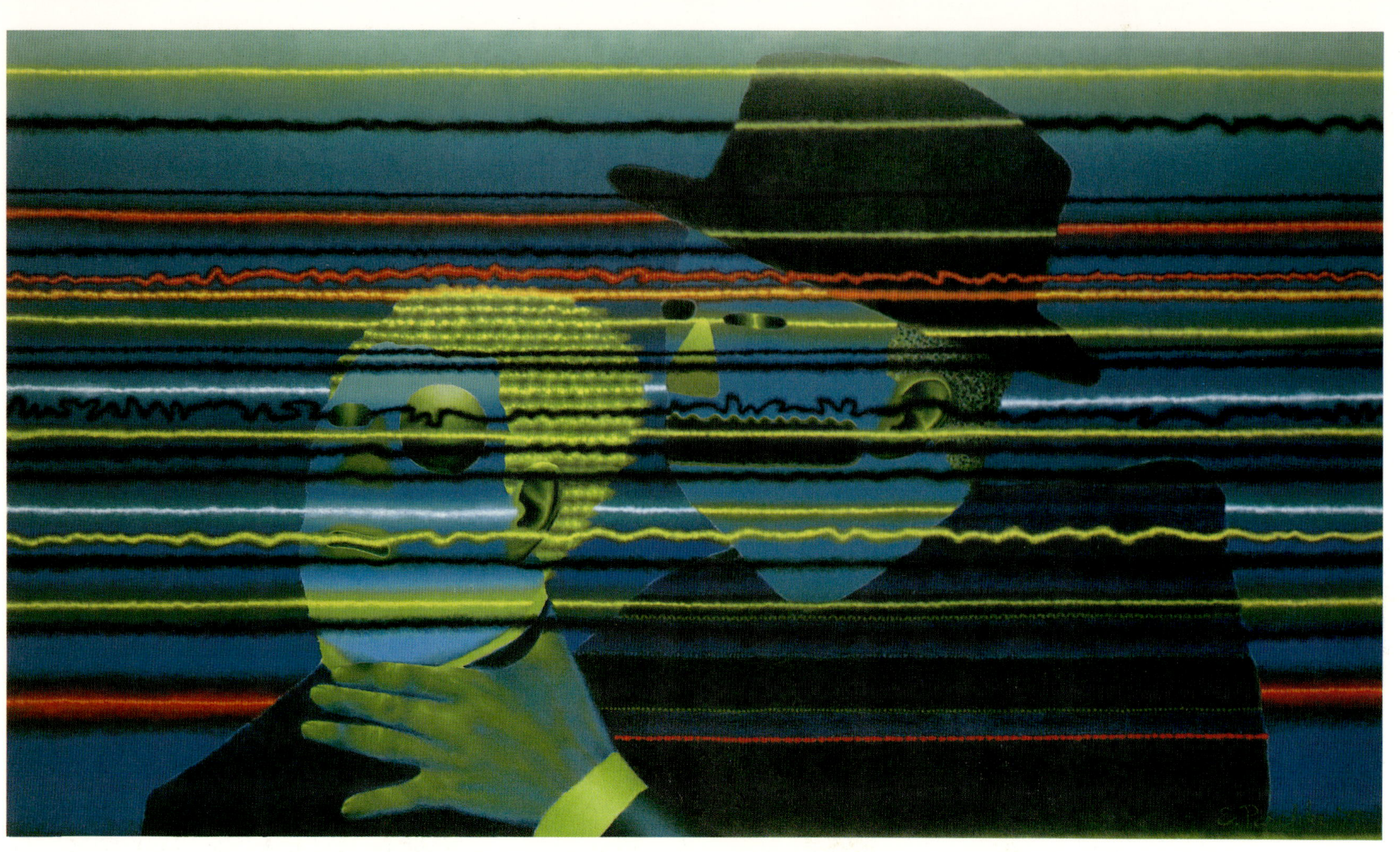

STRANGULITA, 1979

NERVOSA, 1980

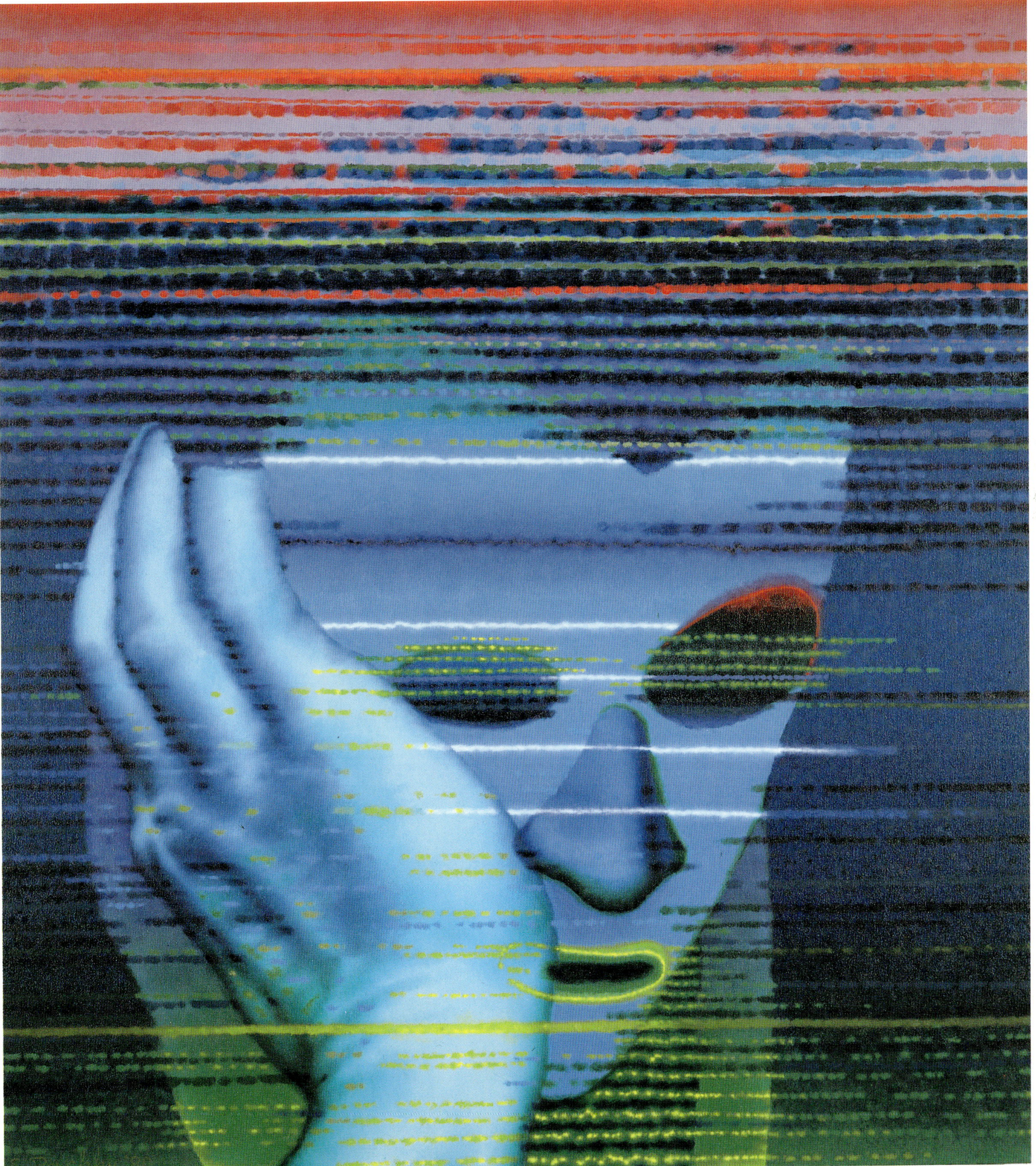

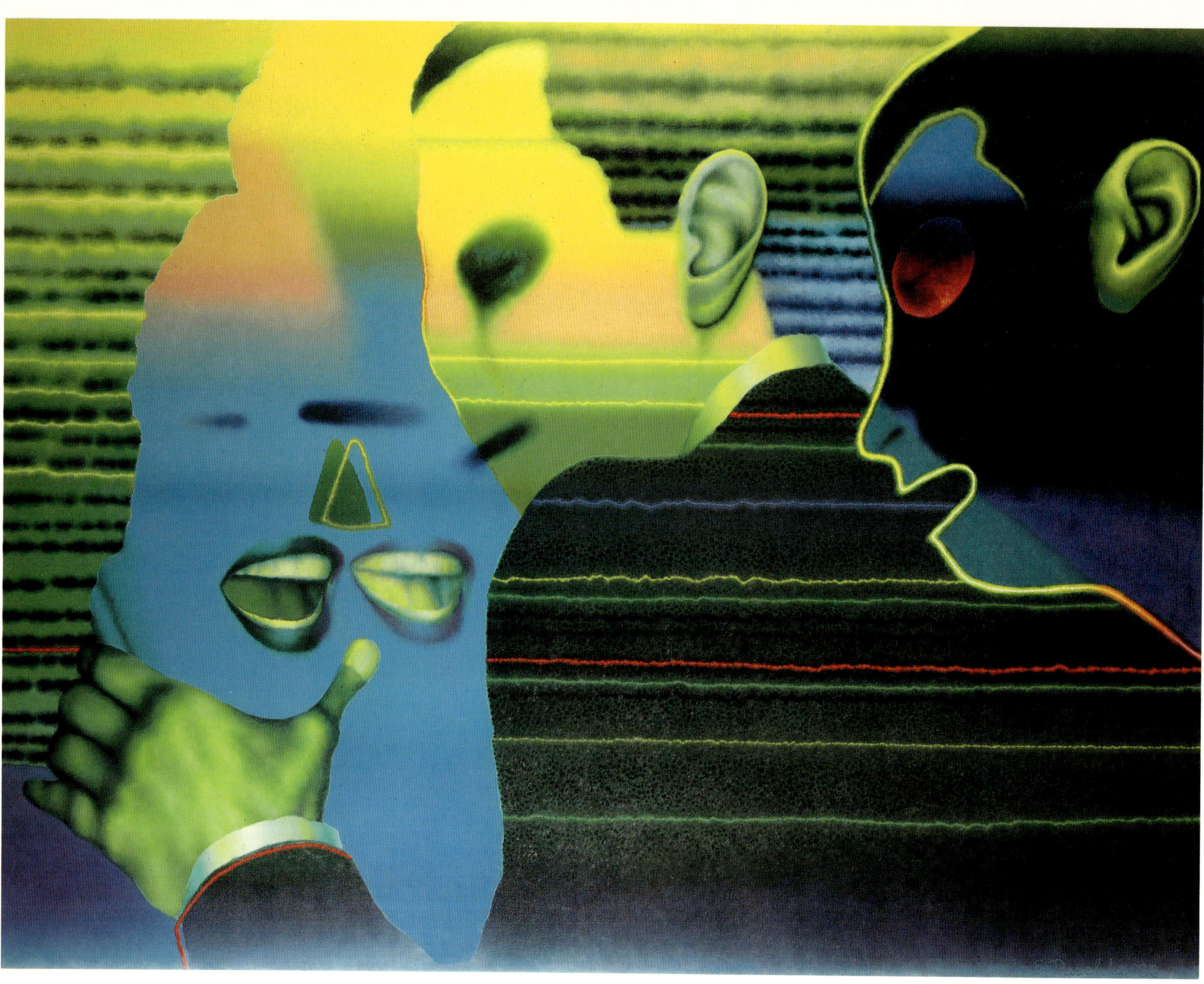

31
VIOLENCIA, 1980

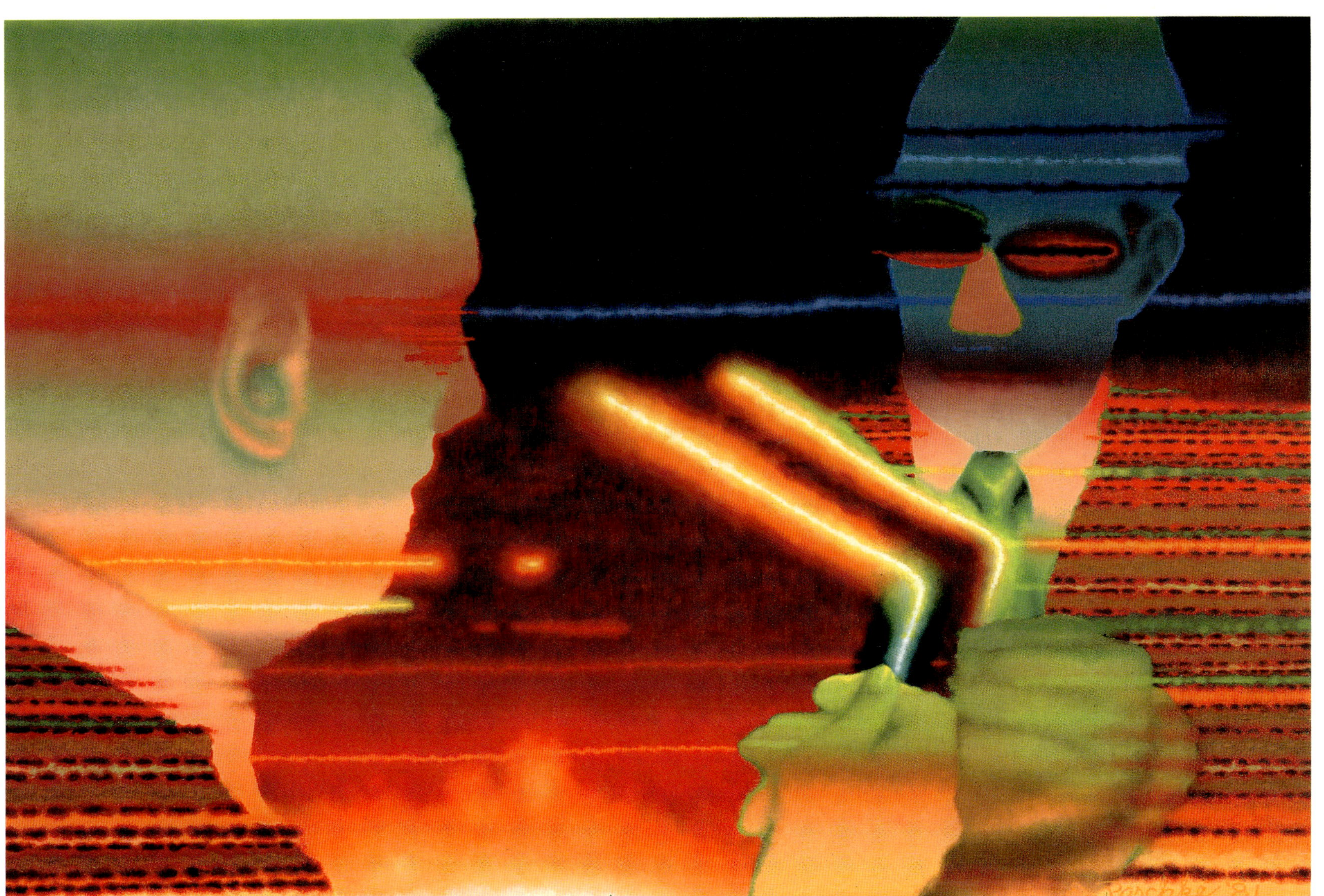

32
L'IMPRESSION, 1981

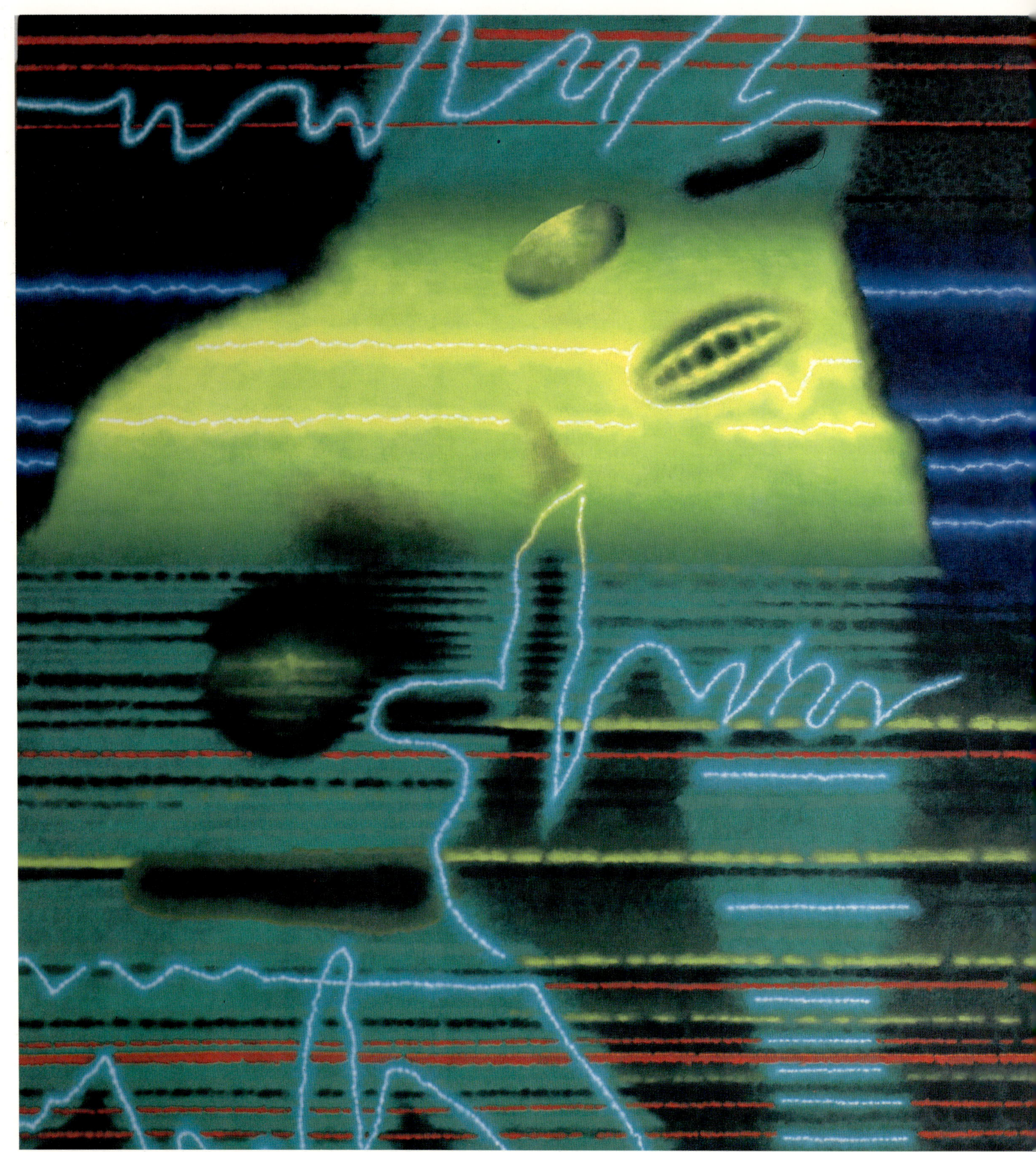

TELEVISMO, 1981

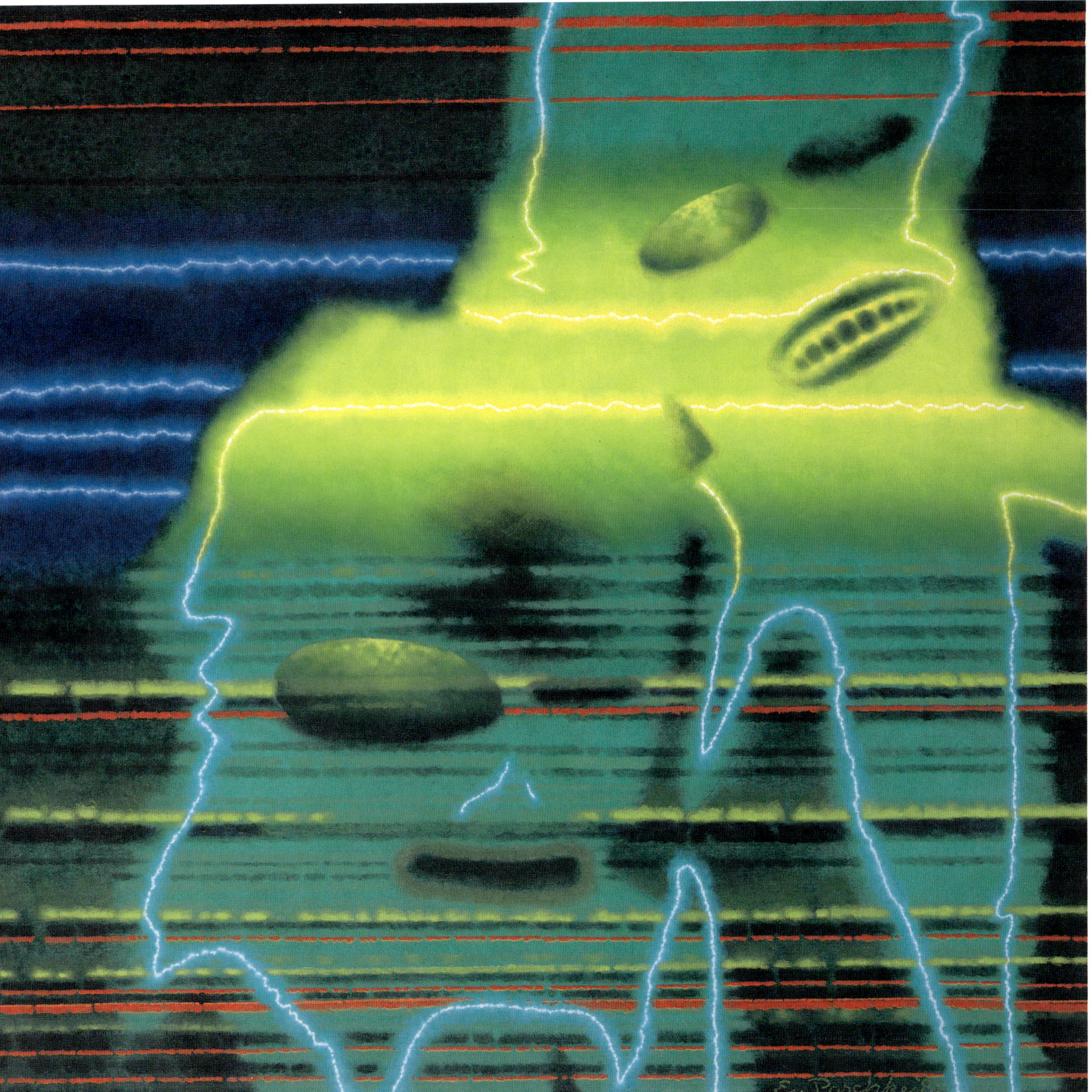

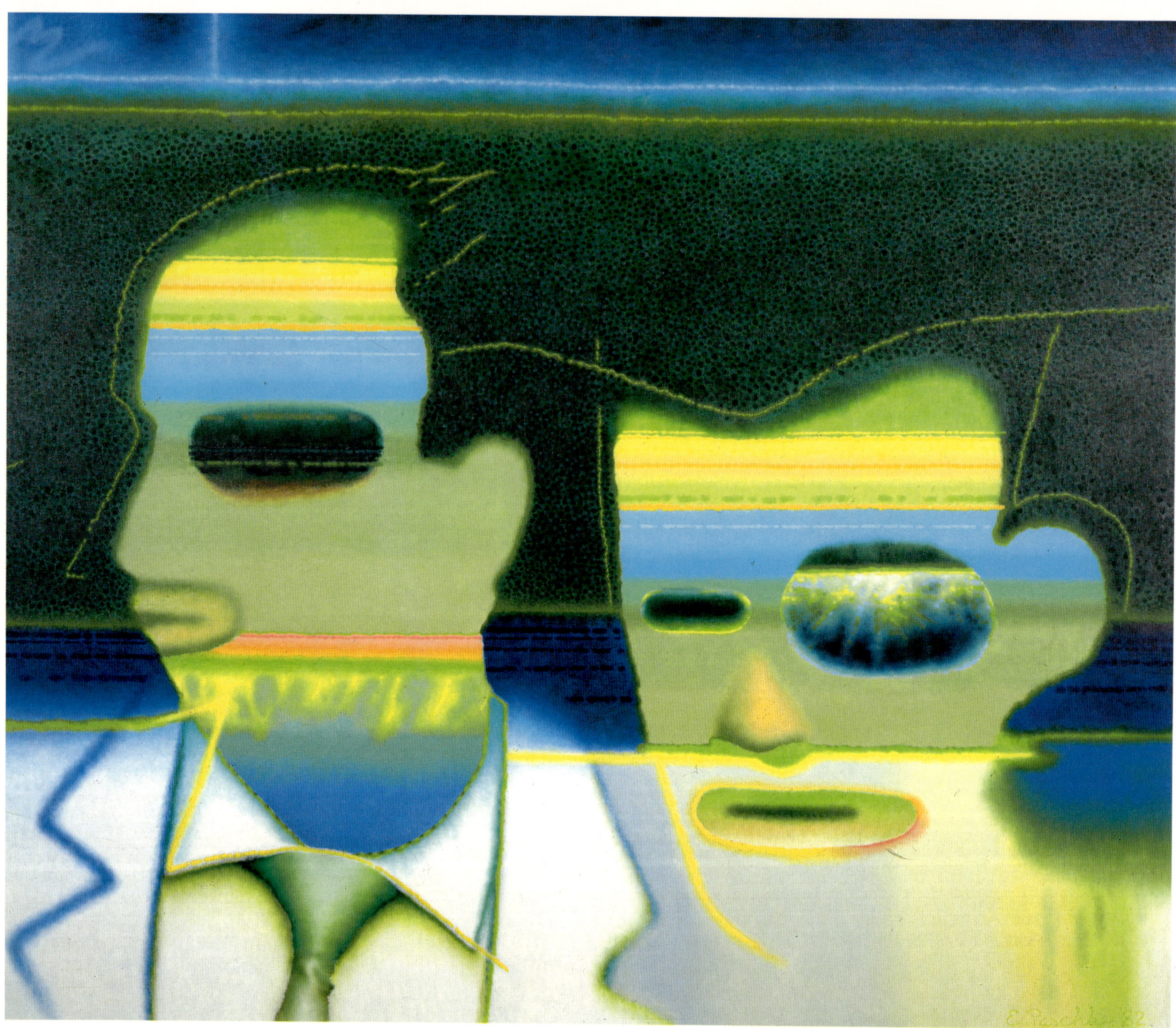

34
BIBUTSU, 1982

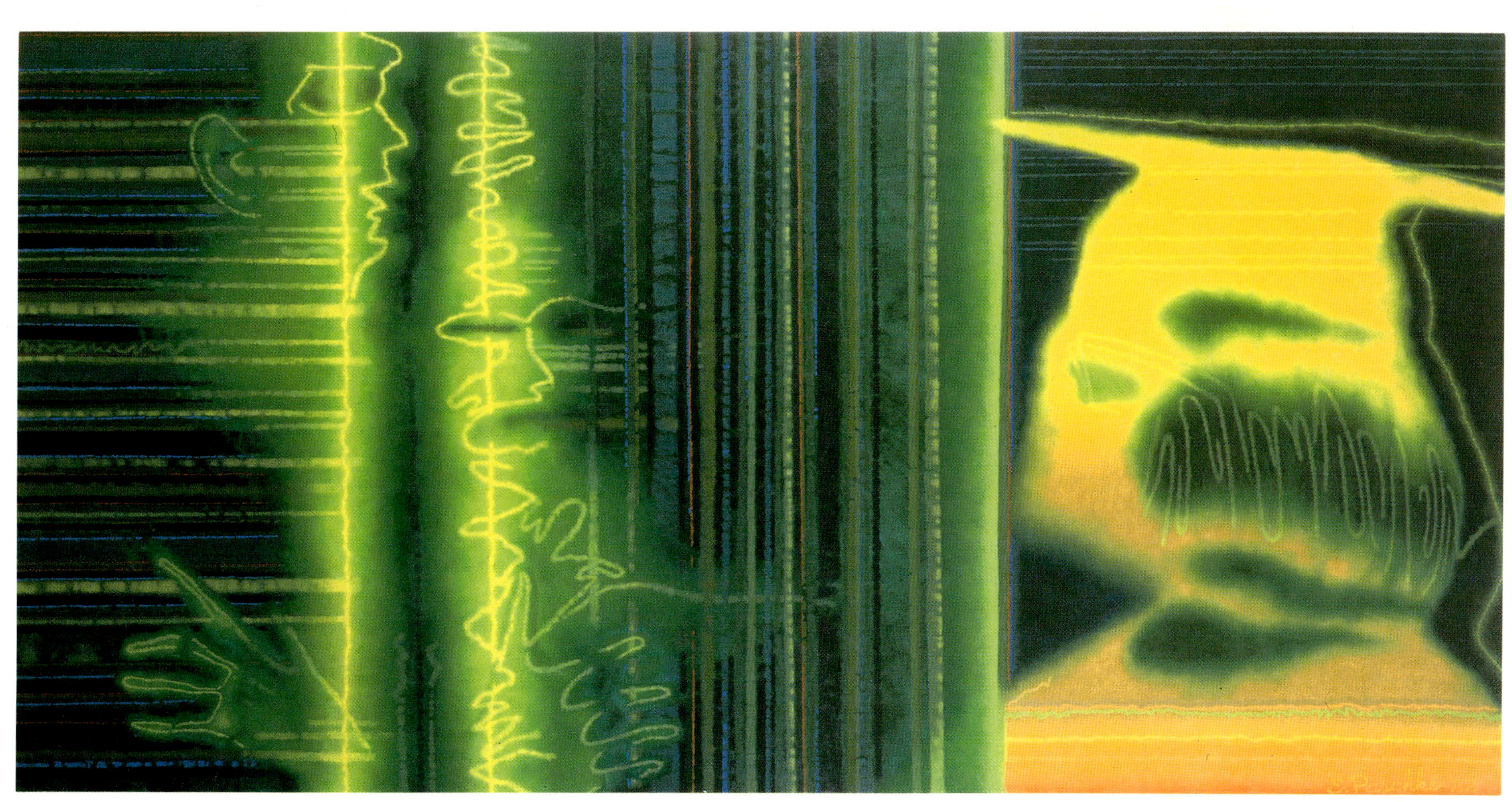

35

FERNSEHEN, 1982

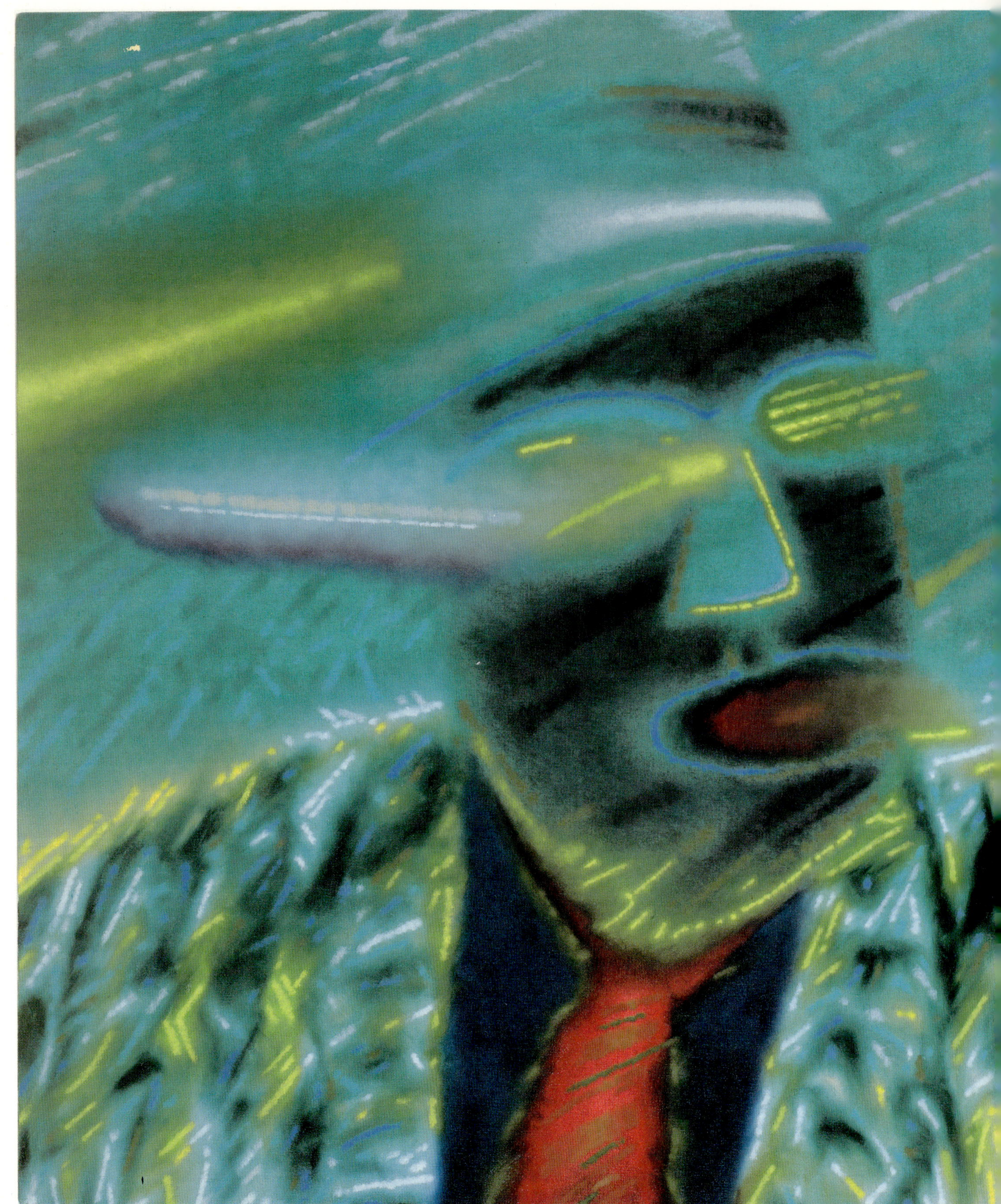

36
MECHANIQUE, 1982

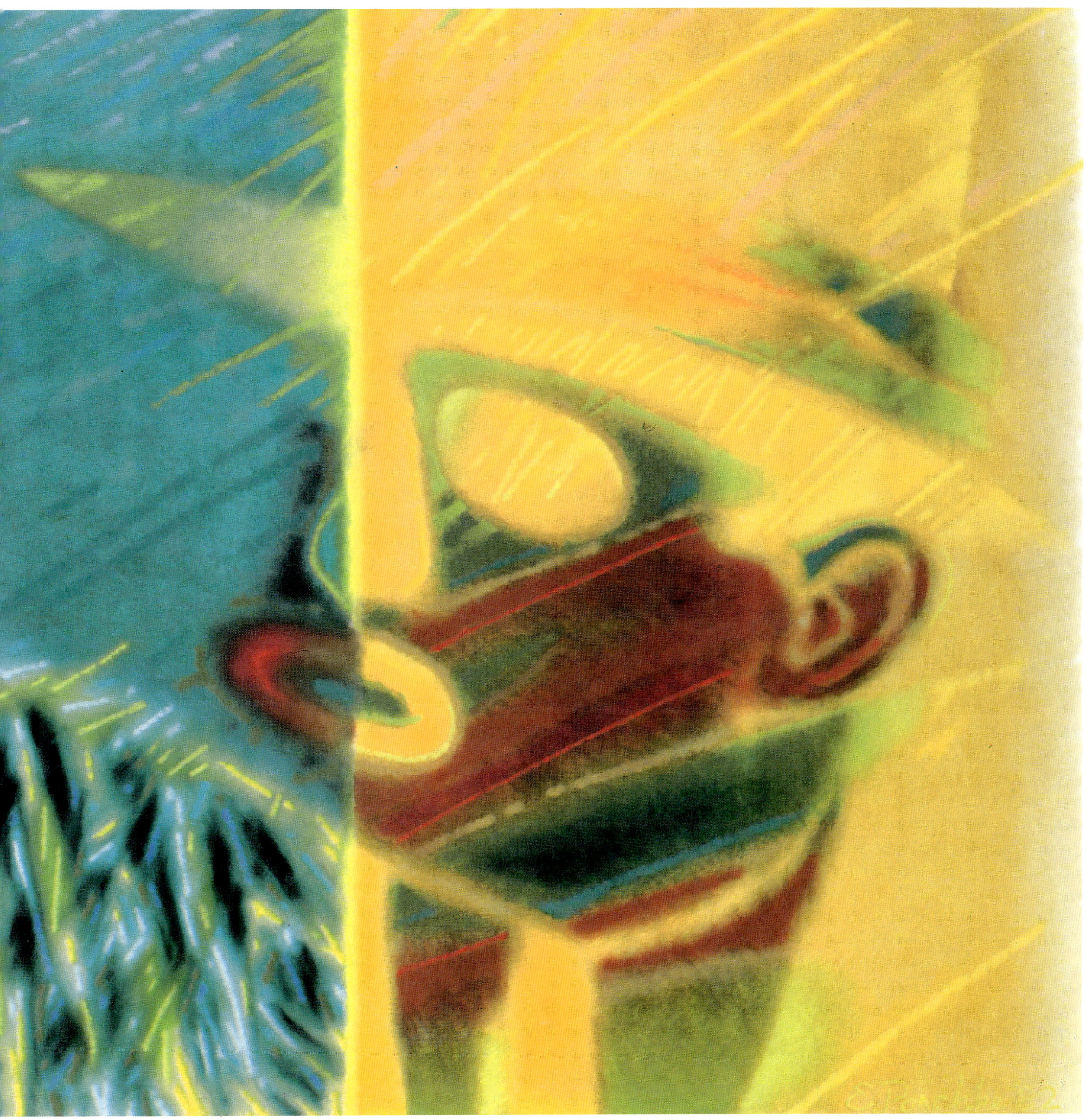

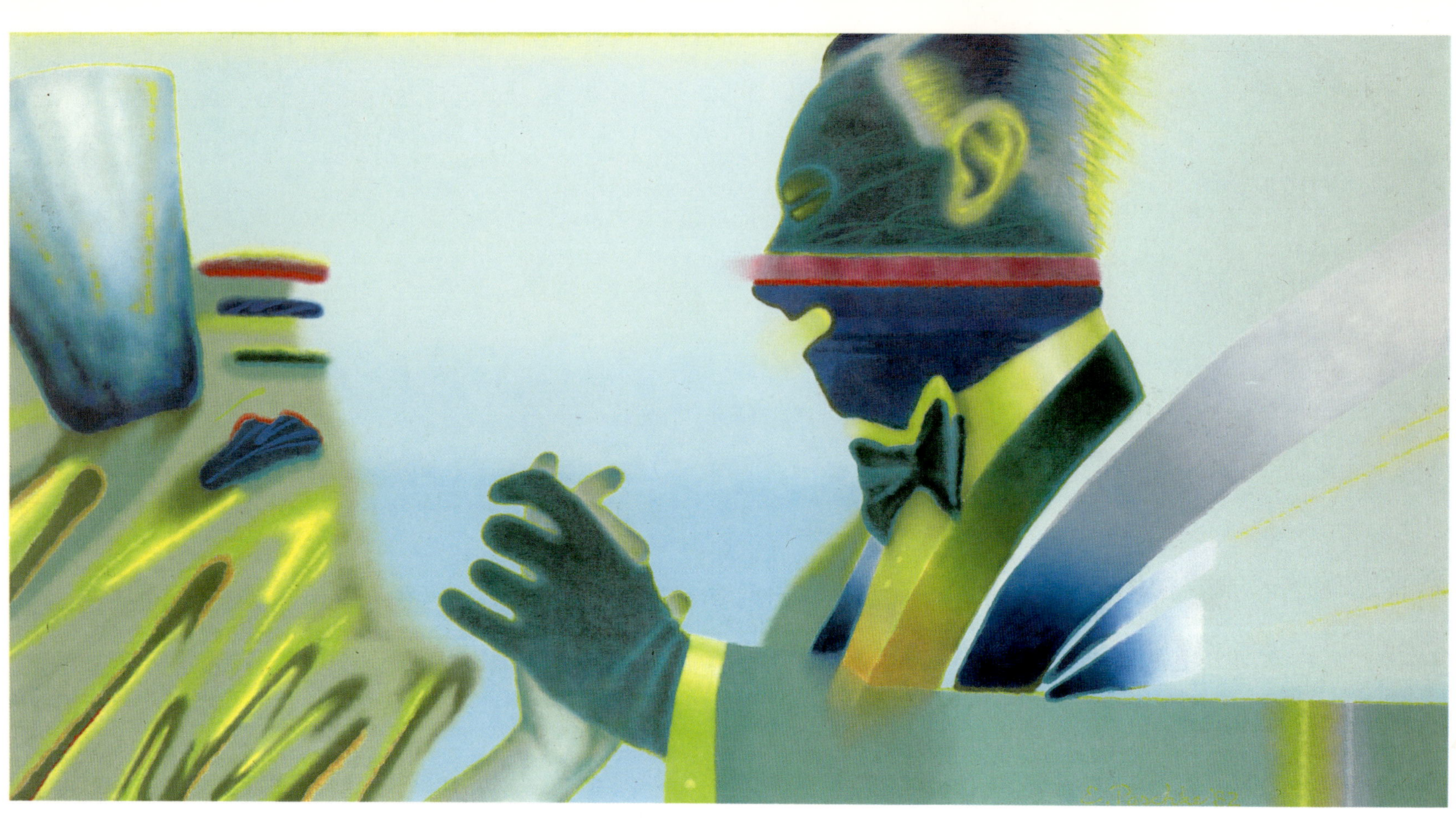

37
DER TANZ, 1982

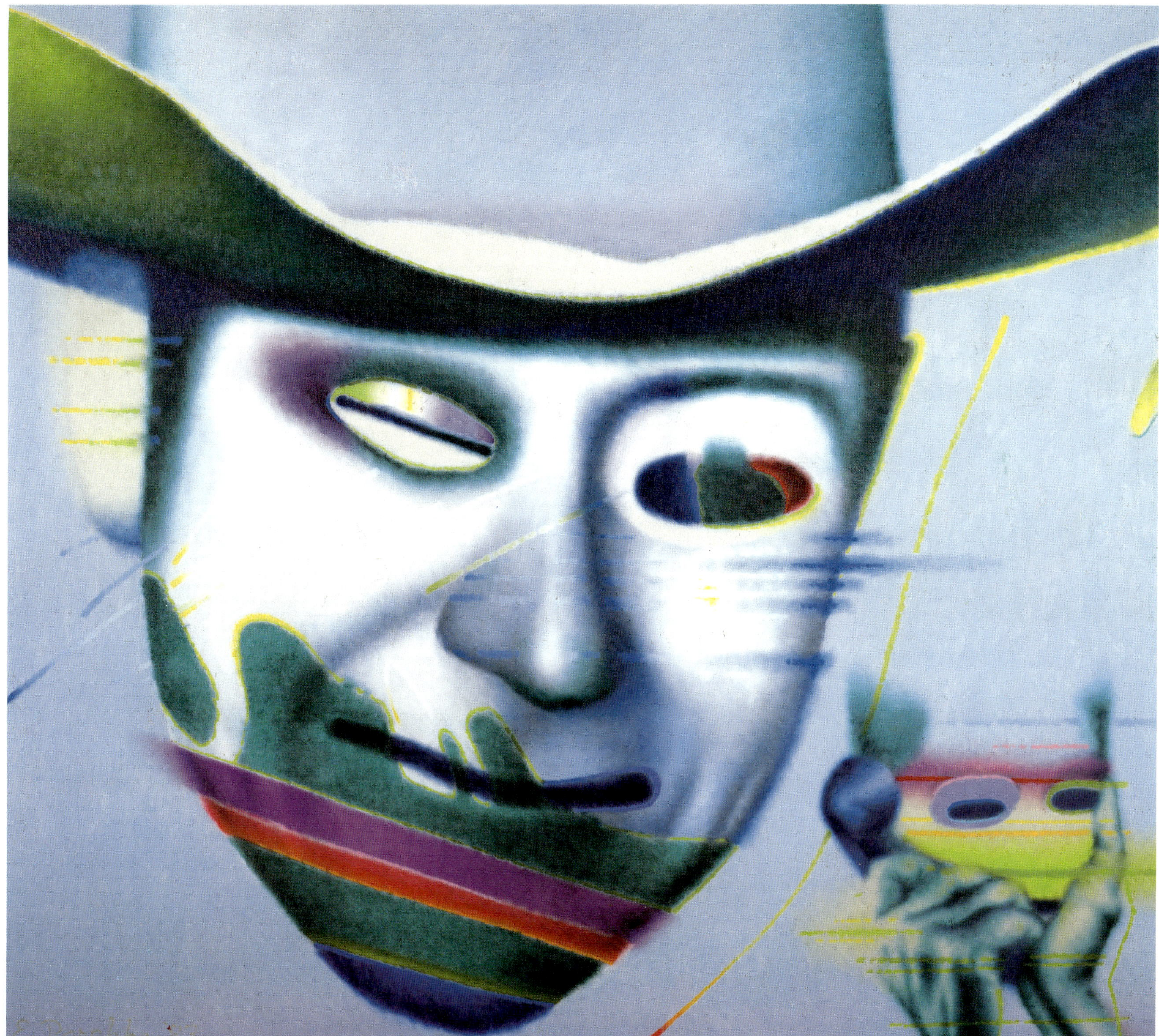

BAHAMAS, 1983

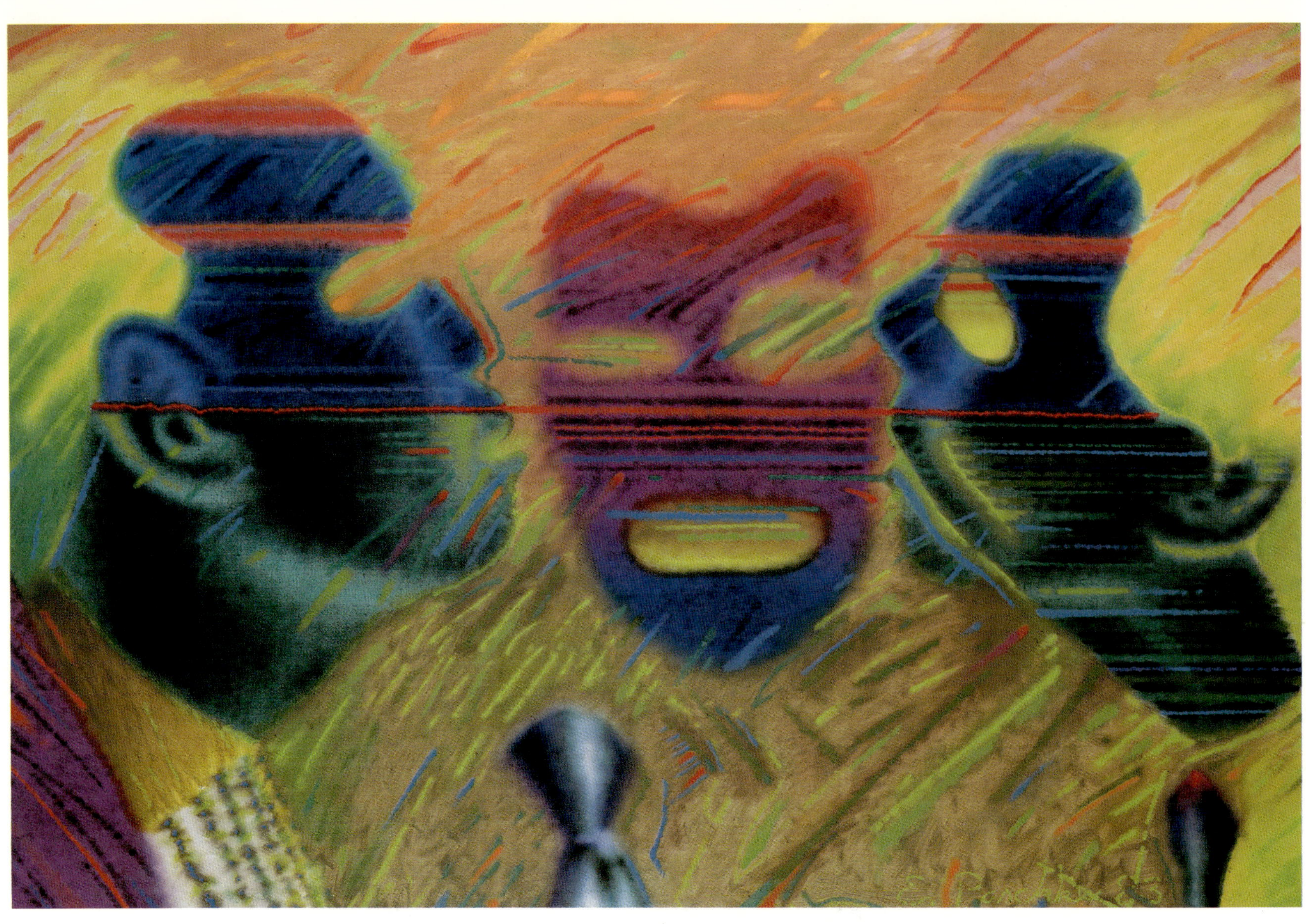

39
LE SAC, 1983

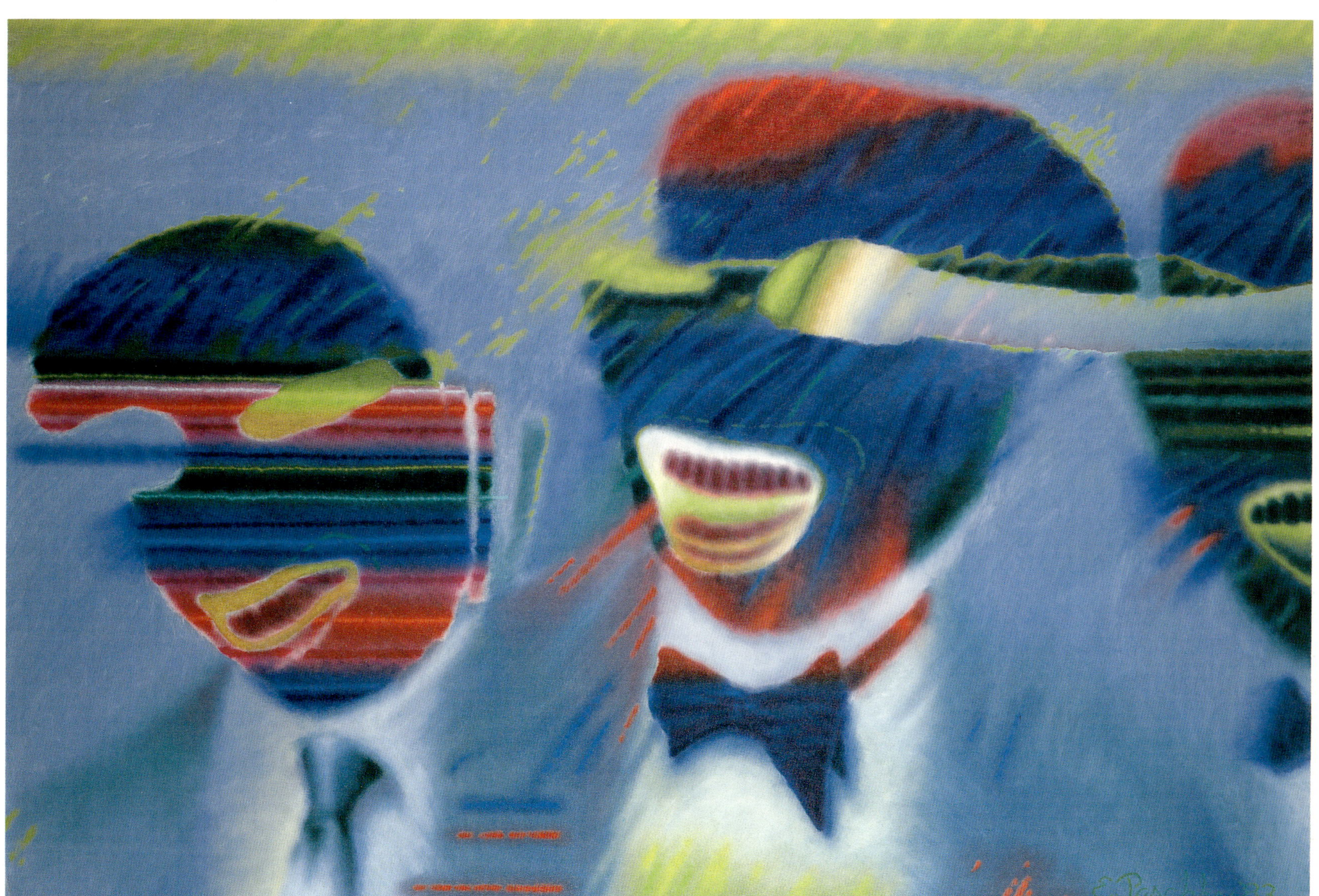

TOWANDA, 1983

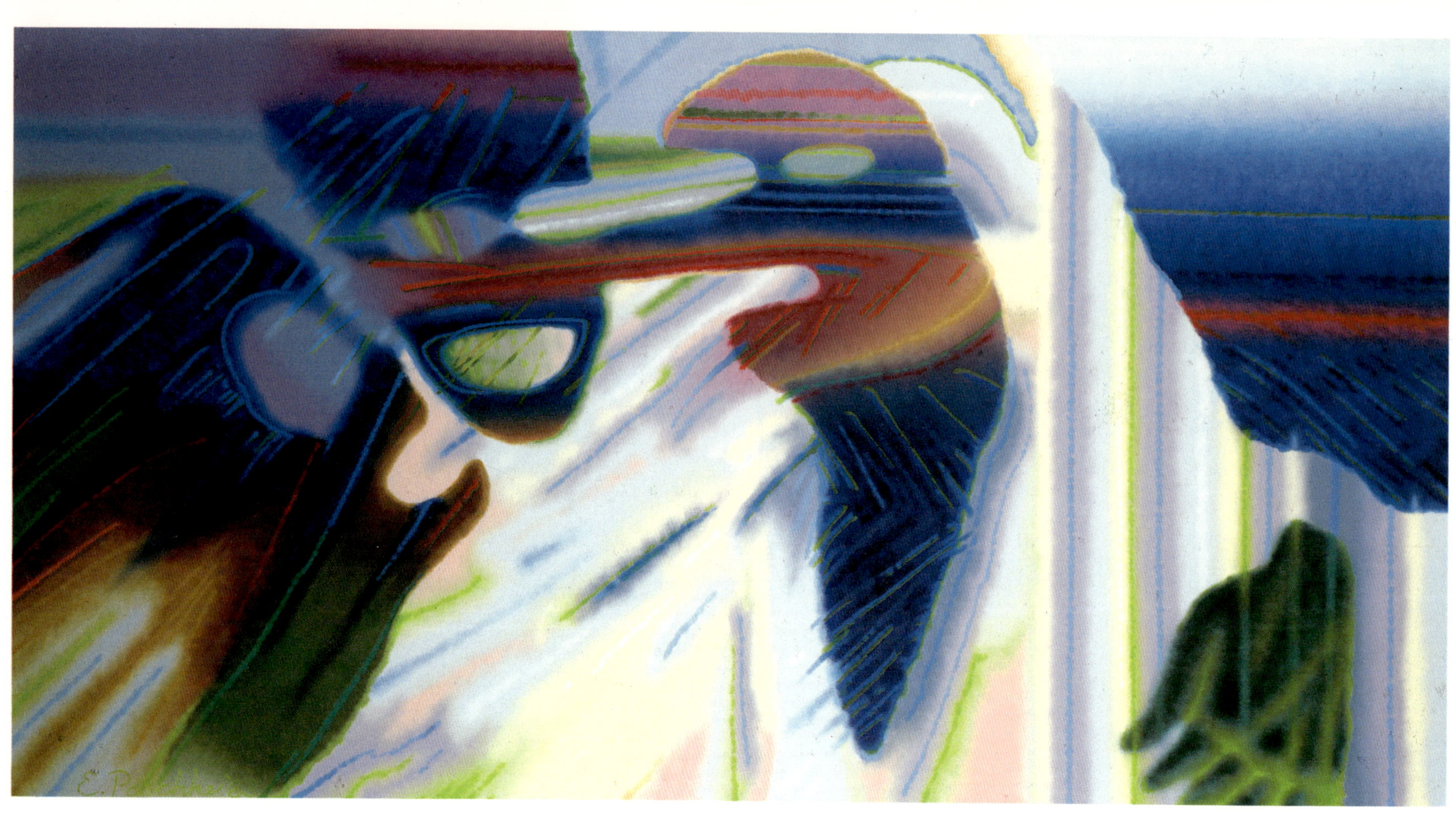

41
VOSOTROS, 1983

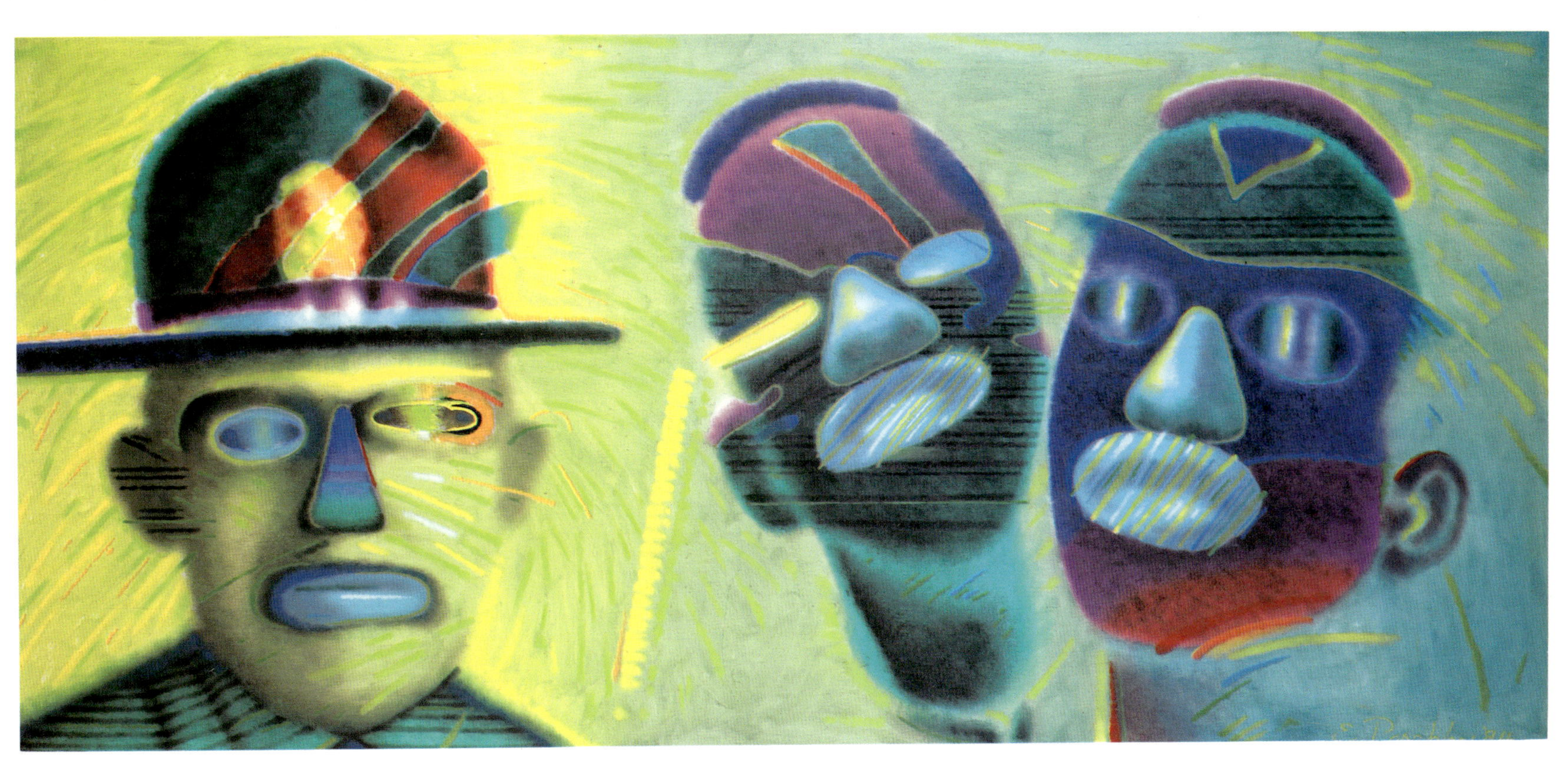

42

AFRIQUE, 1984

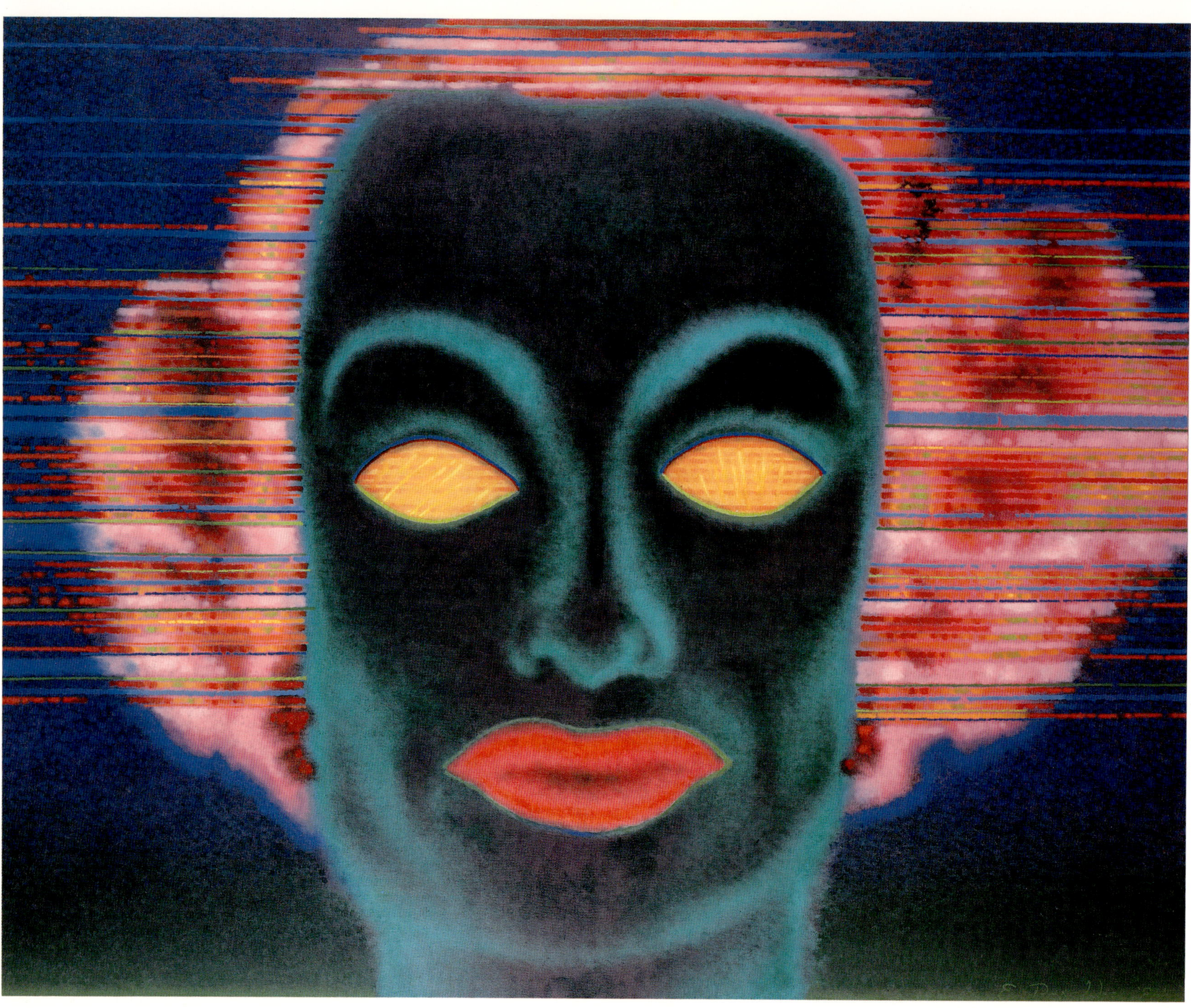

ELECTALADY, 1984

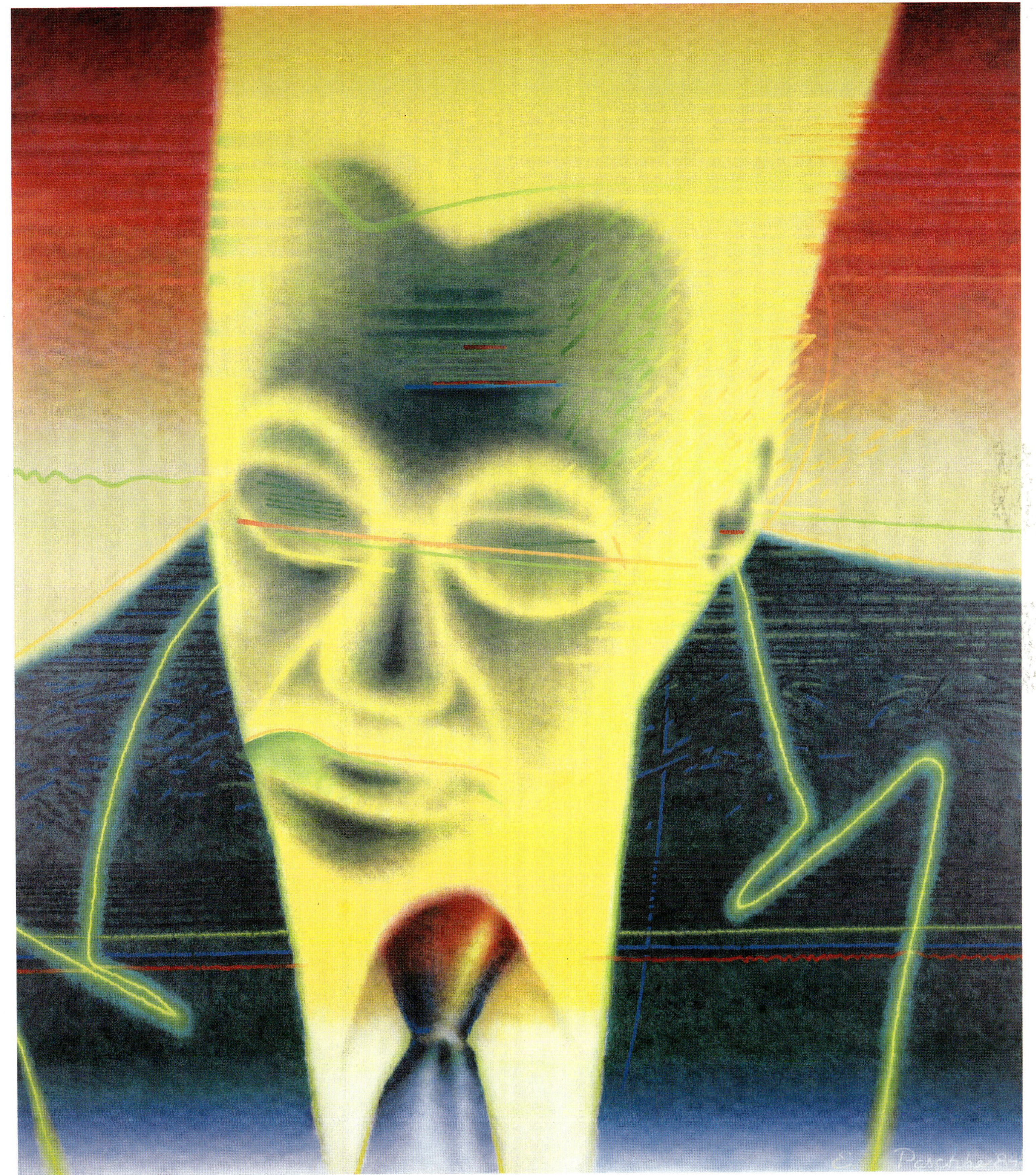

MALIBU, 1984

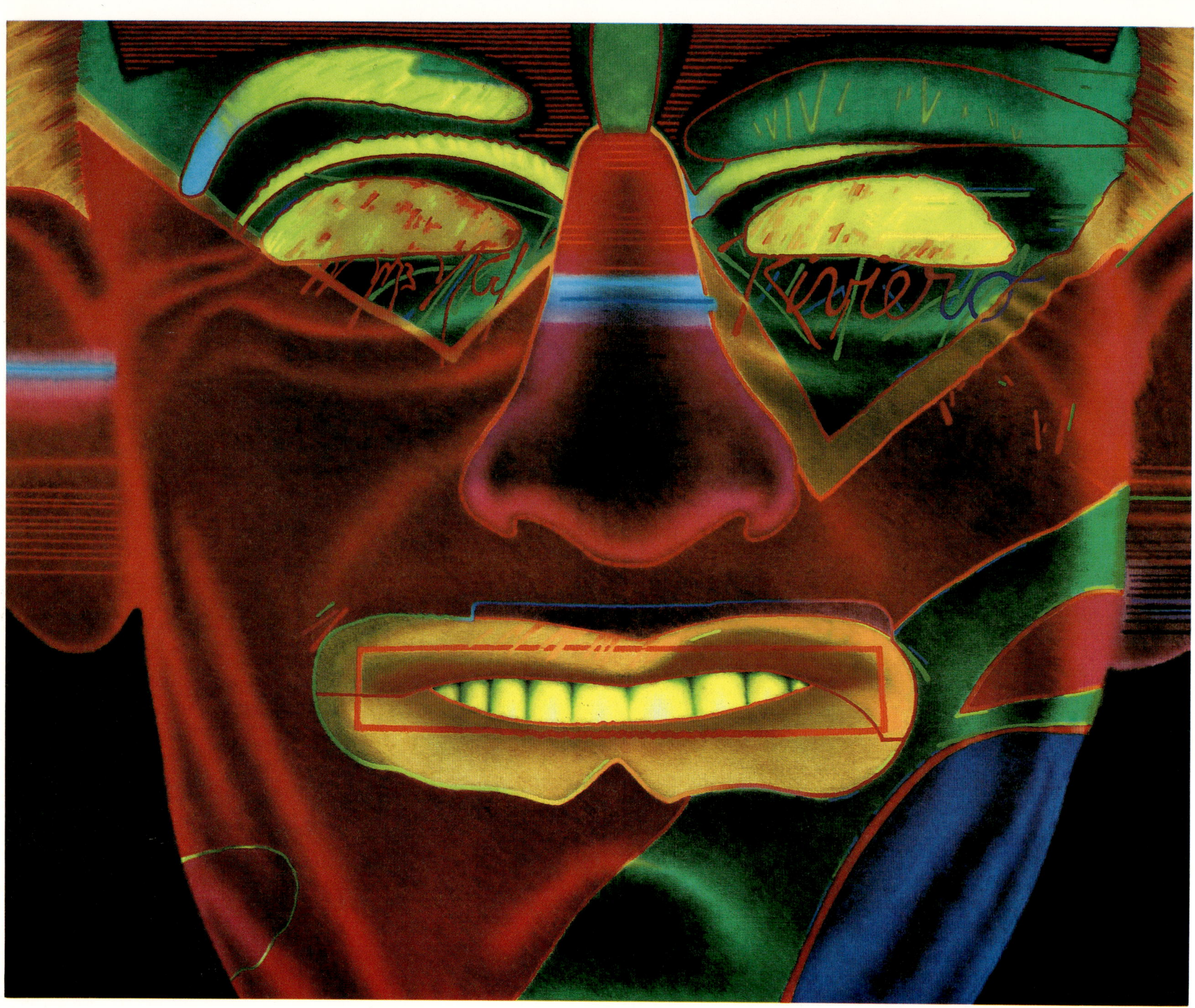

45
CALIENTE, 1985

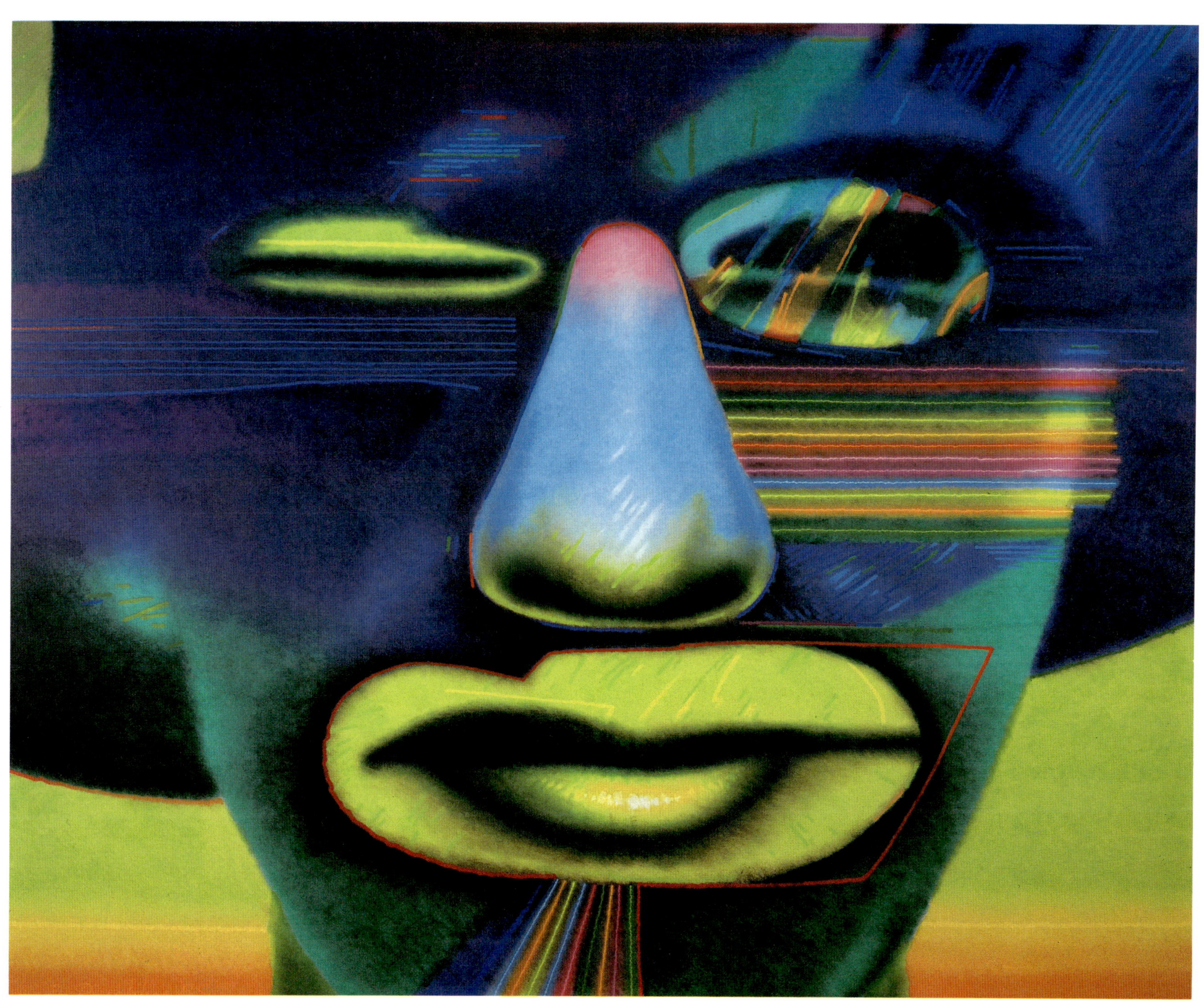

46

FRIO, 1985

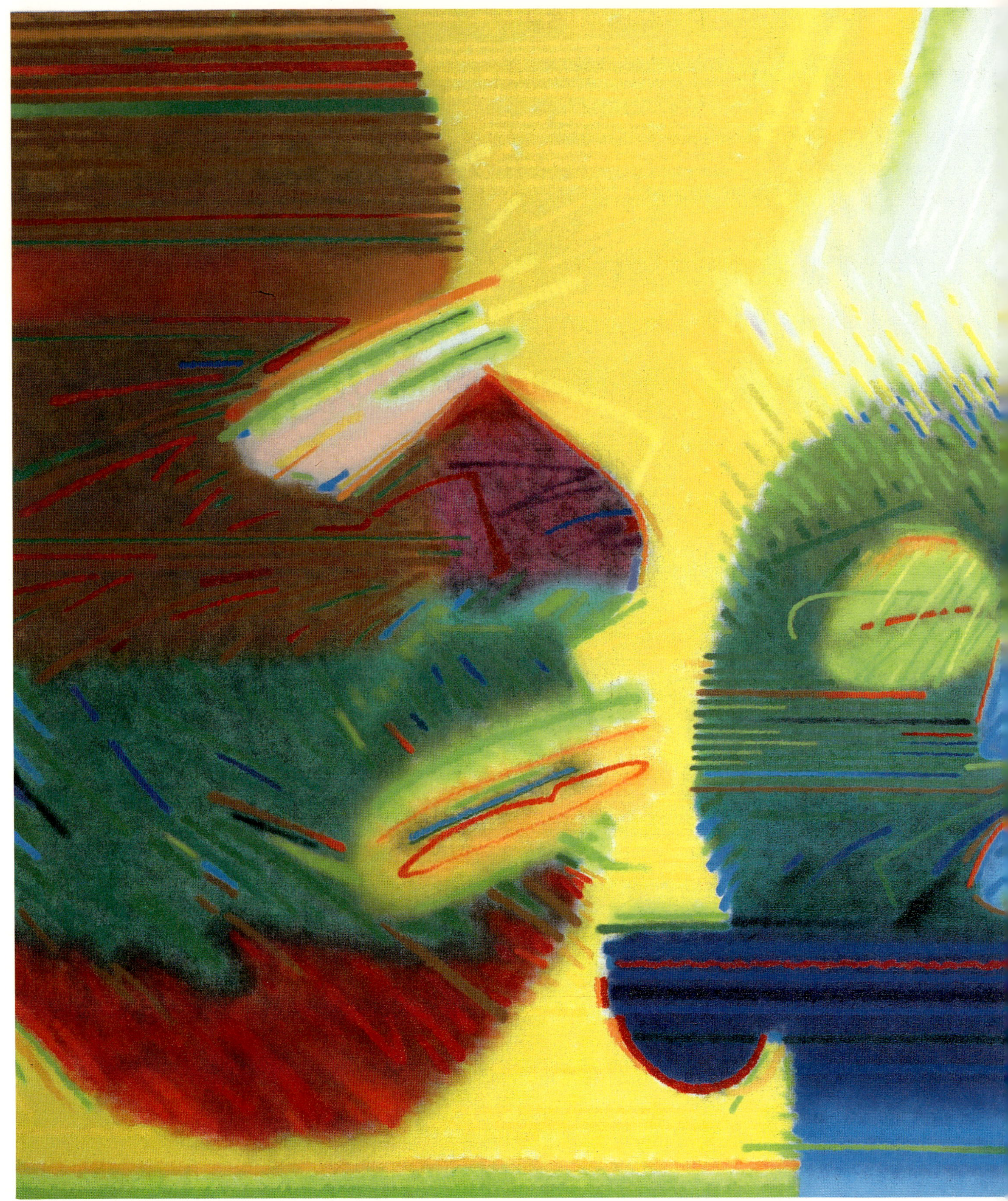

47
TROIKA, 1985

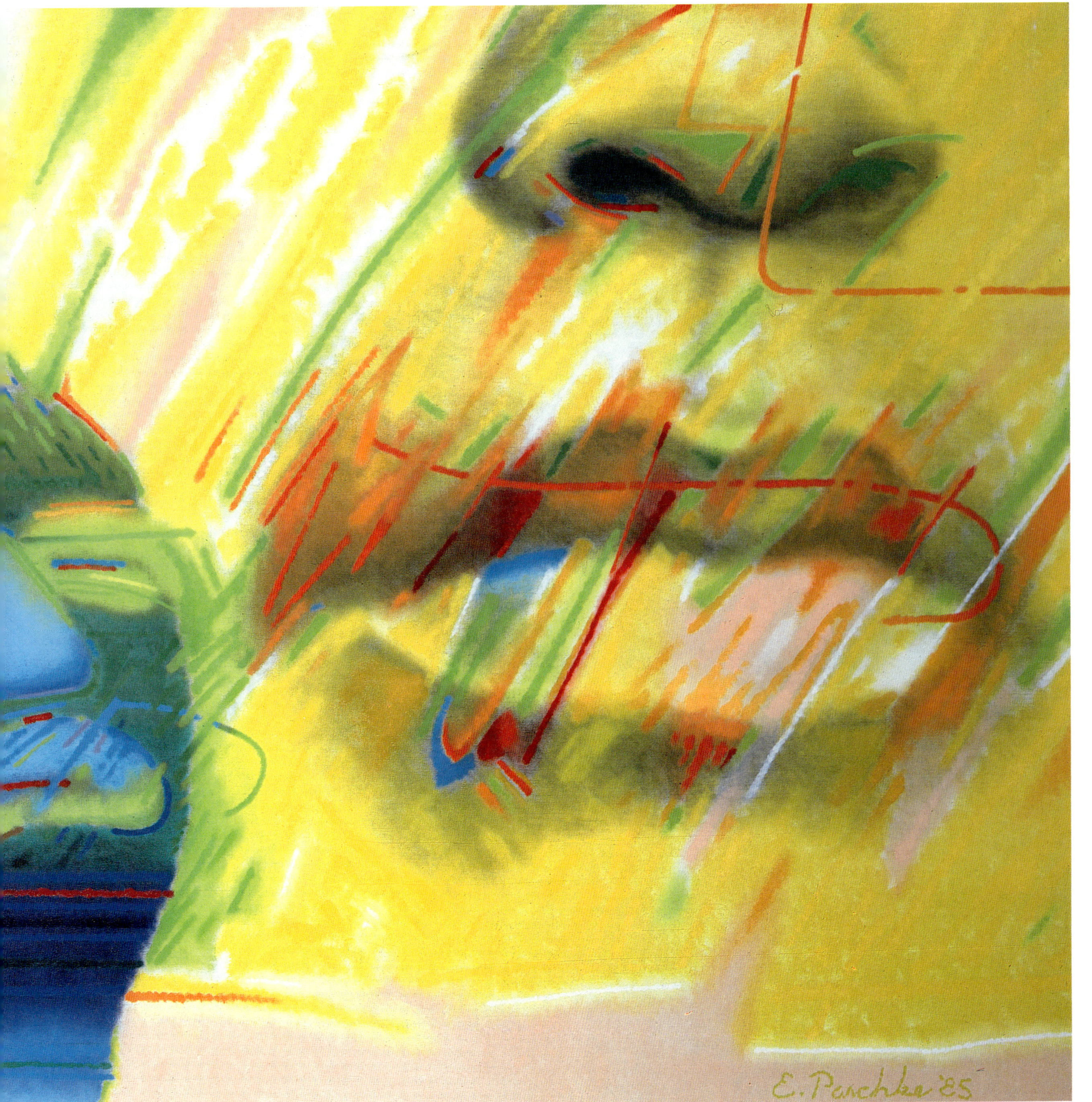
E. Paschke '85

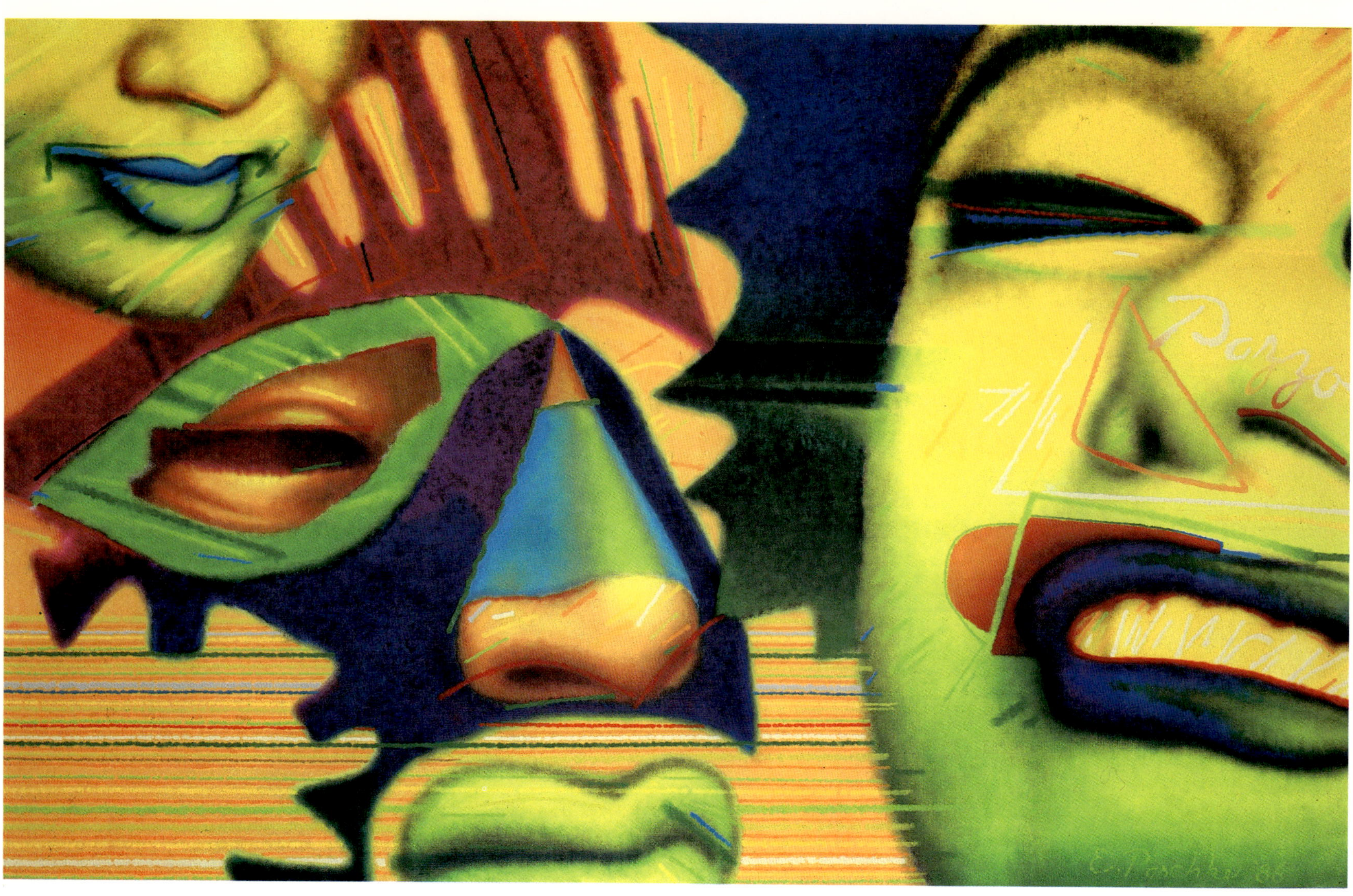

48
PAZZO, 1986

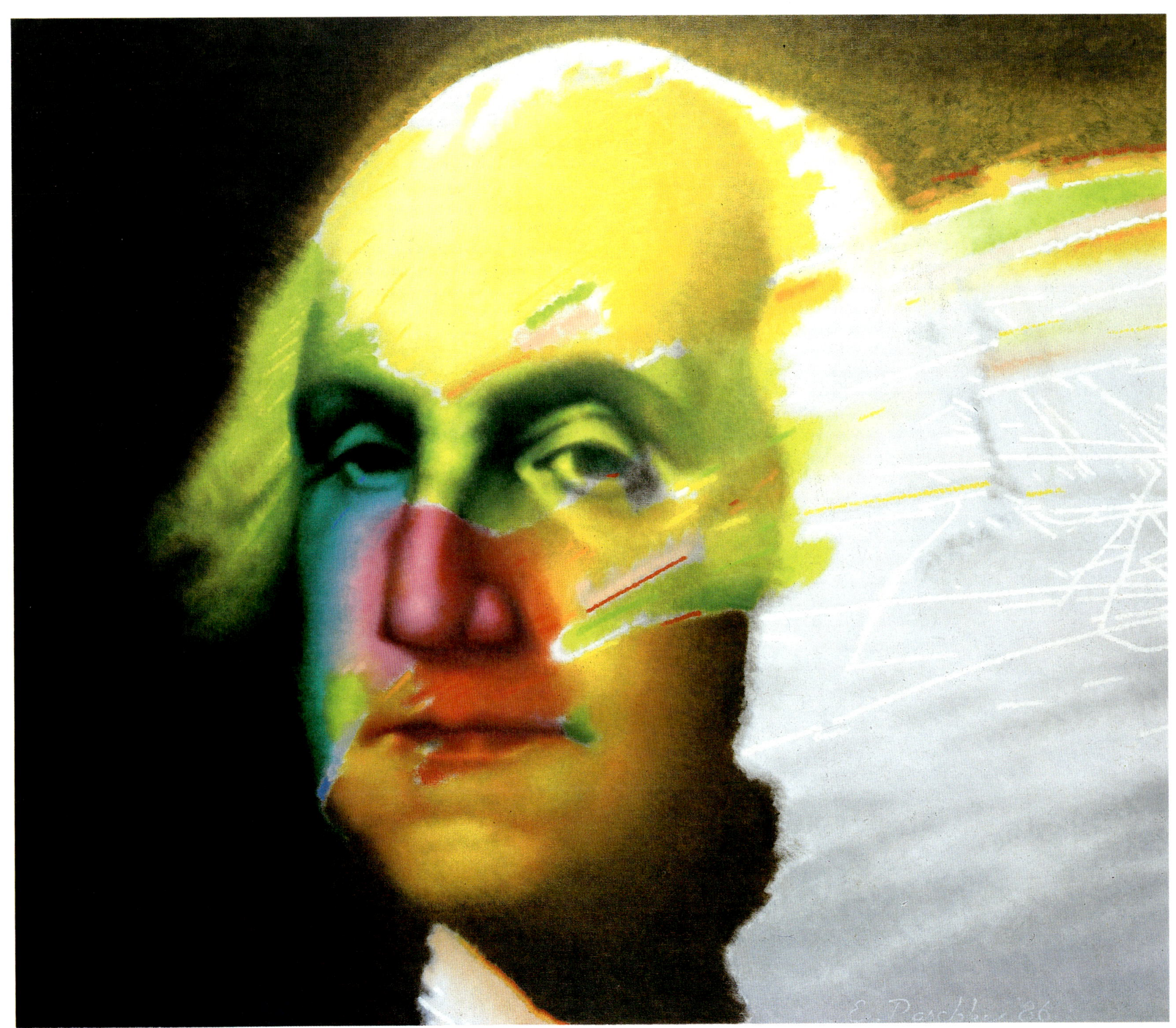

PRIMA VERE, 1986

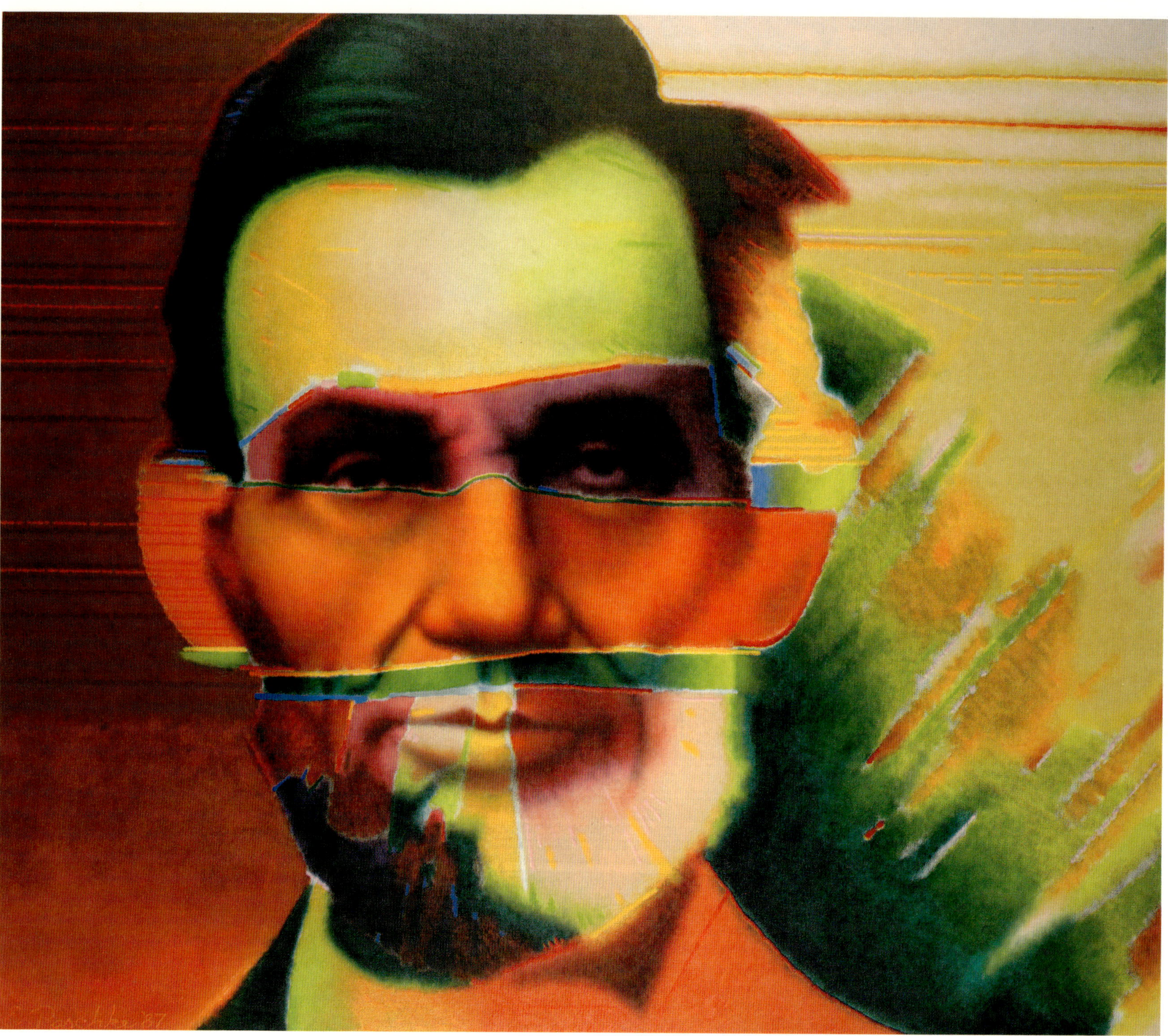

52
LIBREDO, 1987

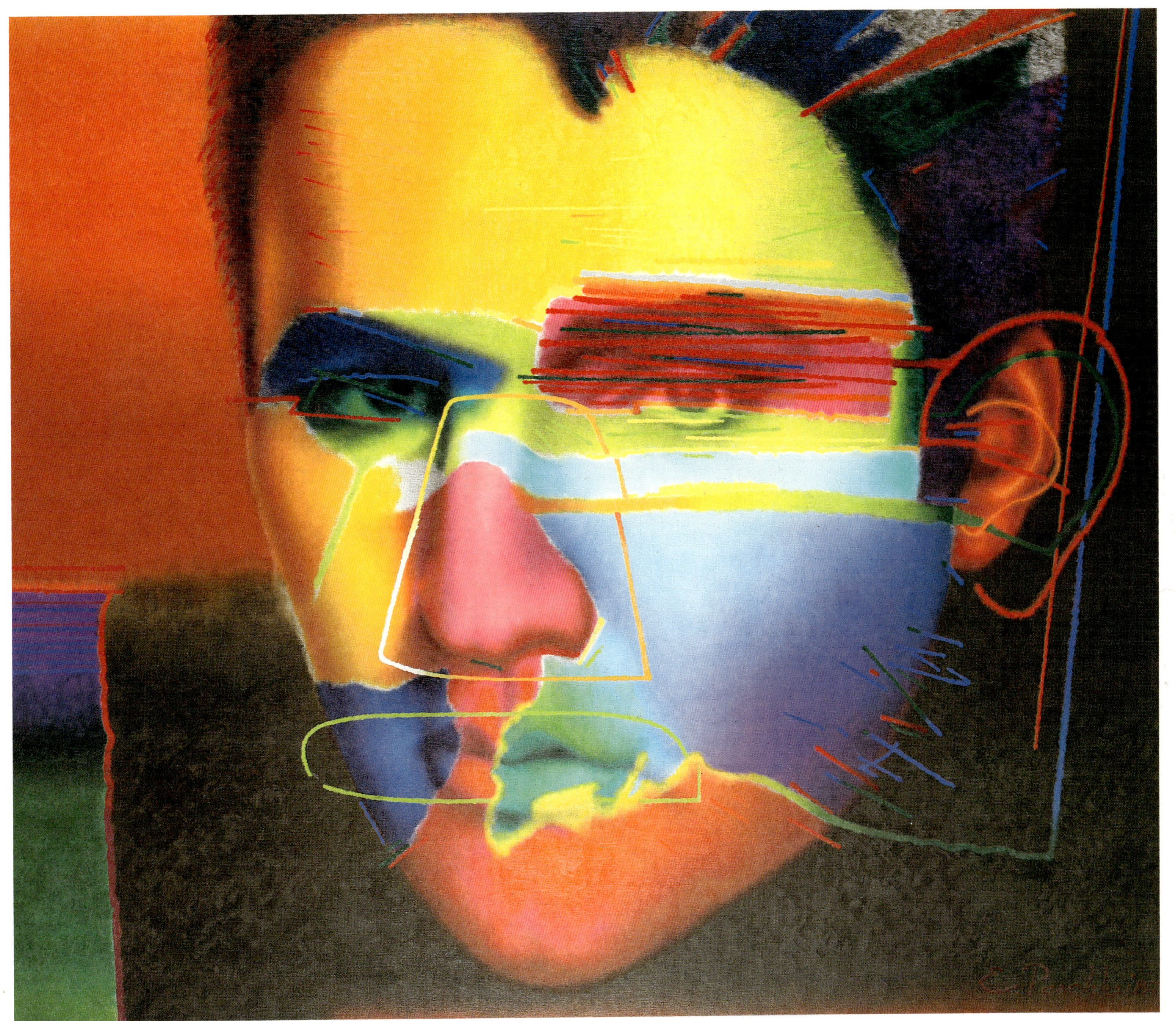

MATINEE, 1987

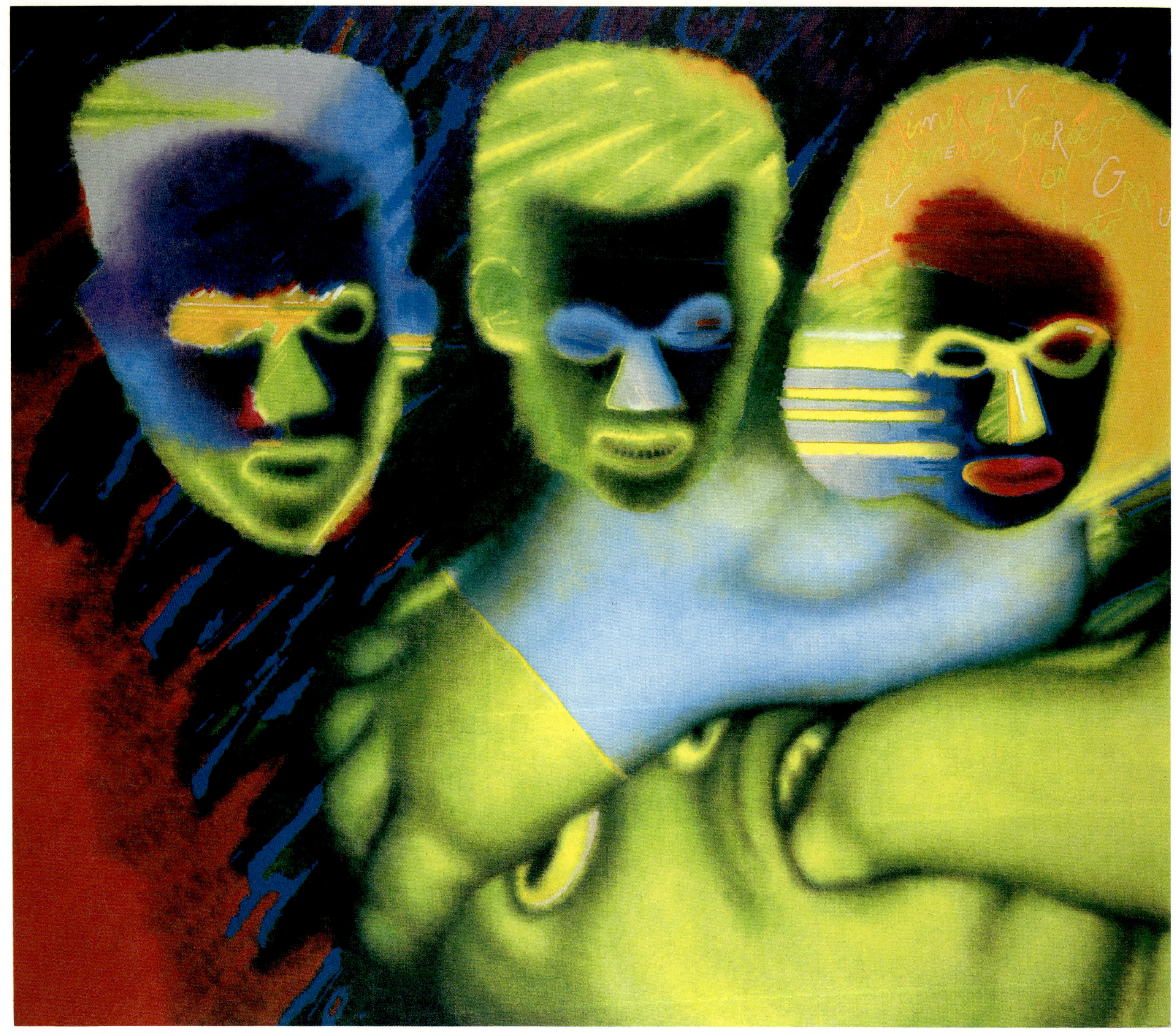

54

PAPAL LUNACY, 1987

OIL ON LINEN

172.7 × 203.2 CM (68 × 80 IN.)

COLLECTION KAREN AND TONY BARONE,
VENICE, CALIFORNIA

55

PEDIFEM, 1987

OIL ON LINEN

203.2 × 203.2 CM (80 × 80 IN.)

MILWAUKEE ART MUSEUM, PURCHASE WITH
NATIONAL ENDOWMENT FOR THE ARTS
MATCHING FUNDS

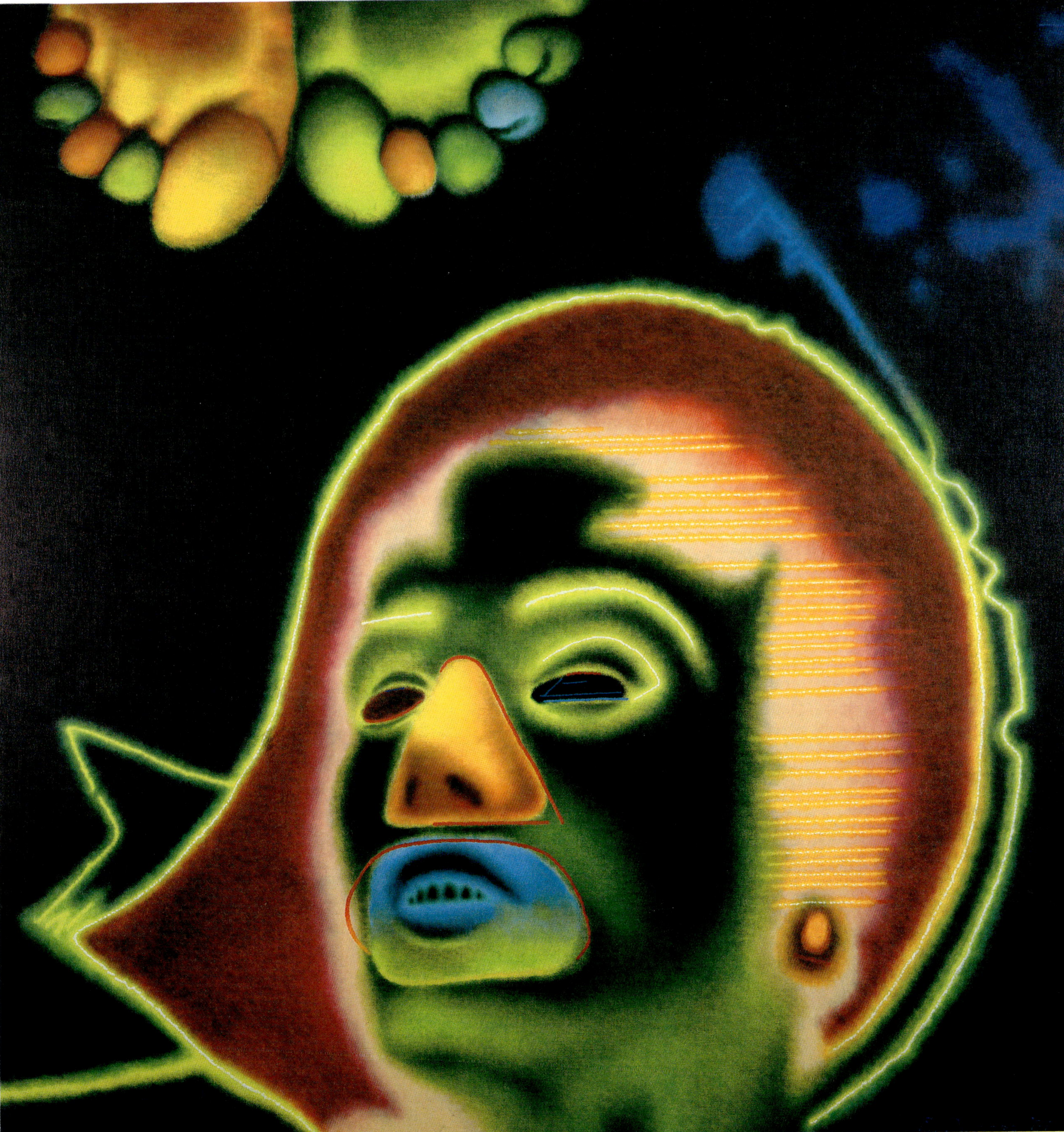

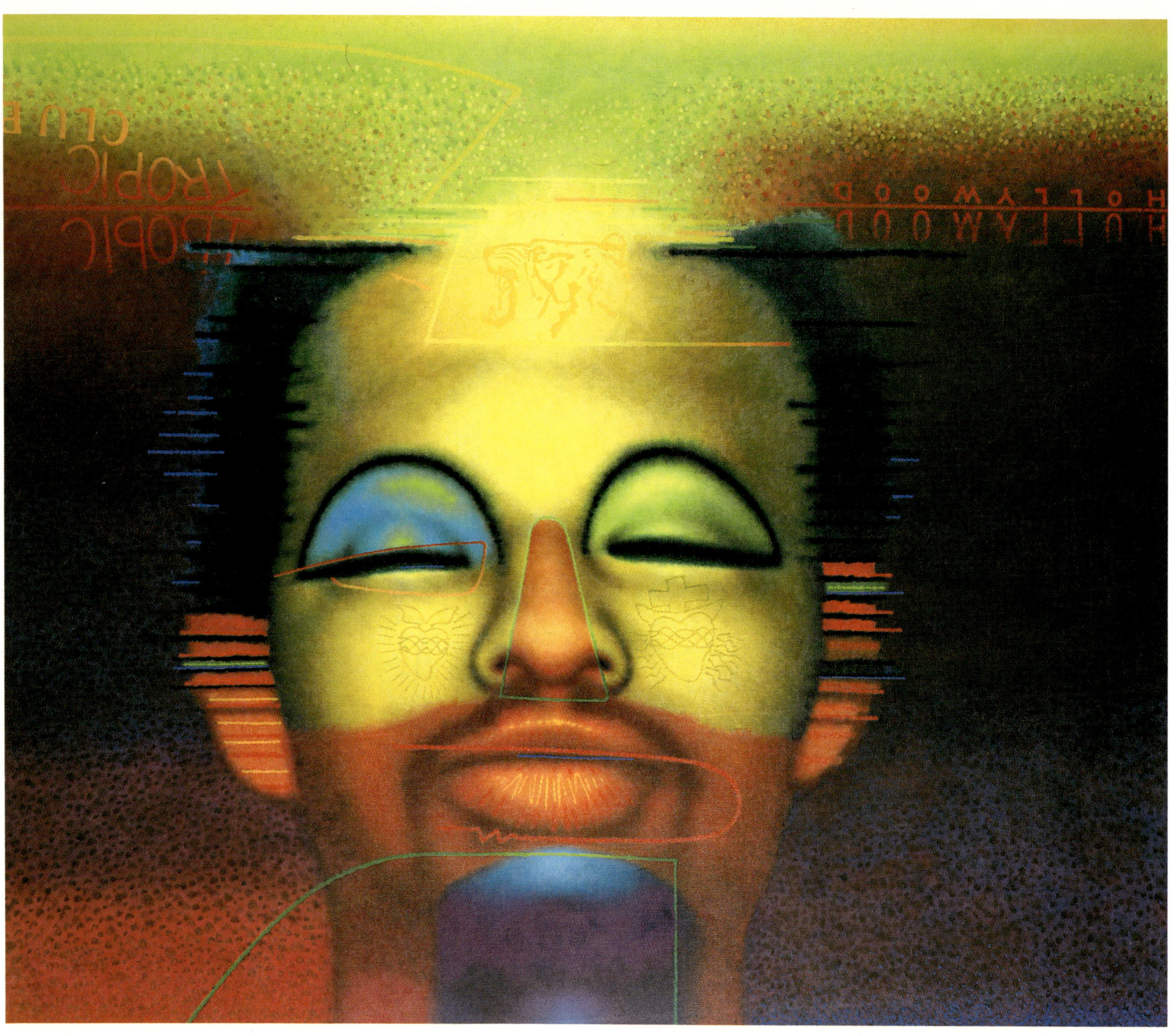

BLACKSTONE, 1988

NEGRETTE, 1988

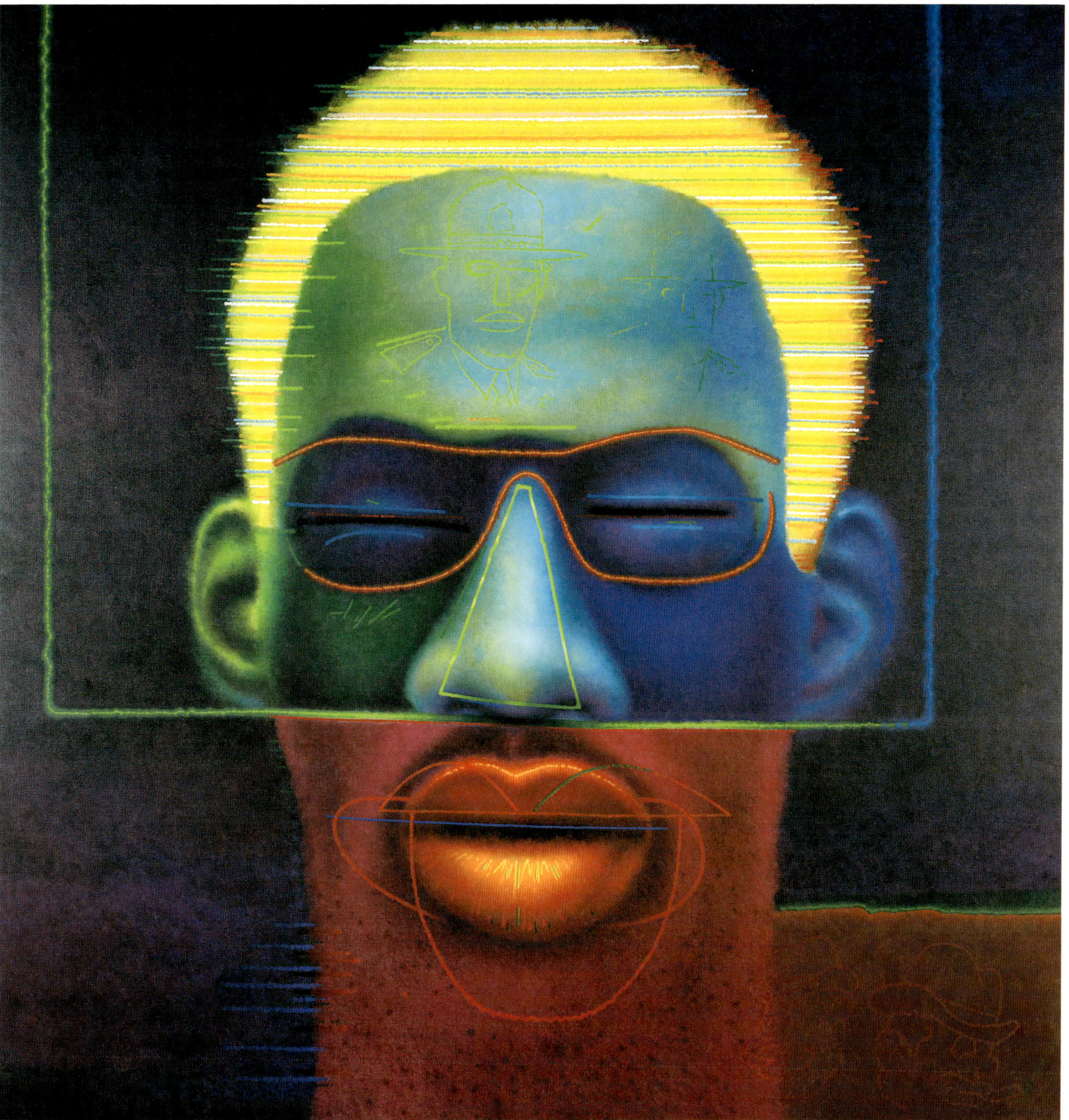

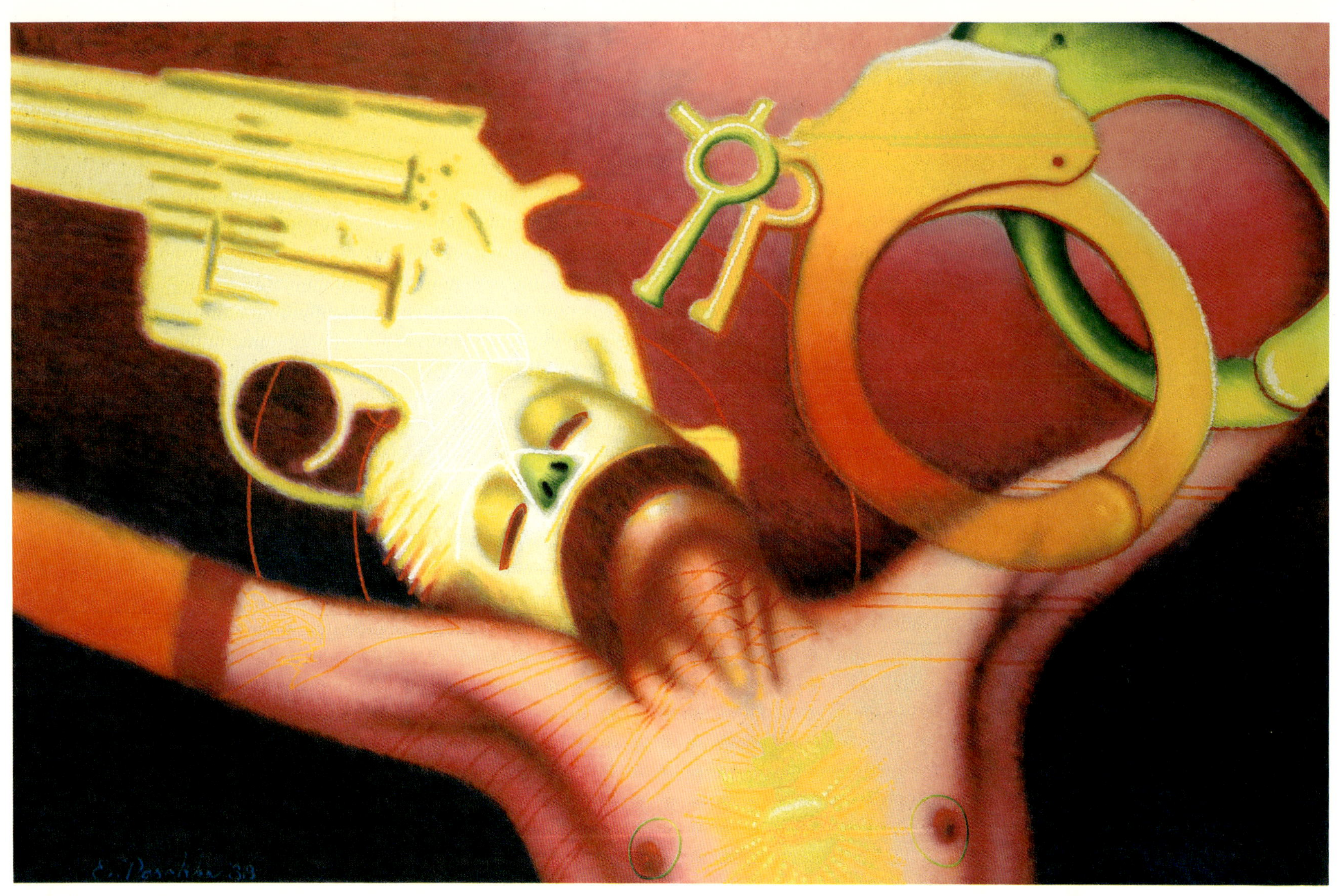

SANTA CABALLO, 1988

YIN AND YANG, 1988

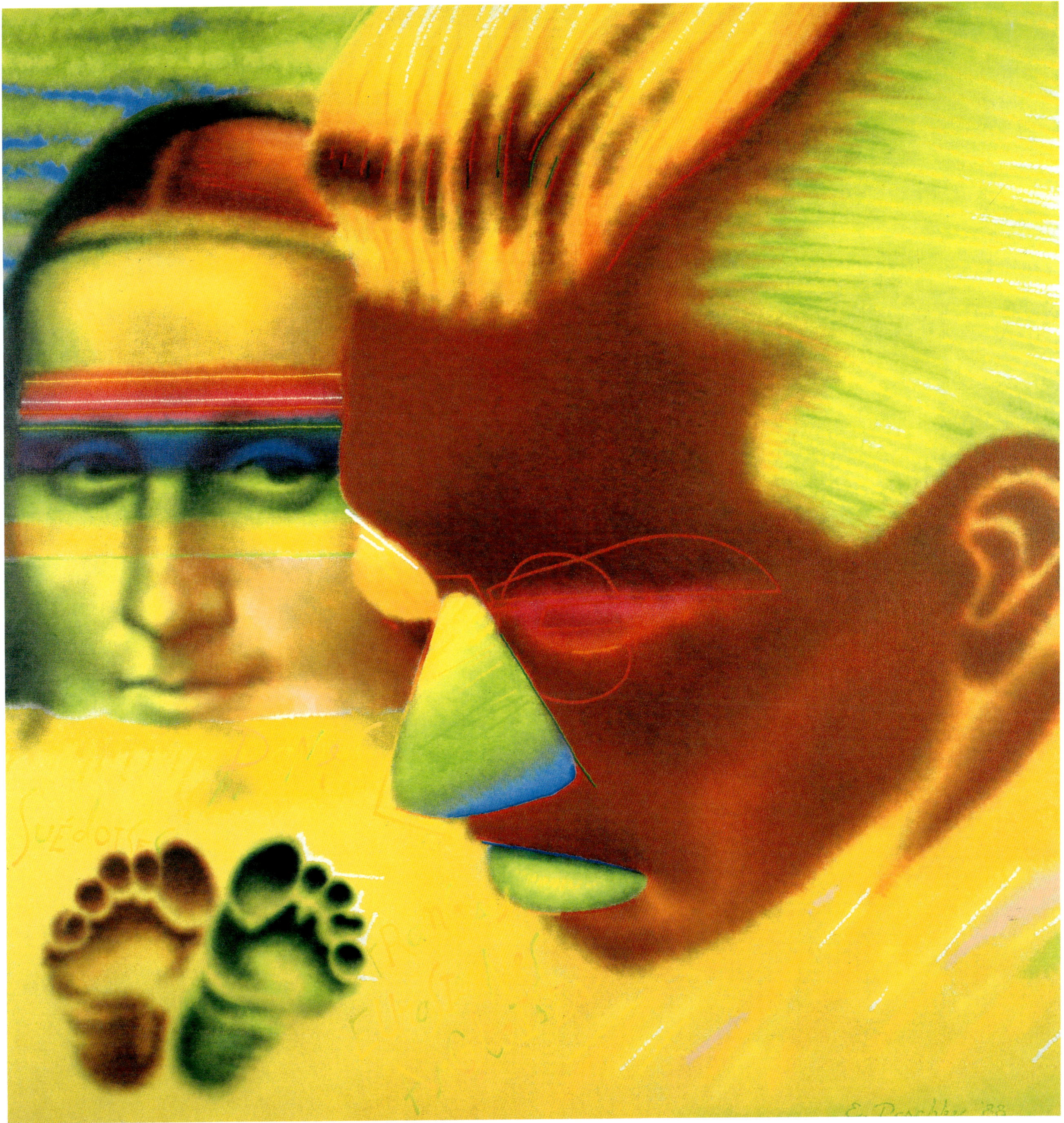

Suéootsé

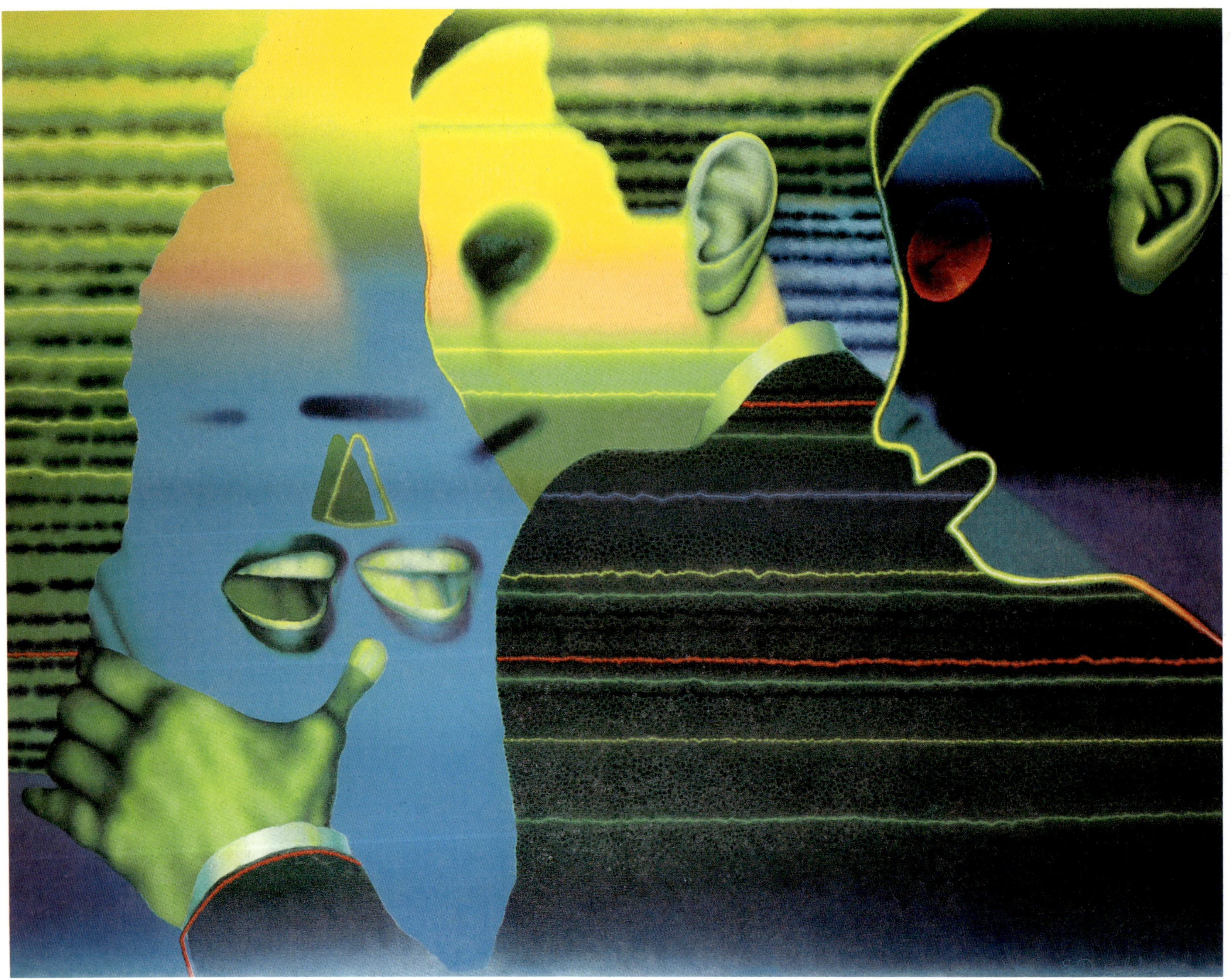

VIOLENCIA, 1980

JOHN YAU

You must know in the first place that everything
with a manifest face also has a secret one.
—Georges Bataille, *Alleluia /
The Catechism of Dianus*

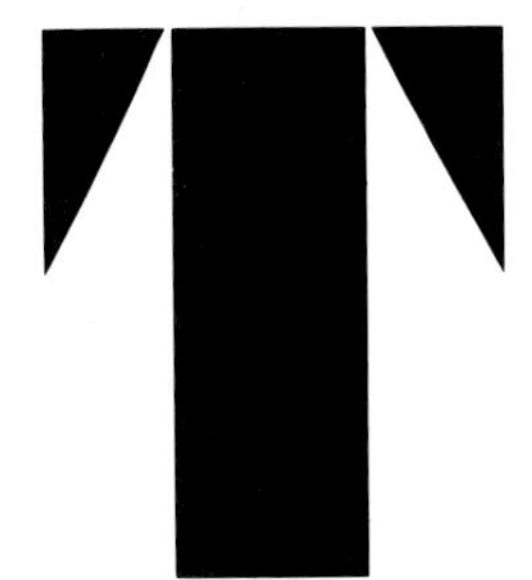

The representation of the Self in the twentieth century is marked by two events: Sigmund Freud's early report of his studies of the subconscious in *The Interpretation of Dreams* (1900) and Pablo Picasso's first use of motifs derived from African sculpture in *Les Demoiselles d'Avignon* (1907). Although working in different areas and for seemingly different purposes and goals, both Freud and Picasso went on to propose that the Self could not only strive toward states of relative freedom, satisfaction, and completion, but that liberation could actually be achieved. In their respective mediums (one in its infancy and not yet respectable, the other ancient and honored), Freud and Picasso were groundbreakers. Each showed society a way to externalize the Psychological or Hidden Self; in this regard, their goals are comparable. The Psychiatrist, for example, aids the Self in its quest to uncover the forces of repression, while the Modernist Artist searches for the means by which the Self can recover its essential shape (a sign of its true potentiality). Ultimately, both these pioneers developed highly articulated paradigms of de-evolution, which enable the Self to recontextualize the bonds of the past. Among other purposes, their paradigms served to represent the nature of the antagonistic relationship between the individual and society.

Now, with a little more than a decade to go before the twentieth century ends, it is clear that the study of the relationship between the individual and society is of increasing significance, particularly in light of the fact that the current objectives of science, industry, and consumerism are undergoing a process of redefinition and reorientation. How and in what condition shall we reach the future is one of the questions contemporary society must find a way to face. Or, to put it another way: what is the legacy our descendants shall inherit? Certainly, the age-old argument between the individual and society (whose most efficient agent has become the mass media) is still over how to arrive at mutually acceptable definitions of the Self.

One of the by-products of consumer culture, however, seems to be the diminishment of this argument. Having gained an enormous and seductive power with the recent invention and development of the electronic media, consumer culture presently offers the individual a variety of continuous narrative illusions, each of which conveys the message that he or she can reach an idealized state of perfection. Such states, the pulsating, heartlike ads tell us, are within our grasp; we simply have to reach for them. In becoming synonymous with the mass media, consumer culture has enabled itself to continually propose the correct inscriptions (clothes, for

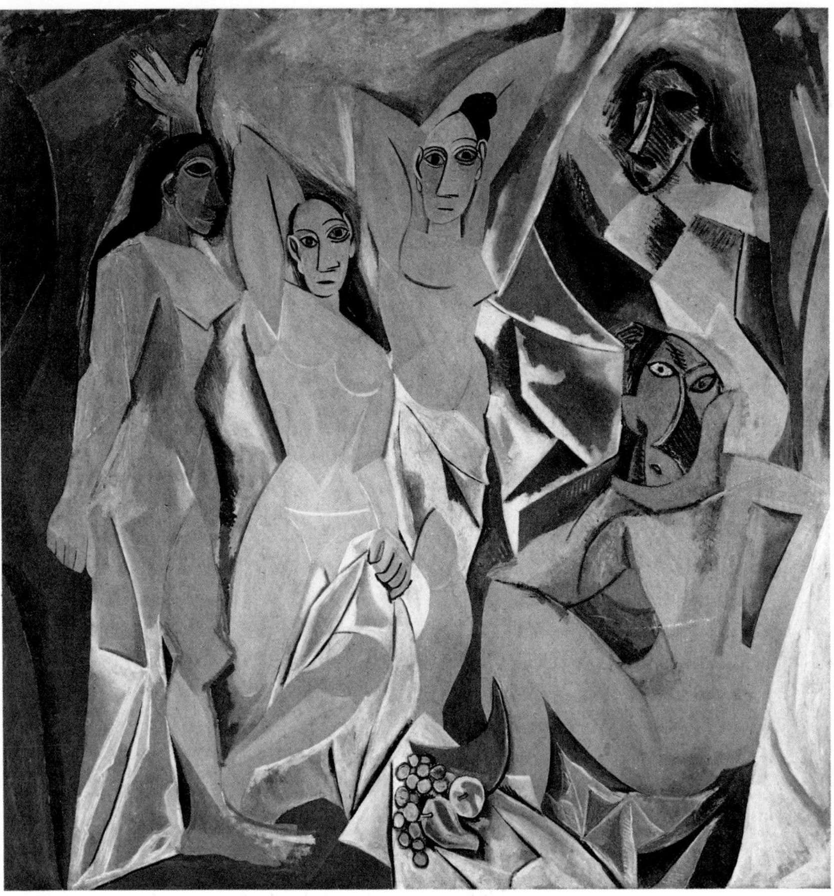

example, or liquids to imbibe, bathe in, and wear) by which one can recognize and be recognized by the other. It broadcasts messages and defines choices. Its sole purpose is to sell the signs one needs to possess if one wishes to become an efficient member of a social group. By making membership in a group a desirable goal, society is able to define and limit the kinds of individuality one can achieve. We have become a nation of statistical types who fit into designated slots; we are nothing more than numbers in a survey.

The relationship between the individual and consumer culture is symbiotic. By choosing from the wide variety of brand-name objects, the individual permits the Self to be absorbed into one of the recognized and productive currents of mainstream society. If meaning is arrived at through difference, as deconstructionist theoreticians have proposed, then consumer society's goal is to name, limit, and measure the range of available differences. In order to achieve this power to name and measure, to circumscribe, society has transformed itself into a highly adaptable agent of repression. In this realm, the world of consumerism, a place we inhabit in one way or another, all the acceptable and therefore valuable forms of individualism can only be reached by obtaining and follow-

ing the proscribed acts of deformation: buy this and become beautiful, handsome, free, and spontaneous. Everywhere one turns, even in dreams it seems, one's life is marked by these and other familiar narratives.

Given the immense power consumer culture has to inscribe and deform its individuals continuously, then Picasso's choice of an African mask and scarification marks to articulate simultaneously both the facial features of the prostitutes and the surface of the composition seems prophetic, particularly in regard to the view of the Self as a deeply inscribed site. Although his use of the scarification marks has been analyzed by Formalist critics and historians as the innovative application of a formal device, they can also be seen as evidence of society's power to inscribe and delimit the individual. They are irrefutable signs of culture's ability to mark the individual. Marking, in this instance, is a form of identifying. By using these decorative signs of linear cuts to articulate the women's features as well as the surface of the composition, Picasso transformed the figures into a unified and inviolable field of distinct individuals. Consequently, they achieve an imaginative state of autonomy within the realm of painting.

Although a wide range of thinkers have contested and modified Freud's theories, his fundamental notion—that the public self is a conditioned construct of the inner psychological self—casts one of the largest shadows across the breadth of this century's terrain. At the same time, Picasso's use of scarification to articulate both the women's faces and bodies and the surface of the painting remains both a radical and useful proposition. Certainly, Ed Paschke's paintings of tattooed figures, for example, can be understood as a synthesis of both Freud (his paradigm of inner and outer selves) and Picasso (his conflation of a person's flesh and skin with the body and surface of a painting). For one thing, his figures are a conjoining of inner and outer selves as well as "decorated" skin and the painting's surface.

It is out of this background (Picasso and Freud and their lifelong concern with the nature of the Self, as well as his own deeply critical response to consumer culture's electronic representations of the Idealized Self) that Ed Paschke has developed his work. Moreover, of all the artists to emerge since the end of World War II, he is one of a handful who have chosen to represent the signs of consumer society's

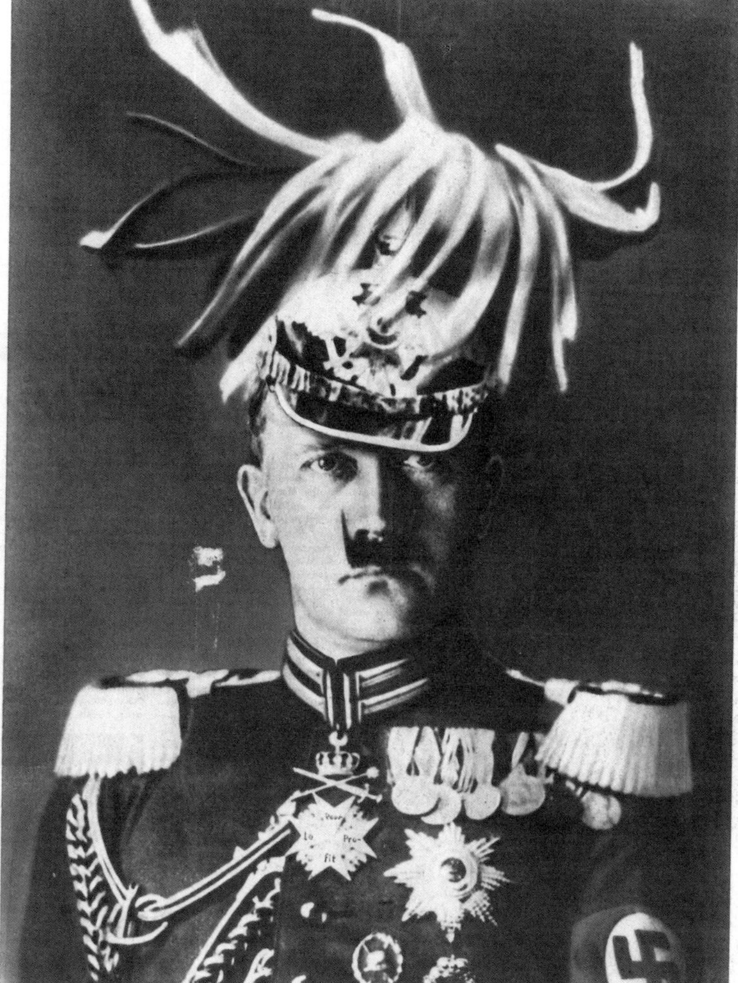

devastating inscriptions of the Self. During the past two decades he has continually found ways to address the disquieting effects of the antagonistic relationship between culture and the individual.

Whereas the highly encoded signs of the Perfect Self have been presented by consumer society as desirable objectives an individual should be motivated to attain, Paschke has both critiqued and revealed the arbitrariness of these electronic mirages by representing the nameless individuals and familiar types who have deformed their bodies and skin in order to achieve recognizable identities. The Self, in fact, has been the focus of his attention since he first emerged as an artist of substance in the mid-1960s. Since then, he has repeatedly lavished his painterly attention on the skin and body of both the painting and the painted. In doing so, he has directed our attention toward the ways society's institutions and consumer culture encourage an individual to deform his or her Self.

II

Ed Paschke's early paintings (1965–68) extend out of the expressive confrontational sociopolitical realm John Heartfield investigated in his critical photomontages. Consisting of phrases taken from languages being used by immigrant cultures existing in America (Spanish and Chinese, for example), a documentary Photo-Realist style, cartoons, and the arbitrarily agreed upon signs of gender coding and encoding, these works are edgy and aggressive. Eschewing the bland ironies that typified the work of many of his contemporaries, Paschke's paintings of the late 1960s can be seen as exposures of come-ons or invitations to a disturbing spectacle. *Amor* (1968), for example, could pass as the garish ad for a grade Z flick on which it is actually based, while *Ramrod* (1969) is suggestive of a poster to a sleazy sideshow (cat. nos. 2, 6). In retrospect, it is clear that during this period of racial strife, the Vietnam War, changing patterns of immigration, and political assassinations, there were two artists who were sensitive to the subtle effects the mass media was having on American life: Andy Warhol (1928–1987) and Ed Paschke (b. 1939).

An innovative member of the preceding or Pop Art generation, Warhol, in his work from the early to the mid-1960s, particularly his "Death and Disaster" paintings, probably exerted the strongest influence on Paschke who was, in the mid-1960s, just beginning his career. However, rather than achieving his identity by following in the footsteps of Warhol and presenting bland, popular images within a suitable Pop Art style, Paschke stuck to oil paint and brushes, while choosing raunchy subject matter and developing a harsh, information-packed, Photo-Realist style. Thus, instead of becoming another practitioner of Pop Art's easy-to-mimic stylizations, Paschke began his career by demanding parity with Warhol. He did so by being critical of, among other things, the older artist's choice of subject matter and mode of presentation.

Warhol, for example, formulated his compositions according to the formalist constraints then dominating the New York art world, while Paschke, a resident of Chicago, did not make such concessions. Warhol arranged his images in grids or repeated them, thus mimicking typical Minimalist compositions. He presented his work in abstract formats (see Benezra, fig. 3). Moreover, Warhol chose his images, many of them of either well-known figures or familiar types, from mainstream sources. He understood mainstream society's largely self-satisfied fascination with being spared from death and disaster, its "It could happen to me, but luckily it didn't" attitude. A modern-day court painter, he understood middle-class White America to be an entity that wished it were distinct, separate, and safe from the rest of America. In the late 1960s Warhol began directing both his attention and his work toward mainstream society. For the most part, his work of the 1970s and 1980s became obsequious and predictable. In taking this direction, he failed to develop beyond his early, ground-breaking work.

Paschke, on the other hand, chose not to align himself with the insular, middle-class values of mainstream society. In contrast to Warhol, who used images he found in daily newspapers, Paschke cast his net into the fantasy realms exploited by the disrespected, disrespectable tabloids and periodicals and chose his information from these seamier sources. One could say that Paschke's sources are located on the underside of Warhol's. It is as if he wanted to have a direct pipeline to the millions of psyches that consulted the *National Enquirer* to learn what was revealed at a seance in Hollywood or the White House. He was interested in uncovering what lay behind such banal gestures as reading the gossip rags one finds in supermarkets. In order to investigate these disquieting areas of American life, where the crackpot and the movie star are often interchangeable identities, Paschke had to solve a pressing formal issue: how was he going to represent both the actual and the fantastic, the psychological depths and the surface presentation?

Instead of transferring the image intact from one medium to another, as Warhol did when he employed the medium of silkscreen, Paschke used the traditional tools of oil paint and brushes to combine various images, languages, and types of representation. In *Ramrod*, for example, he purposefully added cartoon images and abstract stylizations to a realistically rendered figure, whose hirsute upper torso is male and reminiscent of a wrestler, but whose crotch is depicted as female. It is through the deliberate layering of such highly considered interventions as these that Paschke has been able to suggest many of the kinds of differences, contradictions, and paradoxes that exist within America.

Throughout his career, which now extends over three decades, Paschke has had a way of getting right to the heart of the matter, raising questions most of us would rather ignore. His relentless questioning has led him to propose provocative views of America, ones that are, in the final analysis, more directly confrontational and disturbing than Warhol's. It is Paschke's provocativeness that makes the work insistent and fresh. In his lurid, Photo-Realist portrait, *Purple Ritual* (1967), for example, he re-presents a mass-media image of Lee Harvey Oswald (cat. no. 1). Oswald, who is shown holding a rifle and posed like a cowboy, is depicted as a purple figure in and against the purple ground. Paschke's use of a single color to unify the figure/ground relationship recalls Warhol's similar use of monochrome in his early silkscreen paintings of electric chairs and car crashes. Paschke, however, then proceeded to frame this view with a pattern derived from the American flag. Consequently, Oswald is seen both as part of the ground (the surface of the canvas) and part of the cloth of American life. Rather than being depicted as a sign of the other, an alien or the enemy, Oswald is presented within a format that recalls mythic American heroes. In doing so, Paschke gives the good guy/bad guy image of someone like Billy the Kid another twist. His career can be characterized as an attempt to discover irrefutable evidence of the degree to which distinctions between hero and villain have become meaningless.

Whereas Warhol focused largely on victims, heroes, and entertainers, tragic figures like Jackie Kennedy and popular personalities like Elizabeth Taylor, Paschke directed his attention toward the disenfranchised members of America, the petty villains and freaks. The former looked at the main acts, while the latter examined the sideshows. Thus, in 1968, the year Robert F. Kennedy was shot down in the hallway of a Los Angeles hotel, Paschke enfolded Oswald's portrait in an American flag. The demented stars of the sideshows, the painting tells us, are not as different from us as we would like to think. All of us are, as the saying goes, cut from the same cloth.

III

Paschke's development as an artist, his progress, can be measured by the increasing efficiency with which he gets to the essential core of his subject matter. Almost immediately after he formulated his themes in such paintings as *Ramrod, Mid American* (1969) (cat. no. 5), and *Pink Lady* (1970) (cat. no. 8), Paschke reevaluated his approach and shifted his attention from clothed figures in posterlike compositions to shoes in less framed settings. This shift allowed him to give freer rein to his imaginative-critiques of the notion of Self, without jettisoning his earlier themes: the codes used to declare one's identity; the codes used to identify gender; the values associated with being a male or female that are routinely attached to objects; the relationship between the artificial and the natural; the ongoing relationship between the identity and culture. By "imaginative-critique," I mean that his re-presentations of the Self are simultaneously imaginative and critical. Paschke's shoes sprouted acne and hair; they displayed varicose veins and tattoos; they posed; they exhibited both sexual characteristics and personality traits. They were fully realized portraits.

While paintings such as *Hairy Shoes* (1971) and *Bag Boots* (1972) (cat. nos. 9, 10) extend themes first developed in *Ramrod*, they also reveal an artist who is growing increasingly confident about the content he is trying to reveal. In *Joella* (1973) and *Lucy* (1973) (cat. nos. 13, 14), Paschke no longer relied on the built-in safety net of such mediating devices as decorative borders and repetition. Posed frontally, the figures inhabit a no-nonsense, abstract/atmospheric realm. Some of them are physically maimed, while others seem to have maimed themselves. What all of them seem to have in common is their deformity and their humanness, conditions that Paschke sees, one suspects, as either interchangeable or indistinguishable.

During the mid-1970s Paschke again shifted his focus and depicted weirdly costumed figures such as *Rufus* (1974), *Armondo* (1975), *Red Sweeney* (1975), and *Sabreena* (1976) (cat. nos. 15–17, 19). Each of them has objectified his or her body, his subjective existence, with decorative coverings such as tattoos, masks, satin, and leather. By enfolding themselves in highly encoded costumes and thoroughly considered poses, they achieve an unmistakable identity. Like other paintings done during this period, *Red Sweeney* is a portrait of someone who has transformed his Subjective Self into an Idealized Self, a "work of art."

IV

Paschke has accomplished something altogether unexpected in postwar painting; he has extended the perverse or discounted side of Picasso's scarification marks. Instead of reducing them to formal or decorative elements, and thus adhering to the accepted, mainstream view of abstraction's progressive triumph over figuration, he has detonated their psychological implications in new and unforeseen areas. In such paintings as *Ramrod*, *Lucy*, and *Sabreena*, he has successfully expanded the subjective aspects of Picasso's innovative practice in *Les Demoiselles d'Avignon* into the central psychological conflict inhabiting contemporary American society. And in doing so, he has revealed the devastating effects postwar consumer culture has had upon individuals. By expressing their Hidden Self through the decorative use of skins (leather and satin), markings (tattoos), and adornments (sunglasses), figures such as *Rufus* and *Red Sweeney* are able to achieve recognized (and recognizable!) states of liberation. Yet, these signs of liberation are also the clear and unmistakable signs of imprisonment.

While Paschke's men and women are descendants of Picasso's prostitutes, they are neither desirable nor erotic. In fact, the tension between us and them does not revolve around desire, but around repellence. *Joella*, *Lucy*, and *Sabreena* may be entertainers of some kind, but Paschke offers few concrete clues as to what kind. Are they singers and dancers in a club? Or are they freaks in some kinky sideshow act? In either case, who would be their audience? As viewers, we are implicated. Both fascinated and disgusted, we are their audience—the ones who look, and look again.

In *Les Demoiselles d'Avignon* Picasso made the encounter between the viewer and the painting into a standoff between customer and prostitutes. It is the moment of decision, when the customer must choose the one he wants. It is what happens after the come-on, but before the actual contact. It is the moment of negotiation, when one thing is traded for another. In Picasso's painting, the haughty prostitutes stare us down, terminating the negotiation. Distinct entities, they are poised before us, on the brink of merging with both the composition's surface and each other.

In *Sabreena* Paschke made the encounter a standoff between the Subjective Self (the viewer) and Objective Self (the costumed other). Dressed in satin, she has started to emerge from behind the satin curtain. Instead of emphasizing her living skin and erotic presence, Paschke lavished his attention on the dead and sickly skin of her face and clothes. It is as if the marks that Picasso confined largely to the faces of the two prostitutes on the right have spread throughout Paschke's subject, like a virus. They are not marked so much as infected from within.

By using the scarification marks to make the prostitutes (their features and bodies) synonymous with the painting (its surface and objecthood), Picasso equated the skin and body of the women with the skin and body of oil painting. In his lavish attention to such materials as leather, fur, and satin, Paschke widened the realm of Picasso's equation. He went on to make disturbing equations between a painting's surface and tattoos (another kind of scarification mark), different types of masks, costumes, and skin.

In *Les Demoiselles d'Avignon* Picasso made painting, both its materiality and process, into metaphors for the erotic presence, encounter, and act. More than half a century later, Paschke extends the metaphors, but arrives at a very different content. In order to sell convincing signs of the Perfect Self to the members of mainstream society, consumer culture has had to appropriate as many of the paradigms of individualism as it could. We, in turn, are left to inhabit individualism's dead skin. It is this dead skin that Paschke addresses, a world in which Eros is dead.

V

In 1977, about a decade after he first formulated his interest in the properties of skin and identity, Paschke shifted his attention to the body and initiated the second phase of his career. Certainly, his interest in media-shaped perceptions may have influenced his decision to effect television's distortions, holograms' insubstantiality, and cardiographs' linear zigzags. Whatever the reason, the new paintings clarified beyond anyone's doubt that what Paschke had been interested in since the beginning of his career was the myriad ways individuals deform the Self in order to achieve a recognizable image (the electronic age's sign for identity).

In his earlier period Paschke had focused primarily on outsiders—freaks, bit players, criminals, inhabitants of the inner city, and citizens of the Third World. In the second phase Paschke began focusing on members of the middle class and mainstream society, the normal and ordinary citizens. In *Dominant Nurse* (1977) and *Cho Chan* (1978) (cat. nos. 20, 25), the figures have been drained of substance, as if beneath their masks and costumes the flesh has started to become an irradiated field, a bodiless body of garish color and sickly light. Their bodies and faces look like neon electrocardiograms, screens of fatigued yet sinister energy. They embody the possibility that our fields of vision, both psychological and perceptual, have become completely appropriated by the electronic media.

What the paintings seem to be saying is that the Self, so attuned to being persuaded, if not instructed, by electronic media, can no longer see for itself. Thus, the realm of self-reflection and introspection, a private place that was once considered inviolable, no longer exists. Instead, everyone's fantasies (the stylizations of dress, gestures, and modes of contact) have been appropriated by the electronic media's seductive narratives: you too can inhabit these clothes, this body, and this moment is the constant message. Individualism has been replaced by the radiant signs of the Perfect Self. The result: the private and public realms have been crammed together, driving out the body. What these paintings depict is complete depersonalization—alienation taken to its logical extreme. It is not that we have been expelled from Paradise, but from our bodies. We have slid down the evolutionary ladder and become quivering, neon jellyfish.

In *Fumar* (1979) (cat. no. 28), the ovoid shape of the head is outlined by a reddish, neonlike current of color. Both ground and face conform in their spectrographic range of color, threatening to merge. Stylization occurs at both the level of features (face, nose, and mouth) and gesture (a hand holds a cigarette). Depersonalized and pushing toward abstraction, *Fumar*, like Paschke's other paintings of the late 1970s and early 1980s, is a portrait of a contemporary Everyman.

During the late 1970s and early 1980s Paschke alluded to the disturbing possibilities, the neuroses and psychoses, imbedded within the most familiar gestures, poses, and actions. While *Nervosa* (1980) (cat. no. 30) recalls Rodin's well-known sculpture *The Thinker*, it also suggests a close-up of someone who is depressed and unhappy. Is something bothering him or has he just done something he is ashamed of? Is he posing or is his anxiety genuine? Although we cannot name the specific reason he is holding his head the way he is, each of us can identify with the gesture, the pose.

Paschke has an uncanny way of isolating familiar gestures and poses, and making us see them from another point of view. In *Violencia* (1980) (cat. no. 31), for example, is the man's gesture friendly or hostile? Is the woman screaming or laughing? Is the other man, the one looking on, laughing or shouting words of encouragement to his friend? Who is connected to whom? And how? Behind these questions looms a larger question. How does one strive against the effects of depersonalization? By carefully selecting and developing certain gestures and poses, Paschke is able to reveal the extent to which all our actions have been learned and encoded, performed and recorded. His paintings confront us with the disturbing possibility that we have all become emotionless witnesses plugged into a terminal, viewers staring at a screen.

Throughout the early 1980s Paschke depicted two or more figures in many of his paintings, suggesting internal narratives in which stylized gestures echo our own. Irresolvable contradictions are presented. It is as if each figure is unable to go beyond his or her solipsistic state and engage the other. Every gesture seems posed, a mimicry of something else. In a sense, Paschke is also commenting on his ability to turn painting practice into an act of mimicry. In *Les Demoiselles d'Avignon* the prostitutes become accusing figures, and among the viewers they accuse is Picasso, their artist-maker. They have achieved a state of inviolable independence. Staring down at the viewer, Paschke's heads achieve a similar state of independence. Solipsists, rulers of the electronic netherworld they inhabit, they are isolated from everyone, including the artist.

Then, in the late 1980s, Paschke turned his attention to such cultural icons as Elvis Presley, George Washington, Abraham Lincoln, and the *Mona Lisa*. Through his use of glowing color, stylized shapes, and linear arabesques, Paschke raised the question: what constitutes the act of recognition? Paschke's development is connected to the shift he made from the skin to the body, from highly detailed surfaces to fields of light. Behind this attention to skin and body is a deeper interest in the Self. Paschke constantly attempts to reinscribe that which has been inscribed by such mediating institutions as the mass media and consumer culture. In doing so, he opposes mainstream society's belief in the Perfect Self. Instead of offering acceptable variations on the Perfect Self, he confronts the viewer with glowing, fleshless heads, with bloodless intelligence.

Ed Paschke has been developing in a singular way since the late 1960s. Now, a little more than two decades after he began his career, his work can be said to embody, among other possibilities, a creative-critical response to the art world, which has, like mainstream society, been plagued with conformist attitudes. In contrast with most postwar artists, who have been all too willing to accept the body's absence from Modernist and Postmodernist discourse, Paschke's paintings ask: what happens to the Self after dissolution? The end of the twentieth century offers two distinct choices. One can try and become the last artist of this century, or the first artist of the next. Anything else is either nostalgic or a compromise.

The last artist reidentifies the codes by which history has been neatly packaged and sold to the consumer. He or she supports the notion, for example, that the true destination of Picasso's scarification marks was Mondrian's plus-minus paintings and allover abstraction. The first artist, on the other hand, tries to recognize what is in front of him or her. Paschke accomplishes this by being an image maker who examines the deepest currents of the subjected, mediated Self. He strives to re-appropriate what has been thoroughly appropriated by cultural institutions: the inscribed Self.

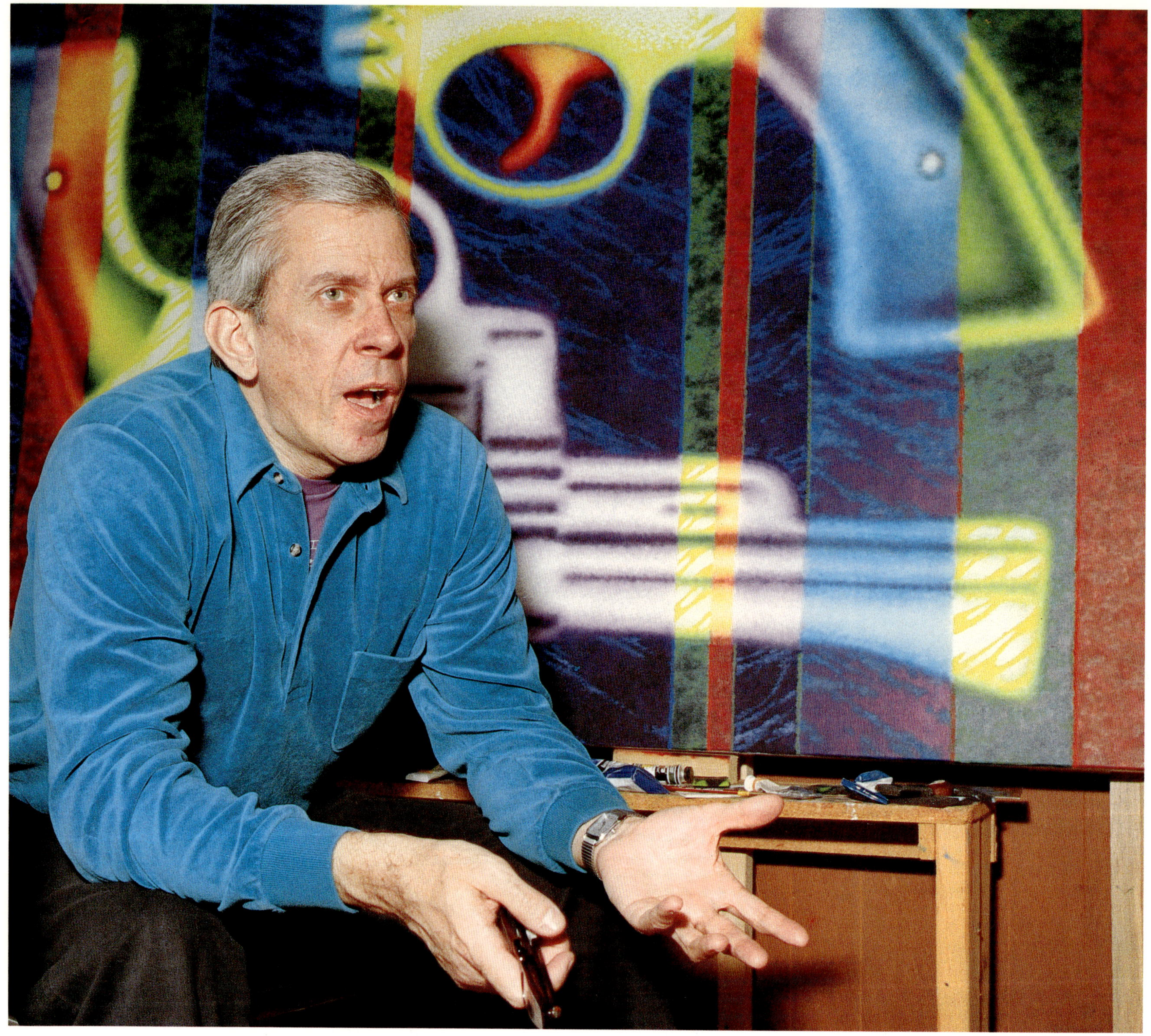

ED PASCHKE IN HIS STUDIO, 1989

DENNIS ADRIAN: I know that you, along with the curatorial staff at The Art Institute of Chicago, were involved in the selection of your show. Did you work with the French museum people too?

ED PASCHKE: I worked with the Art Institute people; we did have a meeting in France. The basic concern there was that the show consist of a substantial number of conceptually related works—the French seemed to feel strongly that you can't just put up works; you have to have some major philosophical premise to manifest in the exhibition.

DA: Did you feel that the exhibition ought to have a certain structure?

EP: It was really difficult for me in such a position to have an overview of my own work. What we tried to do was to put together the strongest possible body of work. There were many considerations flowing through my mind as I tried to do this. One was, should there be a kind of uniform sampling of the work? There might be stronger or weaker periods. Should certain collections, museum or private, be favored in terms of the weight that so doing might give the whole enterprise? But the primary goal was to have the strongest group of paintings.

DA: When you say the stongest possible work, do you mean the most representative *images* of some periods, or is there a level of quality you have aimed at or certain works that you feel to be really at the heart of your artistic and painterly considerations? Specifically, when you think about the early work, what do you think characterizes the most representative and best works?

EP: The very early work was about a kind of confrontational dissonance, a societal dissonance. I think there was an involvement with certain aspects of gender . . . a playing around with issues of gender identification.

DA: The period you're talking about would be 1968 to 1972?

EP: Yes, works such as *Ramrod* and *Hophead* [cat. nos. 6, 7]. This earlier work is sometimes described as being concerned with the underbelly of American society. Then there was the shoe period, the woman series, and the man series. Then there was the couples series. This last series was confrontational. By degrees I was coming closer not only physically but psychologically to the point where in the group of cropped, close-up heads of the mid-1980s I felt I was penetrating the surface, the societal facade, the gamesmanship and the role playing, to get into that subterranean part of the mind that deals with the inner versus the outer self.

DA: Do you feel that these concerns begin really with the works having forms that suggest electronic media, where abstract forms and bandings start to be a kind of language of feeling and begin to articulate a state of mind?

EP: Yes. I think that the media, where all these sources originate, act as a trigger mechanism in my mind. I then project, fantasize, put together various component parts. For a while I was very concerned with the surface appearance of electronic communication. Eventually in my work I came to the point where forms and images disintegrated, broken apart in the fabric of electronic disturbance and its surface. In the most recent work, forms are becoming more solidified, getting back more toward certain kinds of psychological presences or to an edge or tension that characterized some of the earlier work.

DA: In some of the most recent images, bands or rectangles of color appear arbitrarily as though there are overlays or gels over part of the picture; also, there are disjunctively scaled images that recall similar paintings of the late 1960s.

EP: More recently I've been trying to investigate aspects of religion, violence, sexuality, and combinations thereof, stated in a more solidified way.

DA: In other recent works, there are quotations from images having specifically to do with art or even clichés such as the *Mona Lisa*, or images that are related to familiar sculpture and painting. I don't recall any such visual quotations in the earlier work.

EP: I am using the ideas of symbol, metaphor, or icon—ideas that bring with them a baggage of referential information. Certainly Elvis or the *Mona Lisa* are images that have recognizability and a certain referential arrangement that affects the way we see and understand the subjects behind the images. This potential grows out of a cultural fabric, and I guess what I want to do is to take some well-known images as a starting point and maybe try to combine them with others or to break down these images, maybe to dissect what sort of phenomenon broad popular recognizability is.

DA: I've always felt that even some of your early paintings are concerned with making philosophical points about how one sees and understands things, and about elements of painting.

EP: Central to my work is what I refer to as the law of opposites; I believe there are polarities between things; one gets from one extreme to the other by intermediate stages and steps. This law applies to issues of gender identification, which characterize much of the earlier work and which float in and out of my work over the years. Positive/negative, the idea of pacing a painting in terms of complexity and simplicity, the idea of public versus private, are elements that have always interested me and that I've always tried in some way to build into the character of the paintings. In my most recent work, there are ideas concerning religion, which can be seen or used in a positive or a destructive way. I think that the element that makes them united is the pulse of life. I think one of the first thoughts that mystified me when I began to study at The School of The Art Institute of Chicago was a critique about "life in the picture plane." "This painting has life in the picture plane, this one does not; this one has movement, this one does not." It was a year or so before I realized that the "life in the picture plane" had to do with the forces operating between the various elements that create tensions in the eye and mind as the observer investigates and considers all the different facets. All the pictorial elements—some with references, some with overt meanings, some with subliminal ones—somehow play upon the perceptive apparatus of the viewer so that movement, light, and so forth are going on inside his head.

DA: When I look at your paintings, I'm always struck by their formal variety. In certain periods there seem to be sets of compositional concerns that are dominant; they gradually shift or give way to something else. Are these shifts of the formal situation the by-products of these interactive factors you mentioned or is formal structure something you consider independently? From time to time you've changed your way of working or the texture of the paint. You've even had other people introduce things in the paintings in order to alter your process. Do you do these things only in order to change the formal structure?

EP: Sometimes I've been concerned with consciously addressing certain formal issues, and the consequences are various metaphorical, symbolic results. At other times I've been concerned initially with certain metaphorical images and ideas and the formal invention is a consequence.

DA: About 1970–71 I remember the first quite large paintings of yours that I saw, *Pink Lady* [cat. no. 8]. The scale seemed a big change because the earlier works, while not really small, had the scale of easel and cabinet pictures, comfortable or even intimate.

EP: I would compare the bigger scale to the experience of watching something on a movie screen where it's larger than you are. I think people who paint illusionistically have three basic choices of scale: to paint something smaller than it is, the same size it is, or larger than it is. I made a conscious decision to go larger than life because I wanted this almost overwhelming movie-screen scale to happen—and to investigate it.

DA: Monumental figure painting as a category in itself is often considered apart. It's an undertaking not different in artistic quality from smaller-scale works, but it does belong to the upper range. The analogy I've often used is to music. One can write songs, chamber music, concertos, or symphonies and operas. The composer or the artist may want to demonstrate command of the artistic structure in all scales. The big scales often give an amplitude that makes the statement very profound, as well as large.

EP: Yes, the epic scale. It's almost like boxing; the heavyweight division is the one that attracts people because this is as big as you can get: it's more powerful.

DA: Do you ever find that what you're doing picks up some hint or suggestion of something that appeared earlier and is then amplified in a continuation of the initial impulse?

EP: This happens quite often. Some element that I was involved with earlier, but never quite exhausted, is there still.

DA: Artists sometimes discover that issues in their current painting were dealt with earlier. In your own case, do you feel the issues raised are durable enough to sustain this sort of reexploration, or do you feel you might be merely "running the loop" again?

EP: I once heard somebody say that you can break an artist's output or working life into three basic categories. One is when you first strike out; everything is new and there's a first rush of raw ideas. The second phase is characterized by an obsessive concern for technique. The third phase is a regurgitation of phase one. So when these earlier things pop up again I have this panic that. . . . But then I think everybody has a visual vocabulary of elements that always interests him. You may have used a particular element early on and set it aside because you haven't quite exhausted it. I think when you exhaust something, you throw it out of your bag of tricks. One of the cornerstones of my philosophy has always been that painting is not only autobiographical, but as well it's a problem-solving process. Problems feel awkward. . . .

DA: Or they wouldn't be problems.

EP: Right. If you're dealing with issues that are old friends and that feel comfortable and you're not doing anything new, you have to pose problems for yourself. Creativity and innovation are how you solve those problems and, if you're only addressing those you've already solved, you're going to spin your wheels and stay at the same point in terms of growth and development.

DA: Would this open new possibilities that you might not otherwise consider?

EP: Exactly . . . new possibilities. Sometimes, if people are visiting me in my studio, I offer them the opportunity to do something to a painting in the hope that they'll present some awkward problem for me. They usually do.

DA: Some of them probably feel you are presenting an awkward problem to them!

EP: Some people refuse to have anything to do with this suggestion, but some accept the challenge. That's exactly what I want: another mind doing something to my painting that I would not have thought to do.

DA: It suggests that being a painter, or your sense of yourself as a painter, is a kind of mechanism that occasionally you want to test.

EP: No matter how many times I pose that as a problem, I always have the same degree of anxiety and uncertainty about whether I can "pass." It's almost like proving myself again. . . .

DA: There was a strange transitional period in your work that is not represented in the exhibition, during which you made abstract paintings without figures in a variety of compositional types. Some are quite symmetrical, some appear randomly composed, some have deep spatial effects, some are quite flat, but all seem investigations of pure painterly possibilities without any sense of beings or of the psychologies of individuals that is in all your other work.

EP: That's exactly right. I was getting more and more involved in a concern for surface, ornamentation, texture, and formal development. I decided to take the figure out altogether and just focus on what I could do technically, illusionistically, by playing with surface, texture, and light. It was a short series, and then of course I went back again to the figure but armed with a new awareness of surface and technical possibilities.

DA: Another category of paintings that isn't in the exhibition is the portraits, specifically portraits of private individuals. Why was it decided not to deal with them? How do you feel your portraits fit into the work overall?

EP: One can say they present problems and challenges. The commissioned portrait painting brings with it certain constraints, limitations, or directs one's thinking in a particular way—or at least it does for me.

DA: The invention in them is certainly on a par with your other paintings. Is one of the challenges that you don't necessarily always work directly from the model? There has to be some dealing with the specific personality of the sitters at some point, especially if they are the patrons or you are required to meet them. Is that what puts constraints on your autonomy of invention? Also, I've always felt that there is a distinction between your paintings that are portraits and those that just happen to contain a likeness. In all the portraits,

even if the bodies have been reworked or modified in some way, the body remains within the realm of the physically possible; the pictures that simply contain likenesses often have features that are impossibilities by any stretch of the imagination.

EP: With commissioned portraits, I've always felt a need to adhere to a fairly consistent logical portrayal of the person. In other works, not commissioned portraits, I include the likeness of a specific person within a freer kind of pictorial invention.

DA: When you first approached theater design, doing sets and costumes for Charles Ludlum's *Turds in Hell*, you used slide projections of paintings on paper rather than large-scale designs. Did this experience suggest investigating the possibilities of very large formats?

EP: Those paintings on paper were small scale, but I did them thinking that they would actually be experienced on a large scale through projection. Probably big canvases entered into my thinking then. I think you're right, though I never really made that connection before.

DA: The *Turds in Hell* designs have a lot of inventive and imagistic freedom, which was rather different from the work you were doing just before them. I recall that there were many designs—twenty-three or twenty-four—and they took quite a while.

EP: I think those designs are probably also related to the illustrations I did occasionally for *Playboy* magazine. These also were combinations of my own ideas and some from outside.

DA: For the *Turds in Hell* decor, you designed objects and props such as furniture. Certainly this cannot be described as an excursion into sculpture, but did it get you thinking about objects?

EP: I think so, although I hadn't really had that much experience with objects.

DA: I ask because so many painters of your generation in Chicago have also at some time or other gotten involved with objects. Their paintings are often objectlike. Roger Brown has done it, Philip Hanson, and Karl Wirsum. I wonder if your involvement with objects was different because of your work with the theater company. Was this how it happened?

EP: I think that is true, but also the experience of working in fairly close cooperation with the theater group let me see the underlying principles that relate all art forms. As opening night approaches, all these people are developing and perfecting their contributions. Somehow the various parts congeal into a oneness on opening night.

DA: Has the possibility of again working in the theater intrigued you? Have you had any nibbles? I have often thought that you would be terrific for opera as well as other kinds of theater.

EP: I have done a couple of things with Stuart Gordon at the Organic Theater in Chicago. It wasn't as extensive an experience as I had with *Turds in Hell*. I have never had an opportunity to do anything with opera, although I'm always intrigued by it. I did have the experience of working with some people at the Art Institute a few years ago. We produced a multi-media experience involving a videotape, a performance piece, a band show in Grant Park, and "Dos Egos" in the museum's auditorium. Those kinds of things do interest me a great deal. So, all you playwrights out there, look me up!

I think new things are always a source of rejuvenation, cross-fertilization; although you never know what the by-product is going to be, you know it's going to affect your thinking beyond the present experience. It's an important part of growth to allow oneself to be open to different kinds of experience.

DA: The scope of the exhibition is limited to paintings, but I wanted to ask you about the role of drawing in your work at various periods. Your drawings always seem independently conceived as autonomous works.

EP: A group of large drawings shown in Paris a few years ago are a combination of media—pencil, oil stick, wash, etc. I think I've always had a view of drawing as something very essential to painting. I've never done drawings that led to a painting, although some of my drawings have reflected ideas similar to those in contemporaneous paintings. But for

me drawing is something that exists in its own right. Sometimes after I've done a painting I'll do a drawing based on certain related ideas. If I want to find out more about an idea in a slightly different way, I'll approach it in that fashion.

DA: Some artists feel that there are certain kinds of artistic issues, concerns, or undertakings that don't quite all fit in one work or that have various aspects that require realization in more works in the same medium. Is this part of your idea of the function of drawing?

EP: I think so. A drawing usually doesn't take as long to do as a painting, although certain of my drawings have taken quite a while. There is another way to think about this whole subject of the relationship between drawing and painting: my paintings are developed initially with a black-line underpainting.

DA: At that stage the work is almost a drawing.

EP: Yes. In a sense the drawing is *in* the painting.

DA: Well, it's a very economical way to proceed, because if there is any kind of a fiddling around or developing of the idea at that stage, it's at least already on the canvas. I think drawing and painting are closely tied together in your work, although there aren't many elements in the finished paintings that can be called drawing, despite the presence of some writing or a detail that is in itself linear. The underpainting is a kind of tonal drawing beneath the color that affects the final hue because the layers of pigment often remain transparent.

EP: Some of the underpaintings and the drawings mentioned earlier have an intricacy similar to the finished paintings. Now, I often try to force myself to do things that are more haphazard, more quickly stated, in order to capture the initial nervous impulse, the gesture and its spontaneity. I have felt that I was excessively involved with drawing to the point where I might lose the spontaneity of the lines, and that I should somehow learn to limit myself to a shorter period of time in which to work on a drawing.

DA: The recent paintings seem to have even more intense color than before. There is a more resonating clang to the colors of the work now. Is this something that you have consciously developed?

EP: I'm using more layers of colors on top of the black-and-white underpainting now; as a result, I think there is a patina or build-up of multiple layers, sometimes two or three layers of the same color, that gives the hues a depth or richness. In the earlier years I would just put one layer of color over the black-and-white underpainting.

DA: Have you thought of this layering as a conscious analogy to techniques such as glazing or older techniques of slowly developing the color by means of washes or thinned pigment layers of this kind?

EP: It took a few years for me to realize that I am doing underpainting and glazing—like the "big guys" used to do. I didn't always use black underpainting. I used various dark colors. When I really became aware of it, I began to try to play to that as a strength. I explored and experimented with the idea of two, three, and four layers of the same color over a given spot to see what depth and luminosity one could achieve with such a multiple layering.

DA: Because such a technique probably takes more time, do you feel that you have to slow down to the pace of the development of the invention as it evolves on the canvas?

EP: When I do the underpainting, I intentionally try to avoid the presence of detail. I use larger brushes so that I can't really get much fineness but can see the major things.

DA: Then not many of the image's grosser aspects are changed or developed later? Once you get it where you want it in the black, then things are set to a certain degree?

EP: Because I use oil paint, it takes time for one layer to dry; only then do I go on to the next one. I work on several paintings at the same time to use my time more efficiently. Because the process occurs over a wide range of time, I feel there is also a possibility for more layering of *ideas* to take place; I hope the layers of ideas are being built into the layers of paint.

DA: With this kind of layering and more intricate technique, do you find that at a certain point you pretty much know the final form? How exactly do you know when the work is finished?

EP: That is one of the most intriguing questions of artistic involvement: how do you know when the thing you're working on is finished? That question always comes up in art class, and it's one of the most difficult to answer. The best answer I can give is that the work is done when there is a sense of completeness there. It goes back to my earlier mention of the art-school question: "Is there life in the picture plane? How do you know when it's alive?" It's like the moment in *Frankenstein* when a lightning bolt comes out of the sky. Within a painting, a film, a book, or a dance, lots of decisions are collectively built up and everything affects everything else. When there has been engendered a sense of interdependency, a sense of completeness to this circuitry and all is connected in some way, then the work is self-sustaining and you can walk away from it. After that point I realize I don't have to support it any more; it can stand on its own. I don't think I can calculate it and say: "Well, in ten minutes I'm going to be done when I get this one psychological element in place." It just suddenly strikes me that it's all there. I have to be responsive to the work, to listen to its ability to say that it is finished. For me there has to be the possibility of invention every step of the way; even though I set up the major elements with underpainting, critical decisions still remain.

DA: Right up to the last touch?

EP: Right. Sometimes those decisions are the most difficult of all because it's just some little twist of something and it's there. . . . It's a magical thing.

DA: Some painters I've known finish a group of works in a period in which they're working very well and hard, and it is the period itself that comes to an end. Then they keep the paintings around, looking at them critically for quite a while, editing, perhaps rejecting some. Does this ever happen to you, that something you thought was alive was only artificially maintained or on batteries as it were?

EP: There are variations in any artist's work; some are not so good, some are good. Some paintings I feel are not as functional as others. Dealing with them at this stage is a challenge. Such work provides me with an opportunity to do things I might never otherwise try in a painting; it's a desperation move. In an attempt to bail out a painting, I'll reach out for something that perhaps I've never done before and possibly find a new element for my bag of tricks.

DA: What would you say is the success rate of your emergency-room technique?

EP: I would say nine times out of ten the results are very exciting to me and they provide me some of the most important breakthroughs in terms of growth and development.

DA: Have you ever had a memorable struggle with a problem painting?

EP: There's a painting in the show called *Mid American* [cat. no. 5]. I gave up on that painting three or four times, then tried to revive it—mouth-to-mouth resuscitation—several times over a period of about a year or more. I finally arrived at the state that it's in now. I think painting is·an autobiographical activity. Sometimes one takes on certain challenges, certain problems, at a given time yet is not equipped to finish them at that time. Later, perhaps because of greater maturity, experience, or a different perspective, one can complete the painting. The kind of mind-games one plays with oneself are very interesting. One may at times have to trick oneself into a state of thinking or into doing the things necessary to solve a problem.

DA: Your recent exhibition at the Phyllis Kind Gallery here in Chicago [1988] seemed very aggressive.

EP: The paintings shown are high-impact paintings.

DA: These recent paintings bear annotations or graffiti. It looks as though there are notes on them, such as an artist might write on a drawing, when he makes notes about color or wants to remember this or that. These handwritten notes are quite small in scale in relation to the rest of the image.

EP: They create sort of an aftereffect. The intention here is to set up a kind of time-release factor, giving different levels of information There are certain things one doesn't confront immediately in these paintings. The first impact is there, followed by a delayed perception or realization of other aspects.

DA: In these paintings, particularly the large ones, the effect is so striking and splendid that one doesn't on first sight just march right up and start examining the surface for small things. One wants to take it in at one focal distance. Then curiosity about the facture brings one closer. Have you deliberately varied the handling of paint to refresh the compositional gambits?

EP: I think that some of those kinds of changes are motivated by an interest in formalistic change of pace; in other cases, if I want something to be more ethereal, less concretely stated, I'll intentionally alter the technique to be loose, tight, or varied, as the case might require.

DA: Like a number of other artists of your generation from Chicago, you've shown internationally for quite a long time. You showed in Scotland—in 1973, wasn't it? When you have traveled occasionally to exhibitions abroad in France or Switzerland or the United Kingdom, do you find that your paintings are perceived differently there than they are in America?

EP: Because the work reflects societal forces or elements —dynamics—in this culture that may vary in respect to another culture, I think that abroad there might be an absence of some of the associational information that is contained in the painting. This information might go unperceived, or unresponded to. Conversely, some things in the work might provoke a more acute reaction.

DA: But recently you have incorporated likenesses of universally recognized figures such as Elvis and Hitler.

EP: I did those to try to transcend societal and regional differences. I start with the premise that everybody knows who this is, everybody has a certain framework for this, and then I go from there. It's a societal, iconic, almost religious significance that some of these faces have in terms of how widely distributed images of that face have been. We all have a certain way of associating with them. From that as starting point, I proceed to destroy the image by what I do to it. I purposely painted Hitler with pastel colors; it's almost like the musical number "Springtime for Hitler" in Mel Brooks's film *The Producers*. I did Washington and Lincoln twice and tried to set up a time-release factor with parts of the painting intentionally colored to look almost like the work of an Old Master and other parts painted with the garish glow of more contemporary color.

DA: Now that the exhibition of your work is more or less set except for a few final choices and issues to be resolved, would you characterize what you think the exhibition is about? In other words, what does this selection of your work address in a broad way?

EP: I think it shows what I was all about at all these different times during my development as an artist starting in 1968 or so. I think one way to look at an exhibition is that just as the component parts that go into the making of one individual work all produce a totality, an exhibition can be thought of as component parts, a totality of various ideas that have concerned the artist. It's a reflection of the interests, the hang-ups, the preoccupations that I had at different times. Some of these things perhaps were a response to what was happening around me. The social unrest and upheaval that characterized the late 1960s show up in the work from time to time. I think it's just my path, my journey as a human being evolving within this sociological/societal framework.

DA: If you were describing your evolution as a kind of progress, what territories have you gone through and where do you find yourself now? You mentioned the impact of societal forces and events that all of us were responding to at the end of the 1960s, where the exhibition begins. Are there philosophical, metaphysical, and other private concerns in it too?

EP: I would say the early work was about my relationship as a young adult emerging into the turbulence of those times. In the intervening years I've gone through these various changes and have become more introspective; therefore the work has as well, in terms of psychological motivations and other concerns.

DA: After the societal issues of the 1960s, what would you say have been your overriding concerns and where do you find yourself now?

EP: Well, this is probably one of the hardest questions one could possibly try to answer, but I'll try because in a sense I feel that whatever my work is about is perhaps better judged by others rather than by myself. I'm too close to it. I think as the work progressed up through the 1970s, it was involved in various aspects of role playing, societal role playing, gamesmanship, interpersonal relationships, and gradually evolved into more and more of an inward, introspective, psychological sort of thing. What I feel is happening recently, or beginning to happen, is that maybe there is developing a little bit more of a concern for issues outside of self toward religion, weapons, societal violence, and art. I think that there had been a swing of the pendulum in terms of early societal concerns that progressed into inward concerns. Now the pendulum is swinging back out again.

AUTHOR'S NOTE

This conversation with Ed Paschke is drawn from a single interview session lasting about two-and-one-half hours that took place at the artist's home on the evening of October 19, 1988. The conversation commenced without an agenda and without notes but with the understanding that the topics would range over the artistic and interpretive issues raised by the retrospective exhibition at The Art Institute of Chicago, the Centre Pompidou in Paris, and the Dallas Museum of Art. Paschke asked the interviewer to "put the text into English," excising repetitive sections, clarifying ambiguities, and deflating windiness.

In accordance with the artist's instructions, the present text is an assembled reduction of the interviewer's questions and the responses and remarks of the artist. Instead of a record of the actual conversation, it is a concentrated and rectified presentation of Ed Paschke's thoughts about his work in its artistic and technical aspects and some of his reflections on the scope and nature of his career to date and as it is presented in this exhibition. The artist has read and approved the "interview."

1

PURPLE RITUAL, 1967
Oil on canvas
121.9 × 81.3 cm (48 × 32 in.)
Collection Robert H. Bergman, Chicago

2

AMOR, 1968
Oil on canvas
128.3 × 107.3 cm (50½ × 42¼ in.)
Collection Illinois Bell, Chicago

3

DOS CRIADOS, 1968
Oil on canvas
121.3 × 114.9 cm (47¾ × 45¼ in.)
Collection Robert H. Bergman, Chicago

4

ACCORDION MAN, 1969
Oil on canvas
121.9 × 96.5 cm (48 × 38 in.)
Collection of the artist

5

MID AMERICAN, 1969
Oil on canvas
114.3 × 152.4 cm (45 × 60 in.)
The Art Institute of Chicago, Gift of the Society for Contemporary
Art (1970.415)

6

RAMROD, 1969
Oil on canvas
111.7 × 66 cm (44 × 26 in.)
Jones/Faulkner Collection, Chicago

7

HOPHEAD, 1970
Oil on canvas
114.3 × 152.4 cm (45 × 60 in.)
Collection Dennis Adrian, Chicago

8

PINK LADY, 1970
Oil on canvas
161.3 × 127 cm (63½ × 50 in.)
Collection Thunder Thurm, Chicago

9

HAIRY SHOES, 1971
Oil on canvas
96.5 × 121.9 cm (38 × 48 in.)
Collection Thunder Thurm, Chicago

10

BAG BOOTS, 1972
Oil on canvas
127 × 127 cm (50 × 50 in.)
Collection Mrs. Edwin A. Bergman, Chicago

11

FRANCINE, 1973
Oil on canvas
152.4 × 127 cm (60 × 50 in.)
Fond National d'Art Contemporain, France

12

JEANINE, 1973
Oil on canvas
152.4 × 127 cm (60 × 50 in.)
Museum Moderner Kunst, Vienna

13

JOELLA, 1973
Oil on canvas
152.4 × 127 cm (60 × 50 in.)
Private Collection, Paris; courtesy Galerie Darthea Speyer

14

LUCY, 1973
Oil on canvas
152.4 × 96.5 cm (60 × 38 in.)
Museum of Contemporary Art, Chicago, Gift of Albert J. Bildner

15

RUFUS, 1974
Oil on canvas
139.7 × 139.7 cm (55 × 55 in.)
Collection Sonia Zaks, Chicago

16

ARMONDO, 1975
Oil on canvas
213.4 × 101.6 cm (84 × 40 in.)
Collection Lawrence and Evelyn Aronson, Glencoe, Illinois
(Chicago only)

17

RED SWEENEY, 1975
Oil on canvas
188 × 101.6 cm (74 × 40 in.)
Collection Mr. and Mrs. Francis E. Spiezer, Northbrook, Illinois

18

MACHINO, 1976
Oil on canvas
243.8 × 188 cm (96 × 74 in.)
Museum Boymans-van Beuningen, Rotterdam

19

SABREENA, 1976
Oil on canvas
243.8 × 188 cm (96 × 74 in.)
Collection Darthea Speyer, Paris

20

DOMINANT NURSE, 1977
Oil on linen
121.9 × 177.8 cm (48 × 70 in.)
Collection Marshall and Sophia Marcovitz, Glencoe, Illinois

21

MANDRIX, 1977
Oil on linen
177.8 × 101.6 cm (70 × 40 in.)
Collection Andrew and Betsy Rosenfield, Chicago

22

MELON-LAMÉ, 1977
Oil on linen
116.8 × 167.6 cm (46 × 66 in.)
Collection Albert A. Robin, Chicago

23

METAL DE BLEU, 1977

Oil on linen

81.3 × 55.9 cm (32 × 22 in.)

Collection Mr. and Mrs. Bernard Nath, Highland Park, Illinois

24

TERMINALE, 1977

Oil on linen

121.9 × 177.8 cm (48 × 70 in.)

Collection Peter and Eileen Broido, West Chicago, Illinois

25

CHO CHAN, 1978

Oil on linen

116.8 × 243.8 cm (46 × 96 in.)

Collection Sherry and Alan Koppel, Chicago

26

DURO-VERDE, 1978

Oil on linen

121.9 × 243.8 cm (48 × 96 in.)

Virginia Museum of Fine Arts, Richmond, Gift of The Sydney and Frances Lewis Foundation, Virginia

27

AMBROSIA, 1979

Oil on linen

132.1 × 152.4 cm (52 × 60 in.)

Collection Mrs. Edwin A. Bergman, Chicago

28

FUMAR, 1979

Oil on linen

152.4 × 116.8 cm (60 × 46 in.)

Collection Mr. and Mrs. Richard Sandor, Chicago

29

STRANGULITA, 1979

Oil on linen

116.8 × 203.2 cm (46 × 80 in.)

Collection Martin Sklar, New York

30

NERVOSA, 1980

Oil on linen

116.8 × 108 cm (46 × 42½ in.)

Collection Judith and Edward Neisser, Chicago

31

VIOLENCIA, 1980

Oil on linen

188 × 245.1 cm (74 × 96½ in.)

Whitney Museum of American Art, New York, Gift of Sherry and Alan Koppel in memory of Miriam and Herbert Koppel

32

L'IMPRESSION, 1981

Oil on linen

81.3 × 121.9 cm (32 × 48 in.)

Collection Darthea Speyer, New York

33

TELEVISMO, 1981

Oil on linen

106.7 × 213.4 cm (42 × 84 in.)

Collection William H. Plummer, Chicago

34

BIBUTSU, 1982

Oil on linen

203.2 × 243.8 cm (80 × 96 in.)

Collection Joseph D. and Janet M. Shein, Merion, Pennsylvania

35

FERNSEHEN, 1982

Oil on linen

106.7 × 213.4 cm (42 × 84 in.)

The Metropolitan Museum of Art, New York, Kathryn E. Hurd Fund, 1984

36

MECHANIQUE, 1982

Oil on linen

106.7 × 203.2 cm (42 × 80 in.)

Collection Joseph D. and Janet M. Shein, Merion, Pennsylvania

37

DER TANZ, 1982
Oil on linen
106.7 × 203.2 cm (42 × 80 in.)
Collection Albert A. Robin, Chicago

38

BAHAMAS, 1983
Oil on linen
203.2 × 233.7 cm (80 × 92 in.)
Collection Laura-Lee W. Woods, Los Angeles

39

LE SAC, 1983
Oil on linen
121.9 × 182.9 cm (48 × 72 in.)
Birmingham Museum of Art, Museum purchase with funds provided
by the Birmingham Art Association, Mr. and Mrs. Jack McSpadden,
Dr. and Mrs. Warren W. Arrasmith, and Bruce and Lois Berry

40

TOWANDA, 1983
Oil on linen
137.2 × 203.2 cm (54 × 80 in.)
Collection Robert H. Bergman, Chicago

41

VOSOTROS, 1983
Oil on linen
106.7 × 203.2 cm (42 × 80 in.)
Collection Robert Fulk, Chicago

42

AFRIQUE, 1984
Oil on linen
106.7 × 208.3 cm (42 × 82 in.)
Collection Laura and Marshall B. Front, Chicago

43

ELECTALADY, 1984
Oil on linen
188 × 233.7 cm (74 × 92 in.)
Collection James and Maureen Dorment, Rumson, New Jersey

44

MALIBU, 1984
Oil on linen
193 × 172.7 cm (76 × 68 in.)
Acquisition Trust, Jacksonville Art Museum, Florida

45

CALIENTE, 1985
Oil on linen
203.2 × 254 cm (80 × 100 in.)
The Art Institute of Chicago, Gift of the Staff (1986.92)

46

FRIO, 1985
Oil on linen
203.2 × 254 cm (80 × 100 in.)
Collection Robert H. Bergman, Chicago

47

TROIKA, 1985
Oil on linen
106.7 × 203.2 cm (42 × 80 in.)
Collection Mr. and Mrs. H. Arnold Steinberg, Westmount, Quebec

48

PAZZO, 1986
Oil on linen
127 × 203.2 cm (50 × 80 in.)
Collection Paul Tomlinson, Minneapolis

49

PRIMA VERE, 1986
Oil on linen
172.7 × 203.2 cm (68 × 80 in.)
Collection John L. Stewart, New York

50

PURISMA, 1986
Oil on linen
172.7 × 203.2 cm (68 × 80 in.)
Collection John L. Stewart, New York

51

COSMETICA, 1987
Oil on linen
172.7 × 203.2 cm (68 × 80 in.)
Collection John L. Stewart, New York

52

LIBREDO, 1987
Oil on linen
172.7 × 203.2 cm (68 × 80 in.)
Collection John L. Stewart, New York

53

MATINEE, 1987
Oil on linen
172.7 × 203.2 cm (68 × 80 in.)
Collection Robert H. Bergman, Chicago

54

PAPAL LUNACY, 1987
Oil on linen
172.7 × 203.2 cm (68 × 80 in.)
Collection Karen and Tony Barone, Venice, California

55

PEDIFEM, 1987
Oil on linen
203.2 × 203.2 cm (80 × 80 in.)
Milwaukee Art Museum, Purchase with National Endowment for
the Arts Matching Funds

56

BLACKSTONE, 1988
Oil on linen
172.7 × 203.2 cm (68 × 80 in.)
Collection Robert Rowan, Pasadena, California

57

NEGRETTE, 1988
Oil on linen
203.2 × 198.1 cm (80 × 78 in.)
Private Collection, Paris; courtesy Galerie Darthea Speyer

58

SANTA CABALLO, 1988
Oil on linen
127 × 198.1 cm (50 × 78 in.)
Collection James and Maureen Dorment, Rumson, New Jersey

59

YIN AND YANG, 1988
Oil on linen
203.2 × 198.1 cm (80 × 78 in.)
Collection Mr. and Mrs. Pierre-Pascal Bruneau, Paris

CHRONOLOGY

1939

Edward Francis Paschke, Jr., is born June 22, the second son of Waldrine and Edward Stanley Paschke; his brother, Richard, is two years his senior. The Catholic family resides in a middle-class neighborhood on the northwest side of Chicago (near Central Park and Diversey), where Edward Stanley drives a bakery truck.

1944—48

His father serves with the U.S. occupation forces in Germany following World War II; Paschke is fascinated by the Thurberesque cartoons decorating the letters his father mails home. On his father's return home, father and son work together crafting small objects in clay and wood; remembered especially is a crèche decorated with colored lights. The family moves a half mile north, near Belmont and Milwaukee avenues. Paschke attends public school. He is particularly awed by Walt Disney's film *Snow White and the Seven Dwarfs* and sends a collection of his cartoons to the Disney Studios; they respond with an encouraging letter of rejection: he is "too young."

1948—50

The family moves to a 160-acre farm in Lyndon Station, Wisconsin, population four hundred (approximately ten miles north of the Wisconsin Dells). Only four acres are used for raising crops, chickens, and turkeys; Paschke's father is employed building a dam on the Wisconsin River. Paschke feels "different" from the other children in his rural school.

1950—53

The family returns to Chicago and resides with Paschke's grandmother and uncles. He watches wrestling matches on television; the painting *Red Ball* (1971), depicting the Italian fighter "Little Flower," recalls this exposure. Paschke's parents buy a house near the intersection of Addison Street and Harlem Avenue; Paschke attends the local public school. His father and uncles construct a house in Mount Prospect; it remains unsold, so Paschke's father buys it himself and moves his family to the suburbs in the early spring of 1953. Paschke finishes eighth grade in the city.

1953—57

As a student at Arlington Heights High School, Paschke struggles through academic classes but excels in art and athletics. Although he does not play on the school team, he creates a highly praised series of cartoon strips on football players. Personally, he longs for tough and sophisticated urban surroundings. He engages in minor acts of delinquency; the breaking of a food store's plate-glass window results in a job bagging groceries to compensate for damages. Upon graduation from high school, he takes a job with a wrapping-paper factory in Bellwood. Paschke is intrigued by the flamboyant dress and "macho" conversations in Spanish of the Latino factory workers. He plays on their baseball team as pitcher.

1957

Paschke enrolls in The School of The Art Institute of Chicago in the Department of Drawing, Painting and Illustration. He excels in figure drawing (which he practices on the commuter train) but is unprepared to deal with formal concepts of composition; he is particularly mystified by theories of abstraction. At school Paschke paints expressionistically, but in private he draws realistically. Frequently he visits the Art Institute galleries where he admires paintings by Edouard Manet that depict figures in a "posterlike" manner against a black background—thereby violating the rules taught in class. Paschke also responds to compositions by Edgar Degas, particularly *The Millinery Shop* (1879/84) with its "repetition of shapes." Other favorite works include Peter Blume's *The Rock* (1948) and Jack Levine's *The Trial* (1953–54), which he finds "amazingly well painted with an economy of means." He is appreciative of J.-A.-D. Ingres's depictions of flesh and fabrics but is emotionally drawn to Rembrandt's self-portrait. The "Picasso: 75th Anniversary Exhibition" is an important experience for Paschke, as is the work of Richard Lindner included in the "62nd American Exhibition of Painting and Sculpture." In conjunction with academic classes, Paschke reads Charles Dickens, Aldous Huxley, H. L. Mencken, Franz Kafka, and Jack Kerouac.

1958

Favorite classes are two in life drawing: lineal with instructor John Fabion, and volumetric with Isobel Steele MacKinnon, a former student of Hans Hofmann. He also takes a class in lettering and magazine illustration. "Seurat Paintings and Drawings" introduces Paschke to the master's Conté-crayon works, which later serve as stylistic models for his own black-and-white drawings, such as the *Queen Dido* illustration for *Playboy* (see figs. 8, 9). Paschke exhibits *Commutism* (1958), a work based on his daily train rides, in the "1958 Chicago Artists Exhibition." He receives commendation for figure drawing from the School of the Art Institute.

1959–61

Paschke is exposed to the work of Ivan Albright, Leon Golub, Hans Hofmann, Jack Levine, and H. C. Westermann in the "63rd American Exhibition" at The Art Institute of Chicago. He also sees work by Bruce Conner, Robert Rauschenberg, and Larry Rivers in the "64th American Exhibition." He receives Faculty Honorable Mention for Advanced Painting and Figure Drawing (1960–61) and Class Honorable Mention for Figure Painting. He graduates from the Art Institute and wins the Anna Louise Raymond Foreign Traveling Fellowship ($1,500), which he uses for a three-month trip to Mexico with SAIC colleagues Karl Wirsum and Bert Phillips. In August 1961 he returns

to Chicago with slides, a pet parrot named Flaco, and a "visual written journal which locked the experience into my conscious or subconscious."

1961–62

In September Paschke takes an apprentice position at the Pace Studios, Chicago, where he cleans brushes and fetches coffee for the established commercial artists but receives no assignments of his own; he leaves after six months. He receives three commissions from *Playboy* (which include *Queen Dido*, fig. 8) and establishes a continuing relationship with the magazine (twenty-eight of his illustrations are published from 1962 to 1989). In May Paschke seeks employment in New York as a magazine illustrator. During his week there (staying near the Greyhound Station in Times Square), he visits Birdland and museums but is unsuccessful in obtaining a job. Back in Chicago and sensing an impending draft notice, he takes a civil-service examination and works (June–August) as a psychiatric aide at the Dunning Psychiatric Center (Chicago-Read Mental Health Center) to satisfy a long-standing curiosity concerning mental abnormality.

Returning to New York, Paschke rents a room on the Upper West Side and experiments with filmmaking, surreptitiously shooting the neighborhood derelicts. He rewards them with drinks for "mugging" and "acting" in his films. Later he splices this footage with professional movie clips: the interspersed visuals, which the artist had seen repeatedly as a child, are for him "a collage of early life."

1962–64

Paschke is drafted into the Army, November 4, 1962, and sent to Fort Polk, Louisiana. As a Specialist Fourth Class, he illustrates training aids to explain weapons and procedures to incoming troops. The images include diagrams on how to load a gun as well as full-scale renderings of guns; in retrospect, they remind him of Pop Art. Paschke's own proficiency with a .45-caliber revolver qualifies him for the job of pursuing AWOL soldiers across the South into Georgia and Texas. Personally, he is surprised by the tough brutality of several fellow draftees whose aggressive demeanor and life experiences significantly contrast with his own. Released from the Army on November 4, 1964, he returns to Chicago.

1965

In January he spends the remainder of his fellowship funds on a trip to Europe, visiting Rome, Florence, London, and Paris. Glad to be back in the United States, "where things were happening," he spends March and April in New York, where he sublets a room on the Lower East Side in an abandoned synagogue. To keep warm, he stuffs old *New York Times* in the cracked window frames; the most appealing images he cuts out and pastes on cardboard, inking over some parts and painting out others (see fig. 11). The resulting collages—many with duplicate figures—serve as prototypes for paintings. At The Museum of Modern Art's "Recent Painting and

Sculpture Acquisitions'' exhibition, he is impressed by Andy Warhol's *Gold Marilyn* (1962). Paschke returns to Chicago in April. He rents space in a condemned building (near North Avenue and Halsted Street) and paints—living on three dollars a day—until the money runs out. He sees exhibitions of works by Max Beckmann and Stuart Davis at The Art Institute of Chicago. He exhibits in ''Phalanx 3'' at the Illinois Institute of Technology with, among others, Tom Palazzolo, a colleague from the School of the Art Institute, whose work has interested him for its theatrical subject matter and depictions of amusement-park freaks. In October he takes a job at the Wilding Studio working with a team of draftsmen rendering a map to be used in training astronauts for the Apollo moon mission.

1966

Paschke leaves Wilding Studio in June to work for Silvestri, a display company, painting a Piranesi-style scene on the temporary facade around the first-floor windows of the Carson, Pirie, Scott and Company department store (fig. 10); he notes how ironic it is to be covering Louis Sullivan's architectural landmark with an imitation of art. Paschke explores the inner city's ethnic neighborhoods and historic shrines, including sites of infamous crimes and favored underworld hangouts. Occasionally he deposits an assortment of jackets on the back seat of his parents' car and, cruising from bar to bar, changes clothes to harmonize with the local clientele. He sees various exhibitions of work by Jack Levine, René Magritte, Robert Rauschenberg, and James Rosenquist and feels ''an affinity for their Surrealistic juxtapositional strategy.'' Paschke attends the first of the ''Hairy Who'' exhibitions at the Hyde Park Art Center. Seeing his former Art Institute colleagues James Falconer, Art Green, Gladys Nilsson, Jim Nutt, Suellen Rocca, and Karl Wirsum professionally engaged and organized causes him to question his own potential.

1967

Paschke stops work in June to give himself time to paint. *Large Round Open* (1965) (fig. 12) is exhibited in the ''Seventieth Annual Exhibition by Artists of Chicago and Vicinity.'' Paschke sees works by Claes Oldenburg and Dan Flavin at the newly opened Museum of Contemporary Art, Chicago.

1968

Paschke takes the role of ''leading man'' in Red Grooms's film *Tappy Toes*, which is staged in Grooms's room-sized construction, *Chicago* (1967–68). He joins with Sarah Canright, Edward C. Flood, Robert Guinan, and Richard Wetzel in the ''Nonplussed Some'' exhibition at the Hyde Park Art Center; Paschke shows nine works, including *Amor* (1968) and *Dos Criados* (1968) (cat. nos. 2, 3). *Purple Ritual* (1967) (cat. no. 1) and *Tet Inoffensive* (1968) are included in the Museum of Contemporary Art's exhibition ''Violence in Recent American Art.''

In the spring Paschke meets Nancy Cohn, a former Art Institute student he had dated during his undergraduate years. They are married November 22, and he adopts Marc, her three-year-old son from a former marriage. The couple takes an apartment at Clark Street and Oakdale Avenue; Paschke attends graduate school at the Art Institute on the GI Bill; a master's degree will enable him to obtain a teaching position that will support his family and still leave him time to paint.

1969

Paschke studies silkscreening with Sonia Sheridan at The School of The Art Institute of Chicago, where he prints *Budget Floors* (1968–69) (fig. 19). He enters a variety of national juried print and drawing shows as a means of obtaining exposure for his images; practically, he finds that works on paper can be most easily and inexpensively transported. He exhibits in ''Nonplussed Some Some More'' at the Hyde Park Art Center and in ''Don Baum Sez 'Chicago Needs Famous Artists''' at the Museum of Contemporary Art. Paschke is taken on by Deson-Zaks Gallery in Chicago. For ''Art by Telephone,'' an exhibition organized by the Museum of Contemporary Art, Chicago, he follows phoned instructions from British artist Richard Hamilton. *Dos Criados* (1968) is among three works included in ''Human Concern/Personal Torment: The Grotesque in American Art,'' organized by the Whitney Museum of American Art, New York.

1970

Paschke sees a retrospective exhibition of works by Andy Warhol —the artist whom he deems to be the most significant postwar American painter—at the Museum of Contemporary Art, Chicago. He exhibits *Accordion Man* (1969) (cat. no. 4) and other works at the Hyde Park Art Center in ''Marriage Chicago Style'' (see fig. 21). Paschke continues graduate studies at the School of the Art Institute where he is a Ponte del Arte Fellow. He receives his Master of Fine Arts on June 22, 1970 (his thirty-first birthday). In May he has his first one-person show, at the Deson-Zaks Gallery, Chicago. *Mid American* (1969) (cat. no. 5) is exhibited in the ''30th Society for Contemporary Art Exhibition'' at The Art Institute of Chicago and is acquired by the museum. The canvas is one Paschke has struggled with over an extended period of time, and which he had considered a failure prior to repainting its left side. One of Paschke's few repainted works, the painting conceals an image of a young boy beneath the now-visible baseball mitts.

Moving to St. Louis in the late summer, Paschke begins in September teaching at Meramec Community College, Kirkwood, Missouri. He shows Marshall McLuhan's documentary film *The Medium Is the Message* to his painting classes and is as impressed by the film's visual effects—which feature the superimposition of colored gels on live action—as he is by the content.

1971

Paschke continues to teach at Meramec through the spring term. A daughter, Sharon, is born in April. Paschke obtains a teaching position at Barat College, Lake Forest, Illinois, for the following year and returns to Chicago with his family. He rents an apartment in Rogers Park on the North Side near Loyola University; Nancy's younger brother, Daniel Cohn, a student at the school, moves in with them. Paschke uses the living room as a studio; he paints canvases of leather objects (see cat. nos. 9, 10) in order "to get away from the figure." Related imagery appears in his first lithograph, *Hairy Shoes* (1971), which he prints at Landfall Press, Chicago. Paschke exhibits with Sarah Canright, Edward C. Flood, Suellen Rocca, Barbara Rossi, and Karl Wirsum in the exhibition he names "Chicago Antigua" (subtitled "The Artful Codgers") at the Hyde Park Art Center. In April Paschke has his first one-person exhibition in New York, at the Hundred Acres Gallery. Unfavorable reviews deter him from a considered relocation to New York. In late fall Paschke exhibits paintings of shoes and other leather objects at Deson-Zaks Gallery. He "tattoos" himself with marking pens and poses with piles of shoes for the poster announcing the show.

1972

Paschke continues to teach at Barat College. *Amor* (1968) and *M.A. Lady* (1970) are among the works exhibited at the Museum of Contemporary Art in "Chicago Imagist Art." *Fantastic Images*, Franz Schulze's book accompanying the show, formally establishes an identity for Chicago artists. The exhibition travels to New York and is reviewed by Robert Hughes for *Time* magazine (further solidifying the group identity). Mac McGinnes, actor-manager of the Kingston Mines Theater in Chicago, asks Paschke to design sets—in the form of a series of drawings to be projected on a scrim—for Charles Ludlum's play *Turds in Hell.*

1973

In addition to teaching at Barat College, Paschke teaches an evening painting class at the Deerpath Art League in Lake Forest, Illinois. He buys a house in Chicago (on Estes Avenue near Damen Avenue) with a detached two-car garage he intends to remodel as a studio; the plan fails and instead he utilizes a room at Barat where he paints larger-than-life show girls (see cat. nos. 11–14). Paschke exhibits *Ruby Jo* (1973) at The Art Institute of Chicago's "Seventy-fourth Exhibition by Artists of Chicago and Vicinity"; it wins the Logan Prize. The painting is one in which he has utilized a "mistake"—a splashing mark caused by a falling brush—to create a fanciful "fringe" composed of numerous "splash" marks. His work is included in "Made in Chicago," organized by Don Baum, which travels to the XII Bienal de São Paulo, Brazil. Paschke teaches a summer session at The School of The Art Institute of Chicago, where he continues to hold teaching positions through the spring of 1976. He has his first one-person exhibition in Europe, at the Richard de Marco Gallery, Edinburgh; the show travels throughout England. He exhibits show-girl paintings at Deson-Zaks Gallery in late fall; he photographs Nancy in theatrical garments and draws tattoos on the image for the poster announcing the exhibition. The show is reviewed in the *Chicago Tribune* by Franz Schulze and in the *Chicago Daily News* by Alan G. Artner; both note the "revulsion" experienced in viewing the paintings but consider them worthy of serious discussion.

1974

Paschke has his first exhibition at Galerie Darthea Speyer, Paris. He also exhibits the show-girl paintings at Hundred Acres Gallery in New York. He has a one-person exhibition at the Contemporary Arts Center, Cincinnati, Ohio. In addition to continuing with the paintings of women, he begins a group of pencil drawings of men (see figs. 24, 25). In the fall he rents his first "official" studio: two rooms above the Adelphi Movie Theater on Clark Street (two blocks from his home). He begins work on paintings of men (see fig. 26 and cat. nos. 15–18).

1974–75

Lucy (1973) (cat. no. 14) and *Minnie* (1974) are among Paschke's six paintings exhibited in "Made in Chicago," an expanded version of the XII Bienal de São Paulo, organized by the National Collection of Fine Arts, Smithsonian Institution, Washington, D.C.; the show travels to the Museum of Contemporary Art, Chicago (1975). *Rufus* (1974) (cat. no. 15) is included in the "Seventy-fifth Exhibition by Artists of Chicago and Vicinity" at The Art Institute of Chicago. Paschke continues teaching at the School of the Art Institute and also teaches a series of critique classes at the Deerpath Art League (through summer 1978).

1975

Paschke's pencil drawings of men based on politicians (including Richard M. Nixon, fig. 24, H. R. [Bob] Haldeman, John Mitchell, fig. 25, and Herbert Kalmbach) are exhibited at the Pyramid Gallery in Washington, D.C. He explores "abstract" possibilities in his work by creating a series of large-scale paintings based on fabric; these relate to backgrounds in paintings such as *Armondo* (1975) and *Red Sweeney* (1975) (cat. nos. 16, 17). He has his last show at Deson-Zaks Gallery.

1976

Paschke continues teaching at the School of the Art Institute (through spring term) and the Deerpath Art League. He has a show at the Marion Locks Gallery in Philadelphia and a second with Darthea Speyer in Paris. His work is included in "Hyde Park Art Center Retrospective Exhibition: Historic Panoramic Abra Cadabra." In October he begins three lithographs based on drawings of men for Landfall Press, Chicago: *Hubert, Klaus,* and *Tudor* (all 1976–77). He also makes an etching, *Hat* (1976–77).

1977

Paschke begins a new body of work based on anonymous personages. In signing a small painting of a mask, *Signaturo* (1977), he develops a neonlike linear element that suggests involvement with electrical forms of communication; it later serves as an impetus for the "neon" paintings. *Tropicale* (1976) is exhibited in the "35th Society for Contemporary Art Exhibition: Drawings of the 70's" at The Art Institute of Chicago; it is acquired for the museum's collection.

Paschke assumes a full-time faculty position at Northwestern University, Evanston, Illinois. He also teaches at Columbia College, Chicago (February 1977–June 1978), and at the Suburban Fine Arts Center in Highland Park, Illinois (June 1977–June 1978). He has his first exhibition at the Phyllis Kind Gallery, Chicago.

1978–79

Paschke continues teaching at Northwestern University but eliminates other academic posts to give himself more time to paint. He prepares for two one-person shows: at the Galerie Darthea Speyer, Paris, and his first at the Phyllis Kind Gallery, New York. Russell Bowman's review of the New York show in *Arts Magazine* equates Paschke's luminous color with film technicolor or a painting by Mark Rothko. Of the nine group shows in which Paschke's work is exhibited, six specify "Chicago" in the exhibition title, further "regionalizing" his identity at a time when Paschke aspires to universalizing his imagery ("Eleven Chicago Painters," "Chicago: The City and Its Artists 1945–1978," "Contemporary Chicago Painters," "Chicago Collects Chicago," "Chicago: Self-Portraits," "Works on Paper: 77th Exhibition by Artists of Chicago and Vicinity"). Paschke shows at the "Salon de Mai," Grand Palais, Paris. His canvases illustrating Gloria Steinem and three "playgirls" (for Frederick Exley's "Saint Gloria and the Troll," *Playboy* [July 1974]) are included in the exhibition "The Art of Playboy from the First 25 Years."

1980

Inadequate heat forces Paschke to move his studio; he rents space on Howard Street, the Chicago/Evanston boundary. In particular, he is attracted to the area's constant activity centering around its elevated train station and the mixture of ethnic and racial groups. He continues teaching at Northwestern University; he becomes Chairman of the Department of Art Theory and Practice. The Paschke family moves to a larger house in Sauganash on Chicago's Northwest Side, a neighborhood favored by Chicago politicians, police chiefs, and other local officials. The Paschkes are comfortable in the house but dislike the suburban ambience; Paschke later expresses his attitude in *Sauganash* (1983), which depicts two monochromatic and militaristic heads.

1981

Hairy Shoes (1971), *Cho Chan* (1978), and *Fumar* (1979) (cat. nos. 9, 25, 28) are among fourteen works shown in "Who Chicago? An Exhibition of Contemporary Imagists," organized by the Ceolfrith Gallery, Sunderland Arts Centre, Sunderland, England. In addition to teaching at Northwestern University, Paschke accepts various speaking/critiquing engagements at other colleges and universities; he appreciates the opportunity to visit diverse parts of the country. *Violencia* (1980) (cat. no. 31) is included in the "1981 Biennial Exhibition," Whitney Museum of American Art, New York, and acquired for the museum's collection. Paschke's work is included in a group exhibition organized by the Centre d'Art Contemporain, Geneva.

1982

Duro-Verde (1978) (cat. no. 26) is included in "From Chicago," The Pace Gallery, New York; it is reproduced in a review by John Russell in *The New York Times*. Paschke has a retrospective at The Renaissance Society at the University of Chicago. He serves as guest curator for the exhibition "Flip! Flash! Pinball Art!" cosponsored by the Chicago Public Library Cultural Center and the Chicago Council on Fine Arts. *Rufus* (1974) appears on the cover of the October issue of *Art in America*.

1983

Paschke creates a group of loose, expressionistic drawings using oil sticks and paint on large sheets of rag paper. He is commissioned by the Business Committee for the Arts to make a print; *Execo* (1983)—an image of an overweight and presumably self-congratulatory C.E.O.—is unflattering to its intended group but is received without negative backlash. Paschke creates *Viseon*, a lithograph/poster for the 1984 "Chicago International Art Exposition." He has his first exhibition on the West Coast with the Fuller Goldeen Gallery, San Francisco.

1984–85

Paschke exhibits five paintings in "An International Survey of Recent Painting and Sculpture" at The Museum of Modern Art, New York. He designs murals for the Dome Room at Limelight, a Chicago nightclub. The images are appropriated from photographs in Warhol's *Interview* magazine. Paschke resigns the chairmanship of the Department of Art Theory and Practice at Northwestern University but continues to teach as a tenured professor. He assists The Renaissance Society at the University of Chicago in organizing the "Chicago White Sox Baseball Card Portraits." He receives the Academy Honor from The Academy High School for Performing and Visual Arts, Chicago.

1986–88

Violencia (1980) appears as the cover image for a catalogue accompanying "The Figure as Subject: The Last Decade," the inaugural exhibition in the south gallery at the Whitney Museum of American Art at Equitable Center, New York. Ten of Paschke's works appear in an exhibition featuring professors of art at Northwestern University, "Painting at Northwestern: Conger, Paschke, Valerio" (see cat. nos. 39, 40, 44). *Caliente* (1985) (cat. no. 45) is included in the "Seventy-fifth American Exhibition" at The Art Institute of Chicago; it is acquired for the museum's collection. Paschke shows his iconic heads in New York in concurrent one-person exhibitions at the Phyllis Kind Gallery and with a new dealer, Luhring, Augustine and Hodes (see cat. nos. 49–53, 55). He also has his first show with the Dorothy Goldeen Gallery, Santa Monica, California. The Lowe Art Museum, Coral Gables, Florida, organizes a retrospective exhibition of sixteen of Paschke's works (1972–88).

1970

Chicago, Deson-Zaks Gallery (exh. cat.)

1971

Chicago, Deson-Zaks Gallery
New York, Hundred Acres Gallery

1972

Chicago, Deson-Zaks Gallery

1973

Chicago, Deson-Zaks Gallery
Edinburgh, Richard De Marco Gallery (traveled in England and Scotland)

1974

Cincinnati, Contemporary Arts Center
New York, Hundred Acres Gallery
Paris, Galerie Darthea Speyer

1975

Chicago, Deson-Zaks Gallery
Washington, D.C., Pyramid Gallery

1976

Paris, Galerie Darthea Speyer
Philadelphia, Marion Locks Gallery

1977

Chicago, Phyllis Kind Gallery

1978

New York, Phyllis Kind Gallery
Paris, Galerie Darthea Speyer

1979

Chicago, Phyllis Kind Gallery
New York, Phyllis Kind Gallery

1980

New York, Phyllis Kind Gallery

1981

Paris, Galerie Darthea Speyer (exh. cat.)

1982

Chicago, The Renaissance Society at the University of Chicago, "Ed Paschke: Selected Works 1967–1981" (exh. cat.) (traveled to Josyln Art Museum, Omaha, Nebraska; Contemporary Art Museum, Houston)
New York, Phyllis Kind Gallery

1983

New York, Phyllis Kind Gallery
Paris, Galerie Darthea Speyer (exh. cat.)
Pittsburgh, Pennsylvania, Hewlett Gallery, Carnegie-Mellon University, "Ed Paschke: New Paintings 1983" (exh. cat.) (traveled to Phyllis Kind Gallery, Chicago; Kalamazoo Institute of the Arts, Michigan)

1984

Geneva, Galerie Bonnier
New York, Phyllis Kind Gallery
San Francisco, Fuller Goldeen Gallery

1986

New York, Phyllis Kind Gallery
Paris, Galerie Darthea Speyer (exh. cat.)
San Francisco, Fuller Goldeen Gallery

1987

New York, Luhring, Augustine and Hodes Gallery
New York, Phyllis Kind Gallery

1988

Chicago, Phyllis Kind Gallery
Coral Gables, Florida, Lowe Art Museum, University of Miami
Geneva, Galerie Bonnier (exh. cat.)
Paris, Galerie Darthea Speyer (exh. cat.)
Santa Monica, California, Dorothy Goldeen Gallery

1989

London, James Mayor Gallery
New York, Phyllis Kind Gallery
Paris, Galerie Darthea Speyer (exh. cat.)

SELECTED GROUP EXHIBITIONS

1958

Chicago, The Art Institute of Chicago and Chicago Art Organizations, Navy Pier, "1958 Chicago Artists Exhibition" (exh. cat.)

1961–62

Chicago, The Art Institute of Chicago, "First Biennial of Prints, Drawings and Watercolors"

1965

Chicago, Illinois Institute of Technology, "Phalanx 3"

1966

Chicago, The Art Institute of Chicago, "Sixty-ninth Annual Exhibition by Artists of Chicago and Vicinity" (exh. cat.)

1967

Chicago, The Art Institute of Chicago, "Seventieth Annual Exhibition by Artists of Chicago and Vicinity" (exh. cat.)

1967–69

Chicago, Illinois Arts Council, "Six Illinois Painters 67/69: Arcilesi, Ito, Lanyon, Paschke, Rosofsky, Wirsum" (exh. cat.) (traveled throughout Illinois)

1968

Chicago, Hyde Park Art Center, "Nonplussed Some"

DeKalb, Illinois, Northern Illinois University, "National Print and Drawing Exhibition"

Philadelphia, Moore College of Art Gallery, "American Drawing 1968"

1968–69

Chicago, Museum of Contemporary Art, "Violence in Recent American Art" (exh. cat.)

1969

Chicago, Allen Frumkin Gallery, "Chicago Print Show"

Chicago, The Art Institute of Chicago, "Seventy-second Annual Exhibition by Artists of Chicago and Vicinity" (exh. cat.)

Chicago, Hyde Park Art Center, "Nonplussed Some Some More"

Chicago, Museum of Contemporary Art, "Art by Telephone"

Chicago, Museum of Contemporary Art, "Don Baum Sez 'Chicago Needs Famous Artists'"

Philadelphia, Institute of Contemporary Art, University of Pennsylvania, "Famous Artists"

Philadelphia, Institute of Contemporary Art, University of Pennsylvania, "The Spirit of the Comics" (exh. cat.)

1969–70

New York, Whitney Museum of American Art, "Human Concern/Personal Torment: The Grotesque in American Art" (exh. cat.) (traveled to University Art Museum, University of California, Berkeley)

1970

Chicago, The Art Institute of Chicago, "30th Society for Contemporary Art Exhibition"

Chicago, Hyde Park Art Center, "Marriage Chicago Style"

London, Tate Gallery, "Richard Hamilton" (for a collaboration piece)

New York, Richard Feigen Gallery, "Thirteen Chicago Artists"

San Francisco, San Francisco Art Institute, "Surplus Slop from the Windy City" (traveled to Sacramento State College Art Gallery, California)

1971

Barcelona, "III Bienal International del Deporte en Las Bellas Artes"

Carbondale, Illinois, Mitchell Gallery, Southern Illinois University, "National Invitational Drawing Exhibit"

Chicago, The Art Institute of Chicago, "31st Society for Contemporary Art Exhibition: Works on Paper"

Chicago, Hyde Park Art Center, "Chicago Antigua"

Chicago, The Museum of Science and Industry, "Each, in His Own Way: The Commemorative Art Collection of the Florists' Transworld Delivery Association"

DeKalb, Illinois, Northern Illinois University, "Arts USA: 2" (exh. cat.)

1972

Chicago, The Art Institute of Chicago, "32nd Society for Contemporary Art Exhibition: Contemporary Works of Art"

Chicago, Museum of Contemporary Art, "Chicago Imagist Art" (exh. cat.) (traveled to The New York Cultural Center, New York)

Indianapolis, Indiana, Indianapolis Museum of Art, "Painting and Sculpture Today 1972"

1972–73

Ottawa, National Gallery of Canada, "What They're Up To in Chicago" (traveled throughout Canada)

1973

Chicago, The Art Institute of Chicago, "Seventy-fourth Exhibition by Artists of Chicago and Vicinity" (exh. cat.)

Chicago, Illinois Bell, The Lobby Gallery, "Chicago Imagist Art: Drawings—A Postscript"

New York, Whitney Museum of American Art, "1973 Biennial Exhibition: Contemporary American Art"

São Paulo, Brazil, Museu de Arte, "XII Bienal de São Paulo: Made in Chicago" (traveled to Museo de Arte Moderno, Bogotá; Museo Nacional de Bellas Artes, Santiago; Museo Nacional de Bellas Artes, Buenos Aires; Museo de Arte Moderno, Mexico City)

1974

Chicago, The Art Institute of Chicago, "Seventy-first American Exhibition" (exh. cat.)

Chicago, Center for Continuing Education, The University of Chicago, "The Chicago Style: Drawings"

Chicago, Center for Continuing Education, The University of Chicago, "The Chicago Style: Painting" (exh. cat.)

Chicago, The Renaissance Society at the University of Chicago, "Contemporary Still Life"

Urbana-Champaign, Illinois, Krannert Art Museum, University of Illinois, "Contemporary American Painting and Sculpture 1974" (exh. cat.)

Wilmington, Delaware, Delaware Art Museum, "Contemporary American Paintings from the Lewis Collection"

1974–75

Brooklyn, New York, The Brooklyn Museum, "Nineteenth National Print Exhibition" (exh. cat.) (traveled to Fine Arts Gallery of San Diego, California)

Chicago, The Art Institute of Chicago, "Seventy-fifth Exhibition by Artists of Chicago and Vicinity" (exh. cat.)

Washington, D.C., National Collection of Fine Arts, Smithsonian Institution, "Made in Chicago" (exh. cat.) (traveled to Museum of Contemporary Art, Chicago)

1975

Baltimore, Maryland, The Baltimore Museum of Art, Print Exhibition

Peoria, Illinois, Lakeview Center for the Arts, "The Classic Revival"

Springfield, Illinois, Illinois State Museum

1975–76

Normal, Illinois, Visual Arts Gallery, Illinois State University, "Illinois Artists 76: A Bicentennial Invitational Exhibition" (traveled throughout Illinois)

Philadelphia, Moore College of Art Gallery, "North, East, West, South, and Middle: An Exhibition of Contemporary American Drawings" (exh. cat.) (traveled to Pratt Graphics Center, New York; Corcoran Gallery of Art, Washington, D.C.; The Fort Worth Art Museum, Texas; La Jolla Museum of Contemporary Art, California)

1976

Chicago, Hyde Park Art Center, "Hyde Park Art Center Retrospective Exhibition: Historic Panoramic Abra Cadabra" (exh. cat.)

Chicago, Illinois Arts Council, "Koffler Foundation Collection" (exh. cat.) (traveled throughout Illinois)

Chicago, The School of The Art Institute of Chicago, "Visions/Painting and Sculpture: Distinguished Alumni 1945–Present" (exh. cat.)

Hammond, Indiana, Northern Indiana Arts Association Center, "Indiana-Illinois Bicentennial Painting Exhibition"

Lafayette, Indiana, Memorial Union Gallery, Purdue University, "Chicago Art"

Paris, Grand Palais, "FIAC '76: 3ème Foire Internationale d'Art Contemporain" (exh. cat.)

Urbana-Champaign, Krannert Art Museum, University of Illinois, "Painting and Sculpture by Midwest Faculty-Artists" (traveled to Indiana University Art Museum, Bloomington)

1976–77

Sacramento, California, E. B. Crocker Art Gallery, "The Chicago Connection" (exh. cat.) (traveled to Newport Harbor Art Museum, California; Phoenix Art Museum, Arizona; Brooks Memorial Art Gallery, Memphis, Tennessee; Memorial Art Gallery, University of Rochester, New York)

1977

Austin, Texas, University Art Museum, University of Texas, "Recent American Painting"

Chicago, The Art Institute of Chicago, "35th Society for Contemporary Art Exhibition: Drawings of the 70's"

Chicago, The Chicago Public Library Cultural Center, "Masterpieces of Recent Chicago Art" (exh. cat.)

Chicago, Museum of Contemporary Art, "A View of a Decade"

Chicago, The Renaissance Society at the University of Chicago, "Recent Portraiture" (exh. cat.)

Chicago, The David and Alfred Smart Gallery, The University of Chicago, "Artists View the Law in the 20th Century" (exh. cat.)

Columbus, Ohio, Ohio State University Gallery of Fine Art, "Chicago 77"

Greensboro, North Carolina, Weatherspoon Art Gallery, University of North Carolina, "13th Weatherspoon Annual Exhibition: Art on Paper"

Lafayette, Indiana, Memorial Union Gallery, Purdue University, "Critic's Choice"

Madison, Wisconsin, The Madison Art Center, "Contemporary Figurative Painting in the Midwest: An Invitational Exhibition at the Madison Art Center" (exh. cat.)

1977–78

Chicago, Museum of Contemporary Art, "Landfall Press: A Survey of Prints (1970–1977)"

1978

Ann Arbor, Michigan, The University of Michigan Museum of Art, "Chicago: The City and Its Artists 1945–1978" (exh. cat.)

Cedar Falls, Iowa, University of Northern Iowa Gallery of Art, "Contemporary Chicago Painters" (exh. cat.)

Chicago, The Art Institute of Chicago, "Works on Paper: 77th Exhibition by Artists of Chicago and Vicinity" (exh. cat.)

Chicago, Kemper Insurance Companies, "Kemper Art Collection" (exh. cat.)

Chicago, Nancy Lurie Gallery, "Chicago: Self-Portraits" (exh. cat.)

DeKalb, Illinois, Northern Illinois University, "Chicago Collects Chicago" (exh. cat.)

Paris, Grand Palais, "Salon de Mai"

Tallahassee, Florida, Florida State University Gallery of Art, "Eleven Chicago Painters" (exh. cat.)

1978–79

Chicago, The Chicago Public Library Cultural Center, "The Art of Playboy from the First 25 Years" (exh. cat.)

1979

Aspen, Colorado, The Aspen Center for the Visual Arts, "American Portraits of the Sixties and Seventies" (exh. cat.)

DeKalb, Illinois, Northern Illinois University, "Contemporary Images: Selections from the Student Association Art Collection" (exh. cat.)

1979–80

Chicago, The Art Institute of Chicago, "100 Artists 100 Years: Alumni of The School of The Art Institute of Chicago, Centennial Exhibition" (exh. cat.)

Washington, D.C., National Museum of American Art, Smithsonian Institution, "The Koffler Foundation: Chicago Currents" (traveling exhibition)

1980

Annandale-on-Hudson, New York, Proctor Art Center, Bard College, "Images"

Chapel Hill, North Carolina, The Ackland Art Museum, University of North Carolina, "Some Recent Art from Chicago" (exh. cat.)

Chicago, Illinois Bell, The Lobby Gallery, "Professors of Art in Northern Illinois" (exh. cat.)

Chicago, Illinois Bell, The Lobby Gallery, "The Social Mirror: Selections from the Illinois Bell Collection" (exh. cat.)

Chicago, The David and Alfred Smart Gallery, The University of Chicago, "Master Prints from Landfall Press" (exh. cat.)

Evanston, Illinois, Mary and Leigh Block Gallery, Northwestern University, "Collaborations" (exh. cat.)

London, James Mayor Gallery, "Six Artists from Chicago"

Milwaukee, Wisconsin, Milwaukee Art Museum, "American Prints 1960–1980" (exh. cat.)

Urbana-Champaign, Illinois, Krannert Art Museum, University of Illinois, "Selections from the Collection of George M. Irwin" (exh. cat.)

1980–81

Chicago, Illinois Bell, The Lobby Gallery, "Professors of Art in Northern Illinois" (exh. cat.) (traveled throughout Illinois)

Mt. Vernon, Illinois, Mitchell Museum, "Chicago Artists"

1980–82

Sunderland, England, Ceolfrith Gallery, Sunderland Arts Centre, "Who Chicago? An Exhibition of Contemporary Imagists" (exh. cat.) (traveled to Camden Arts Centre, London; Third Eye Centre, Glasgow; Scottish National Gallery of Modern Art, Edinburgh; Institute of Contemporary Art, Boston; Contemporary Arts Center, New Orleans)

1981

Cleveland, Ohio, The Cleveland Museum of Art, "Contemporary Artists" (exh. cat.)

Geneva, Centre d'Art Contemporain

Grand Fork, North Dakota, University of North Dakota Art Gallery, "The Figure: A Celebration" (traveled to Art Museum of South Texas, Corpus Christi)

Munich, Haus der Kunst (curated by the Whitney Museum of American Art), "Amerikanische Malerei 1930–1980" (exh. cat.)

New York, Semaphore Gallery, "The Anxious Figure"

New York, Whitney Museum of American Art, "Biennial Exhibition, Whitney Museum of American Art, 1981" (exh. cat.)

Ridgefield, Connecticut, Aldrich Museum of Contemporary Art, "New Dimensions in Drawing"

1981–82

Chicago, The Art Institute of Chicago, "Prints and Multiples: 79th Exhibition by Artists of Chicago and Vicinity" (traveled throughout Illinois; The National Academy of Design, New York; National Museum of American Art, Smithsonian Institution, Washington, D.C.; Portland Art Museum, Oregon)

Milwaukee, Wisconsin, Milwaukee Art Museum, "Center Ring: The Artist, Two Centuries of Circus Art" (traveled to Columbus Museum of Art, Ohio; New York State Museum, Albany; The Corcoran Gallery of Art, Washington, D.C.)

Newport Harbor, California, Newport Harbor Art Museum, "Inside/Out: Self beyond Likeness" (traveled to Portland Art Museum, Oregon; Joslyn Art Museum, Omaha, Nebraska)

United States International Communication Agency, "Landfall Press 1970–1980" (exh. cat.) (traveling exhibition)

1982

Amherst, Massachusetts, University of Massachusetts, "Contemporary Prints: The Figure beside Itself"

Chicago, The Chicago Public Library Cultural Center, "Flip! Flash! Pinball Art!" (exh. cat.)

Chicago, Museum of Contemporary Art, "Selections from the Dennis Adrian Collection" (exh. cat.)

Kansas City, Kansas, Douglas Drake Gallery, "Hot Chicago"

Kansas City, Missouri, Kansas City Art Institute, "Chicago Imagists" (traveled to Saginaw Art Museum, Michigan)

Milwaukee, Wisconsin, Milwaukee Art Museum, "Recent Directions"

New York, The Art Lending Service of The Museum of Modern Art, "Illuminations" (traveled to Dancer, Fitzgerald, Sample, Inc., New York; General Electric Company, Fairfield, Connecticut; Freeport McMoRan, Inc., New York)

New York, The Pace Gallery, "From Chicago" (exh. cat.)

New York, Whitney Museum of American Art, "Focus on the Figure: Twenty Years" (exh. cat.)

1983

Annandale-on-Hudson, New York, Proctor Art Center, Bard College, "The T.V. Show"

Atlanta, Nexus Gallery, "What Artists Have to Say about Nuclear War" (exh. cat.)

Bloomington, Illinois, Illinois Wesleyan University, "Contemporary Chicago Images"

Chicago, ARC Gallery, "Art on the Edge"

Chicago, Artemisia Gallery, "Looking at Women: Images of Women by Contemporary Artists"

Cologne, Galerie Rudolf Zwirner, "Brown, Nutt, Paschke"

Evanston, Illinois, Terra Museum of American Art, "200 Years of American Painting from Private Chicago Collections"

Fairfield, Connecticut, General Electric Company, "On the Leading Edge: Cross-Currents in the Contemporary Art of the Eighties"

Geneva, Galerie Bonnier, "Gladys Nilsson, Jim Nutt, Ed Paschke, Suellen Rocca, Karl Wirsum" (exh. cat.)

Greensboro, North Carolina, Weatherspoon Art Gallery, University of North Carolina, "20th Century Figural Images on Paper"

New York, American Academy of Arts and Letters, "Painting and Sculpture by Candidates for Art Awards"

New York, Artists' Choice Museum at Marisa del Re Gallery, "Bodies and Souls"

New York, Phyllis Kind Gallery, "Dialect ≠ Dialectic: A Group of Artists with Complex Individual Vocabularies" (traveled to Phyllis Kind Gallery, Chicago)

New York, Monique Knowlton Gallery, "Intoxication"

Pittsburgh, PPG Place, "New York Painting Today—A Three River Arts Festival Exhibition" (exh. cat.)

Reading, Pennsylvania, Friedman Gallery, Albright College, "A Painting Show/Selections from a Private Collection"

1983–84

Austin, Texas, Archer M. Huntington Gallery, University of Texas, "New American Painting: A Tribute to James and Marie Michener"

1984

Athens, Ohio, Trisolini Gallery, University of Ohio, "Chicago Cross-Section"

Chicago, Rhona Hoffman Gallery, "Artists Call against United States Intervention in Central America and the Caribbean"

Chicago, Museum of Contemporary Art, "Selected Gifts from The Joseph and Jory Shapiro Collection" (exh. cat.)

Chicago, Museum of Contemporary Art, "Ten Years of Collecting at the MCA" (exh. cat.)

Fairfield, Connecticut, General Electric Company (curated by the Art Lending Service of The Museum of Modern Art, New York), "Ten Years of Contemporary Art"

Middlebury, Vermont, Johnson Gallery, Middlebury College, "Art in the '80's: Post Avant-Garde"

New York, Freeport McMoRan, Inc. (curated by the Art Lending Service of The Museum of Modern Art, New York), "Selections: Art since 1945"

New York, The Museum of Modern Art, "An International Survey of Recent Painting and Sculpture" (exh. cat.)

New York, Sutton Gallery, "American Drawings 1983 from A to Z"

San Francisco, Fuller Goldeen Gallery, "50 Artists/50 States"

1984–85

Chicago, Phyllis Kind Gallery, "Imagist Update"

Mexico City, Tamayo Museo, "New Narrative Painting"

New York, Whitney Museum of American Art, "American Art since 1970" (exh. cat.) (traveled to La Jolla Museum of Contemporary Art, California; Museo Tamayo, Mexico City; North Carolina Museum of Art, Raleigh; Sheldon Memorial Art Gallery, University of Nebraska, Lincoln; Center for the Arts, Miami)

Seattle, Washington, Henry Art Gallery, University of Washington, "Strange"

Tokyo, Laforet Museum, "Correspondences: New York Choice '84"

Washington, D.C., Hirshhorn Museum and Sculpture Garden, Smithsonian Institution, "Content: A Contemporary Focus 1974–1984" (exh. cat.)

1984–86

New York, The Art Museum Association of America, "Disarming Images: Art for Nuclear Disarmament" (exh. cat.) (traveled to Contemporary Arts Center, Cincinnati, Ohio; University Art Gallery, San Diego State University, California; Museum of Art, Washington State University, Pullman; New York State Museum, Albany; University Art Museum, University of California, Santa Barbara; Munson-Williams-Proctor Institute Museum of Art, Utica, New York; Fine Arts Gallery, University of Nevada, Las Vegas; Baxter Art Gallery, California Institute of Technology, Pasadena; Yellowstone Art Center, Billings, Montana; Bronx Museum of the Arts, New York)

1984–87

New York, Independent Curators Inc., "Large Drawings" (exh. cat.) (traveled to Bass Museum of Art, Miami; Madison Art Center, Wisconsin; Norman Mackenzie Art Gallery, Regina, Saskatchewan; Anchorage Historical and Fine Arts Museums, Alaska; Santa Barbara Museum of Art, California)

1985

Bayside, New York, Queensborough Community College of the City of New York, "The Parodic Power of Popular Imagery" (exh. cat.) (traveled to Freedman Gallery, Albright College, Reading, Pennsylvania; Marion Locks Gallery, Philadelphia)

Chicago, The Art Institute of Chicago, "The Mr. & Mrs. Joseph Randall Shapiro Collection" (exh. cat.)

Chicago, The Renaissance Society at the University of Chicago, "Chicago White Sox Baseball Card Portraits"

New York, Pratt Manhattan Center, "Illuminating Color: Four Approaches in Contemporary Painting and Photography" (traveled to Pratt Institute Gallery, Brooklyn, New York)

New York, Whitney Museum of American Art, "Drawing Acquisitions, 1981–1985" (exh. cat.)

New York, Whitney Museum of American Art, "Biennial Exhibition, Whitney Museum of American Art, 1985" (exh. cat.)

Newark, New Jersey, Robeson Center Gallery, Rutgers, The State University of New Jersey, "The Political Landscape" (exh. cat.)

Philadelphia, Philadelphia Art Alliance, "Psychodrama"

Richmond, Virginia, Virginia Museum of Fine Arts, "Late Twentieth Century Art: Selections from the Sydney and Frances Lewis Collection in the Virginia Museum of Fine Arts" (exh. cat.)

Seattle, Washington, Henry Art Gallery, University of Washington, "Sources of Light: Contemporary American Luminism" (exh. cat.)

Trenton, New Jersey, Hollman Hall Art Gallery, Trenton State College, "Contemporary Issues II"

Washington, D.C., Corcoran Gallery of Art, "The 39th Corcoran Biennial Exhibition of American Painting" (exh. cat.) (traveled to Mary and Leigh Block Gallery, Northwestern University, Evanston, Illinois; The Butler Institute of American Art, Youngstown, Ohio; Contemporary Arts Center, Cincinnati, Ohio)

1986

Chicago, The Art Institute of Chicago, "Seventy-fifth American Exhibition" (exh. cat.)

Evanston, Illinois, Mary and Leigh Block Gallery, Northwestern University, "Painting at Northwestern: Conger, Paschke, Valerio" (exh. cat.)

Flushing, New York, The Queens Museum, "Television's Impact on Contemporary Art" (exh. cat.)

Los Angeles, Los Angeles Contemporary Exhibitions, "T.V. Generation"

New York, Whitney Museum of American Art at Equitable Center, "The Figure as Subject: The Last Decade" (exh. cat.)

New York, Whitney Museum of American Art at Philip Morris, "The Changing Likeness: Twentieth Century Portrait Drawing" (exh. cat.)

1986–90

New York, The Art Museum Association of America, "Focus on the Image: Selections from the Rivendell Collection" (exh. cat.) (traveled to Phoenix Art Museum, Arizona; Museum of Art, University of Oklahoma, Norman; Munson-Williams-Proctor Institute Museum of Art, Utica, New York; University of South Florida Art Galleries, Tampa; Lakeview Museum of Art and Sciences, Lakeview, Illinois; University Art Museum, California State University, Long Beach; Laguna Gloria Art Museum, Austin, Texas)

1987

Berkeley, California, University of California, University Art Museum, "Made in U.S.A.: An Americanization in Modern Art, the '50s and '60s" (exh. cat.) (traveled to The Nelson-Atkins Museum of Art, Kansas City, Missouri; Virginia Museum of Fine Arts, Richmond)

Bowling Green, Ohio, School of Art Gallery, Bowling Green University, "Of New Account: The Chicago Imagists"

Chicago, The Renaissance Society at the University of Chicago, "Drawings of the Chicago Imagists"

Chicago, The David and Alfred Smart Gallery, The University of Chicago, "The Chicago Imagist Print" (exh. cat.)

Chicago, Terra Museum of American Art, "Surfaces: Two Decades of Painting in Chicago—Seventies & Eighties" (exh. cat.)

New York, American Foundation for AIDS Research, Phyllis Kind Gallery, "Art against Aids" (exh. cat.)

1988

Milwaukee, Wisconsin, Milwaukee Art Museum, "1988/The World of Art Today" (exh. cat.)
Milwaukee, Wisconsin, UWM Art Museum, University of Wisconsin, "Realisms" (exh. cat.)

1988–89

Albany, New York State Museum in association with the Smithsonian Institution Traveling Exhibition Service, "Diamonds Are Forever: Artists and Writers on Baseball" (exh. cat.) (traveled to Norton Gallery of Art, West Palm Beach, Florida; Museo de Arte e Historia de San Juan; The Contemporary Arts Center, Cincinnati; Utah Museum of Fine Arts, University of Utah, Salt Lake City; The Museum of Fine Arts, Houston; The Baltimore Museum of Art; The Chicago Public Library Cultural Center; The Oakland Museum, California; The New York Public Library)
New York, The Museum of Modern Art, "Committed to Print: Social and Political Themes in Recent American Printed Art" (exh. cat.) (traveled to The Peace Museum, Chicago; Glenbo Museum, Calgary, Alberta)

New York, Whitney Museum of American Art, "Figure as Subject: The Revival of Figuration since 1975" (exh. cat.) (traveled to Edwin A. Ulrich Museum of Art, State University, Wichita, Kansas; The Arkansas Arts Center, Little Rock; Amarillo Art Center, Texas; Utah Museum of Fine Arts, University of Utah, Salt Lake City; Madison Art Center, Wisconsin)

1989

Lynchburg, Virginia, Randolph Macon Women's College, "Chicago"
Virginia Beach, Virginia, Virginia Beach Center for the Arts, "Made in America" (exh. cat.)

1989–90

Minneapolis, Minnesota, Walker Art Center, "First Impressions: Early Prints by Forty-six Contemporary Artists" (exh. cat.) (traveled to Laguna Gloria Art Museum, Austin, Texas; The Baltimore Museum of Art, Maryland; Neuberger Museum, State University of New York, Purchase)

Adams, Brooke. "The Progress of Ed Paschke." *Art in America* 70, 9 (Oct. 1982): cover, 114–22.

Adams, Lucia. "Ed Paschke's 'Hophead': Primitive Myth Cloaked in Popular Culture." *Nit and Wit Magazine*, Jan.–Feb. 1983, pp. 18–19.

Adrian, Dennis. "And Now, Theater Sees His 'Hell.'" *Chicago Daily News*, July 29–30, 1972, Panorama sec., p. 5.

______. "Drawings of the '70's: A Many-Styled Show." *Chicago Daily News*, Mar. 12–13, 1977, Panorama sec., pp. 12–13.

______. "Ed Paschke: Selected Works, 1967–1981." In *Sight Out of Mind: Essays and Criticism on Art* (Ann Arbor, Michigan: UMI Research Press, 1985), pp. 71–77, also see 16–18, 34–35, 45, 65, 89.

______. "The Chicago Imagist Print." *Dialogue Magazine* 10, 6 (Nov.–Dec. 1987): cover, 16–19.

______. "The Import of Imagism." *Dialogue Magazine* 11, 3 (May–June 1988): 27–29.

Albany, New York State Museum in association with the Smithsonian Institution Traveling Exhibition Service. *Diamonds Are Forever: Artists and Writers on Baseball.* Exh. cat. by Peter H. Gordon, with Sydney Waller and Paul Weinman. San Francisco: Chronicle Books, 1987.

Allen, Jane Adams. "Chicagoan's Exhibit a 'Shoe-In.'" *Now! —Chicago Today*, Nov. 28, 1971, p. 52.

______. "A Country Machine in Need of Energy and Movement." *Chicago Tribune*, Mar. 4, 1973, p. 15.

______. "Stripping the Strippers, An Evening with Ed Paschke." *The New Art Examiner* 1, 3 (Dec. 1973): 3.

______. "The Other Tradition." *The New Art Examiner* 2, 5 (Feb. 1975): 1, 4–5, 15.

______. "Art / The Exhibit of Broad Shoulders." *The Washington Times*, Feb. 1, 1985, pp. B1, B3.

Anderson, Don J. "Medieval Exhibit at the Art Institute." *Now! —Chicago Today*, May 24, 1970, p. 64.

______. "A Funeral Exhibit—Believe It or Not." *Now!—Chicago Today*, Feb. 7, 1971, p. 77.

______. "Art / 'Artful Codgers' Are at It Once Again." *Now! —Chicago Today*, Apr. 11, 1971.

______. "To See Ourselves as Others See Us." *Chicago Magazine* 9, 2 (Mar.–Apr. 1972): 67–69, 80.

Andries, Dorothy. "He Shares Artists' Problems." *Lively Arts, A North Shore Guide*, Dec. 5, 1974, p. 6.

Ann Arbor, Michigan, The University of Michigan Museum of Art. *Chicago: The City and Its Artists 1945–1978.* Exh. cat. by Michael Marlis. Ann Arbor, 1978.

"Art for Everyone's Sake." *Kemper Annual Report*, May 16, 1978, p. 12.

Artner, Alan G. "Picasso's Late Work Seen in a Later Light." *Chicago Tribune*, Dec. 12, 1973, Arts and Fun sec.

______. "Yankee Visions at Age 71." *Chicago Tribune*, June 9, 1974, Arts and Fun sec.

______. "Portraits and Drawings in Pleasing Perspective." *Chicago Tribune*, Mar. 20, 1977, Arts and Fun sec.

______. "New Showings Spotlight the Chicago Artists." *Chicago Tribune*, Oct. 23, 1977, Arts and Fun sec.

______. "Art '77: Old Issues Carry Over into Art's New Year." *Chicago Tribune*, Jan. 1, 1978, Arts and Fun sec.

______. "New Season Promises a Packed Schedule." *Chicago Tribune*, Sept. 7, 1979, sec. 4, p. 11.

______. "Audubon—the Artist Rises above Accuracy." *Chicago Tribune*, Nov. 9, 1979, sec. 3, p. 15.

______. "MCA Rounds Up Dennis Adrian's 'Maverick Herd.'" *Chicago Tribune*, Feb. 7, 1982, sec. 6, p. 8.

______. "Paschke Show: 34 Eye-Openers from a Chicago Master." *Chicago Tribune*, Mar. 14, 1982, sec. 6, p. 15.

______. "So Long, Greenbergian Formalism, Here Come Meaning and Experience." *Chicago Tribune*, Apr. 24, 1983, Arts and Books sec., p. 13.

______. "Paschke's Paintings at Phyllis Kind Clothe Image in Distorted Video Mask." *Chicago Tribune*, Sept. 23, 1983, sec. 5, p. 18.

______. "Art / Terra Incognita." *Chicago Tribune*, Sept. 13, 1987, sec. 13, p. 10.

Art News 88, 6 (Summer 1989): cover.

______. "Exhibit a Record of Paschke's Development." *Chicago Tribune*, Oct. 28, 1988, sec. 7, pp. 62–63.

______. "The Year's Best Art Exhibitions." *Chicago Tribune*, Jan. 1, 1989, Arts sec., pp. 16–17.

Aspen, Colorado. The Aspen Center for the Visual Arts. *American Portraits of the Sixties and Seventies*. Exh. cat. by Phillip Yenawine. Aspen, 1979.

Atlanta, Nexus Gallery. *What Artists Have to Say about Nuclear War*. Exh. cat. by John Howett, Jeff Kipnis, and Chip Reynolds. Atlanta, 1983.

Auer, James. "Northwestern Trio Art Show a Winner." *The Milwaukee Journal*, Feb. 23, 1986, sec. 1, p. 8.

Baker, Kenneth. "The Insider." *Connoisseur Magazine* 214, 865 (Mar. 1984): 126–30.

______. "Ed Paschke at Phyllis Kind." *Art in America* 73, 2 (Feb. 1985): 139–40.

______. "From Chicago." *San Francisco Chronicle*, Nov. 6, 1986, p. 68.

Baldwin, Nick. "Chicago Art at UNI." *Des Moines Register* (Iowa), Apr. 9, 1978, p. B5.

Barnard, Judith. "The MCA, The Little Museum That Grew." *Chicago Daily News*, Sept. 10–11, 1977, Panorama sec., pp. 3, 12.

Barnes, Stephanie Schoenfeldt. "Chicago Collects." *Dialogue Magazine* 11, 3 (May–June 1988): 32–35.

Barry, Edward. "The 'Truths' Bubble Beneath the Surface." *Chicago Tribune*, May 31, 1970, sec. 5, p. 11.

Bates, Steven L. "Ed Paschke: Recent Paintings." *Arts and Sciences* (Northwestern University, Evanston, Illinois) 5, 1 (Spring 1982): 8–13.

Battcock, Gregory. "The Progress of Realism." In *Why Art: Casual Notes on the Aesthetics of the Immediate Past*. New York: E. P. Dutton & Company, 1977, pp. 97–131.

Bayside, New York, Queensborough Community College of the City of New York. *The Parodic Power of Popular Imagery*. Exh. cat. by Lenore Malen. Bayside, 1985.

Beckley, Bill. "Reviews and Previews: Ed Paschke." *Art News* 70, 2 (Apr. 1971): 20, 66.

Bedno, Jane. "A Little Praising with Faint Damns." *Hyde Park / Kenwood Voices* (Chicago), Mar. 1970, p. 6.

Berger, Philip. "Gallery Tripping: Are All Chicago Painters Students of Seurat?" *The Reader* (Chicago), May 1986, p. 23.

Berger, Yves. "Paschke." *Le Figaro* (Paris), Nov. 26, 1976.

Berkeley, California, University of California, University Art Museum. *Made in U.S.A.: An Americanization in Modern Art, the '50s and '60s*. Exh. cat. by Sidra Stitch. Berkeley, 1987.

Blecha, Karen. "Success Hasn't Changed the Kid in Ed Paschke." *The Herald* (Chicago), Apr. 20, 1973, sec. 4, p. 1.

Blinderman, Barry. "Ed Paschke: Reflections and Digressions on 'The Body Electric.'" *Arts Magazine* 56, 9 (May 1982): 130–31.

Blumenthal, Lyn, and Kate Horsefield, eds. *Profile: Ed Paschke*. Chicago: Video Data Bank, The School of The Art Institute of Chicago, 1983.

Bonesteel, Michael. "Hairy, Scary, Odd and Daring—'Selections from the Dennis Adrian Collection at the Museum of Contemporary Art.'" *The Reader* (Chicago), Feb. 12, 1982, pp. 34–36.

______. "Ed Paschke." *Artforum* 22, 5 (Jan. 1984): 81–82.

______. "Paschke's Painting in Perspective." *Pioneer Press* (Chicago), Jan. 23, 1986, p. 22.

Bowman, Russell. "Ed Paschke." *Arts Magazine* 53, 2 (Oct. 1978): 14.

______. "Speakeasy." *The New Art Examiner* 12, 1 (Oct. 1984): 14–17.

Brisset, P. "Ed Paschke." *L'Oeil* 369 (Apr. 1986): 82.

Brooklyn, New York, The Brooklyn Museum. *Nineteenth National Print Exhibition*. Exh. cat. by Jo Miller. Brooklyn, 1974.

Brown, Ellen. "Contemporary Arts Center: News Photos and Nightmares." *The Cincinnati Post*, July 13, 1974, p. 41.

Bruner, Louise. "Chicago Imagists' Show Tough, Fun." *Toledo Blade*, Oct. 27, 1987.

Byrne-Dodge, Teresa. "C.A.M. Show of Paschke's Works Opens." *Houston Post*, Aug. 22, 1982, p. AA14.

Carrol, Paul. "Ed Paschke." *Interview* 10 (Apr. 1980): 52–53.

Carroll, Nancy. "A Conversation with Franz Schulze." *North Shore Art League News* (Winnetka, Illinois) 19 (May–June 1972): 6–9.

Cedar Falls, Iowa, University of Northern Iowa Gallery of Art. *Contemporary Chicago Painters*. Exh. cat. by Sanford Sivitz. Cedar Falls, 1978.

Chandler, Christopher. "Art-rageous Ed." *Inside Chicago Magazine* 1, 6 (Nov.–Dec. 1987): 12–13.

Chapel Hill, North Carolina, The Ackland Art Museum, University of North Carolina. *Some Recent Art from Chicago.* Exh. cat. by Katharine Lee Keefe. Chapel Hill, 1980.

Chicago, The Art Institute of Chicago. *Sixty-ninth Annual Exhibition by Artists of Chicago and Vicinity.* Exh. cat. Chicago, 1966.

______. *Seventieth Annual Exhibition by Artists of Chicago and Vicinity.* Exh. cat. Chicago, 1967.

______. *Seventy-second Annual Exhibition by Artists of Chicago and Vicinity.* Exh. cat. Chicago, 1969.

______. *Seventy-fourth Exhibition by Artists of Chicago and Vicinity.* Exh. cat. Chicago, 1973.

______. *Seventy-fifth Exhibition by Artists of Chicago and Vicinity.* Exh. cat. by A. James Speyer. Chicago, 1974.

______. *Seventy-first American Exhibition.* Exh. cat. by A. James Speyer. Chicago, 1974.

______. *100 Artists 100 Years: Alumni of The School of The Art Institute of Chicago.* Exh. cat. by Katharine Kuh. Chicago, 1979.

______. *Prints and Multiples: 79th Exhibition by Artists of Chicago and Vicinity.* Exh. cat. by Esther Sparks. Chicago, 1981.

______. *The Mr. & Mrs. Joseph Randall Shapiro Collection.* Exh. cat. by Dennis Adrian, Katharine Kuh, and Joseph Randall Shapiro. Chicago, 1985.

______. *Seventy-fifth American Exhibition.* Exh. cat. by A. James Speyer and Neal Benezra. Chicago, 1986.

Chicago, The Art Institute of Chicago and Chicago Art Organizations. *1958 Chicago Artists Exhibition.* Exh. cat. with an introduction by Mayor Richard J. Daley. Chicago, 1958.

Chicago, Center for Continuing Education, The University of Chicago. *The Chicago Style: Painting.* Exh. cat. by Dennis Adrian. Chicago, 1974.

______. *Masterpieces of Recent Chicago Art.* Exh. cat. by Dennis Adrian. Chicago, 1977.

______. *The Art of Playboy from the First 25 Years.* Exh. cat. by Ted Hearne. Chicago, 1978.

______. *Flip! Flash! Pinball Art!* Exh. cat. by Ed Paschke and Carol Schreiber. Chicago, 1982.

Chicago, Deson-Zaks Gallery. *Ed Paschke.* Exh. cat. by Dennis Adrian. Chicago, 1970.

Chicago, Hyde Park Art Center. *Hyde Park Art Center Retrospective Exhibition: Historic Panoramic Abra Cadabra.* Exh. cat. by Goldene Shaw. Chicago, 1977.

Chicago, Illinois Arts Council. *Koffler Foundation Collection.* Exh. cat. by Dennis Adrian. Chicago, 1976.

______. *Six Illinois Painters 67/69: Arcilesi, Ito, Lanyon, Paschke, Rosofsky, Wirsum.* Exh. cat. by Don Baum. Chicago, 1989.

Chicago, Illinois Bell, The Lobby Gallery. *Professors of Art in Northern Illinois.* Exh. cat. by Diane S. Newberry and Michele Vishny. Chicago, 1980.

Chicago, Nancy Lurie Gallery. *Chicago: Self-Portraits.* Exh. cat. by Joanna Frueh. Chicago, 1978.

Chicago, Museum of Contemporary Art. *Violence in Recent American Art.* Exh. cat. by Robert Glauber. Chicago, 1968.

______. *Chicago Imagist Art.* Exh. cat. by Franz Schulze. Chicago, 1972.

______. *Selections from the Dennis Adrian Collection.* Exh. cat. by Dennis Adrian, Mary Jane Jacob, Regan Heiserman, Naomi Vine, and Lynne Warren. Chicago, 1982.

______. *Selections from the Permanent Collection.* Exh. cat. by Mary Jane Jacob, Terry Ann R. Neff, Carol Schreiber, Naomi Vine, and Lynne Warren. Chicago, 1984.

______. *Selected Gifts from The Joseph and Jory Shapiro Collection.* Exh. cat. Chicago, 1984.

Chicago, The Renaissance Society at the University of Chicago. *Recent Portraiture.* Exh. cat. by Dennis Adrian. Chicago, 1977.

______. *Ed Paschke: Selected Works 1967–1981.* Exh. cat. by Dennis Adrian, Linda L. Cathcart, and Richard Flood. Chicago, 1982.

Chicago, The School of The Art Institute of Chicago. *Visions / Painting and Sculpture: Distinguished Alumni 1945–Present.* Exh. cat. by Dennis Adrian. Chicago, 1976.

Chicago, The David and Alfred Smart Gallery, The University of Chicago. *Artists View the Law in the 20th Century.* Exh. cat. by Dennis Adrian. Chicago, 1977.

______. *Master Prints from Landfall Press.* Exh. cat. by Dennis Adrian. Chicago, 1980.

______. *The Chicago Imagist Print.* Exh. cat. by Dennis Adrian and Richard A. Born. Chicago, 1987.

Chicago, Terra Museum of American Art. *Surfaces: Two Decades of Painting in Chicago—Seventies & Eighties.* Exh. cat. by Judith Russi Kirshner. Chicago, 1987.

Christiansen, Richard. ". . . and Don Baum's the Godfather." *Chicago Daily News,* Jan. 11–12, 1975, p. 3.

______. "A Bunny Empire Spawns 'The High Art of Low Art.'" *Chicago Tribune,* Dec. 17, 1978, Arts and Fun sec., p. 3.

Cleveland, Ohio, The Cleveland Museum of Art. *Contemporary Artists.* Exh. cat. by Tom E. Hinson. Cleveland, 1981.

Coburn, Marcia Froelke. "Success in the Abstract No Artful Fluke." *Chicago Sun-Times,* Feb. 5, 1984, Living sec., pp. 3, 7.

______. "The Collector: A Self-Portrait." *The Reader* (Chicago) 14 (Nov.16, 1984), sec. 1.

______. "Rustic Texture and Urban Angst: Chicago Cultivates a Hotbed of New, High-Intensity." *Chicago Scene,* Nov. 1, 1985, pp. 15–17.

______. "The Bad Boy of Art." *Chicago Magazine* 35, 11 (Nov. 1986): 170–75, 212–15.

———. "A Broad Brush Colors Terra's Exhibition of Chicago Art." *Chicago Tribune*, Sept. 11, 1987, sec. 5, p. 3.

Cohen, Ronnie. "Star Quality." *Portfolio* 5, 5 (Sept.–Oct. 1983): 80–87.

Cohrs, Timothy. "Reviews / Ed Paschke." *Arts Magazine* 60, 7 (Mar. 1986): 140.

———. "Reviews / Ed Paschke." *Arts Magazine* 61, 8 (Apr. 1987): 106–7.

Day, Holly T. "Ed Paschke at Phyllis Kind." *Art in America* 66, 2 (Mar.–Apr. 1978): 144.

DeClue, Denise. "Sideshows, Sensations, Perversities, and Paschke." *Chicago Daily News*, July 29–30, 1972, Panorama sec., cover, pp. 4–5.

DeKalb, Illinois, Northern Illinois University. *Arts USA: 2*. Exh. cat. by Norman E. Magden. DeKalb, 1971.

———. *Chicago Collects Chicago*. Exh. cat. by Jack Olson. DeKalb, 1978.

———. *Contemporary Images: Selections from the Student Association Art Collection*. Exh. cat. by Pegee Garrity and Marcia Wellwood. DeKalb, 1979.

DeSantis, Tallio Francesco. "Albright's Avant-Garde Painting Show Signals a Return To Figurative Tradition." *Reading Eagle* (Pennsylvania), Dec. 4, 1983, p. 18.

"Ed Paschke's 'Adria.'" *Chicago Daily News*, Nov. 20, 1976, Wrap-Up sec.

Edelman, Robert G. "Ed Paschke: Selected Works, 1967–1981." *The New Art Examiner* 9, 8 (May 1982): 19.

Elliott, David. "Phyllis Kind: Growing with Chicago's Best Art." *Chicago Sun-Times*, Dec. 7, 1980, Living sec., pp. 3, 5.

———. "Art / Collector Adrian: A Gambler Who Loves Wild Cards." *Chicago Sun-Times*, Feb. 14, 1982, pp. 5, 7.

———. "These Three Artists Paint Modern Visions." *Chicago Sun-Times*, Mar. 14, 1982, sec. 5, p. 22.

———. "Chicago Is Enjoying Its Own Eclecticism." *Art News* 81, 5 (May 1982): 90-94.

"Evanston Art Center Exhibit Is Open Sunday." *Pioneer Press Newspapers* (Chicago), Oct. 18, 1978, Diversions sec., pp. D12–13.

Evanston, Illinois, Mary and Leigh Block Gallery, Northwestern University. *Collaborations*. Exh. cat. by Kathy Foley. Evanston, 1980.

———. *Painting at Northwestern: Conger, Paschke, Valerio*. Exh. cat. by John Arthur, Mary Mathews Gedo, and Michele Vishny. Evanston, 1986.

Flood, Richard. "Reviews, New York: Ed Paschke." *Artforum* 19, 6 (Feb. 1981): 73–74.

Flushing, New York, The Queens Museum. *Television's Impact on Contemporary Art*. Exh. cat. by Marc H. Miller. New York, 1986.

Forgey, Benjamin. "Lucy Clark's Striking Display of Watercolors." *The Washington Star*, May 23, 1975, Portfolio sec., p. C1.

Fox, Catherine. "Nuclear Anxiety Radiates from Nexus." *The Atlantic Journal*, May 22, 1983.

Fox, Terry Curtis. "Murky Muddle in the Mines." *Chicago Daily News*, Aug. 20, 1972, p. 16.

Freeman, Phyllis, Eric Himmel, Edith Pavese, and Ann Yarowsky. *New Art*. New York: Harry N. Abrams, 1984, p. 207.

Frueh, Joanna. "Chicago's Emotional Realists." *Artforum* 17, 1 (Sept. 1978): 41–47.

———. "Victims of the Accident." *The Reader* (Chicago), Nov. 9, 1979, p. 43.

———. "Allegory, An-other-world [the artist-allegorist]." *Art Journal* 45 (Winter 1985): 327–28.

Fuller, Peter. "Who Chicago?" *Aspects: A Journal of Contemporary Art* (Newcastle-upon-Tyne, England) 14 (Spring 1981).

Gage, Richard. "Reviews / Ed Paschke." *The New Art Examiner* 11, 2 (Nov. 1983): 19.

"Gallery Highlights: Chicago's Style Is Here." *Philadelphia Inquirer*, Feb. 22, 1976, p. H11.

Gardner, Paul. "The Electronic Palette." *Art News* 85, 2 (Feb. 1985): 167–73.

Gaskill, Jane. "Paschke's Couples." *Foxylady* 1, 5 (Aug. 1975): 106–9.

Gedo, Mary Mathews. "Dennis Adrian Collection." *Arts Magazine* 56, 8 (Apr. 1982): 9.

Geneva, Galerie Bonnier. *Gladys Nilsson, Jim Nutt, Ed Paschke, Suellen Rocca, Karl Wirsum*. Exh. cat. Geneva, 1983.

———. *Ed Paschke*. Exh. cat. by John Yau. Geneva, 1988.

Gibson, Michael. "Around the European Galleries." *International Herald Tribune*, Oct. 23–24, 1976, p. 7.

———. "Critical View: Patron Saints and Others." *International Herald Tribune*, Oct. 23–24, 1976, p. 7.

Glauber, Robert. "The Effect of American Violence on American Art." *Lerner Skyline Newspaper* (Chicago), July 31, 1968, pp. 14–15.

———. "Marriage Chicago Style." *Lerner Skyline Newspaper* (Chicago), Mar. 4, 1970, p. 4.

———. "Good Show(s)." *Lerner Skyline Newspaper* (Chicago), May 20, 1970.

———. "A Raunchy Exhibit of Sleaziness." *Lerner Skyline Newspaper* (Chicago), Dec. 5, 1973, p. 8.

———. "Bizarre Approach to a Sick Period." *Lerner Skyline Newspaper* (Chicago), Nov. 30, 1974, p. 4.

———. "Savage Truth, Satire in Paschke's Work." *Lerner Skyline Newspaper* (Chicago), Jan. 29, 1975, p. 4.

Glueck, Grace. "Burst of Growth in Chicago's Art World." *The New York Times*, May 12, 1987, Arts / Entertainment sec., p. C13.

———. "The Blossoming Art Scene in Chicago." *International Herald Tribune*, May 18, 1987.

Goldberg, Vicki. "The Bergmans' Treasures." *Saturday Review*, Nov. 1980, pp. 56–59.

"Golden Years with the Artful Codgers." *Chicago Daily News*, Mar. 14–17, 1971, Panorama sec., p. 3.

Hagenberg, Roland, with an introduction by Robert Pincus-Witten. *Untitled '84: The Artworld in the Eighties* (New York: Pelham Press, 1984).

Haggerty, G. "Ed Paschke." *Art News* 85, 4 (Apr. 1986): 155.

Halstead, Whitney. "Chicago." *Artforum* 6, 10 (Summer 1968): 63–65.

______. "Fantasy and Self Expression among Our City's Artists." *Chicago Sun-Times*, Jan. 5, 1975, Showcase sec.

Hanson, Henry. "Upfront / The Art Mart: Paschke's Passion." *Chicago Magazine* 27, 8 (Aug. 1978): 16.

______. "Return of the Natives." *Chicago Magazine* 28, 12 (Dec. 1979): 229–31.

______. "A Man of Modest Means." *Chicago Magazine* 31, 1 (Jan. 1982): 116–17, 159.

______. "Upfront." *Chicago Magazine* 31, 3 (Mar. 1982): 14.

______. "Paschke Mini-Retrospective." *Chicago Magazine* 31, 4 (Apr. 1982): 128.

______. "Phyllis Kind Opens Two New Art Galleries." *Chicago Magazine* 32, 6 (June 1983): 18.

______. "A Pier without a Peer." *Chicago Magazine* 33, 5 (May 1984): 153–55.

______. "Spectator Sport / Seventeen Artists Play Ball with the White Sox." *Chicago Magazine* 34, 8 (Aug. 1985).

______. "NU Professors Show at Block Gallery." *Chicago Magazine* 35, 2 (Feb. 1986): 92, 94.

______. "Upfront-Artworks / Paschke Painting Sells Big at AIDS Benefit." *Chicago Magazine* 36, 7 (July 1987): 28, 94.

______. "Collecting the Collectors." *Chicago Magazine* 37, 4 (Apr. 1988): 114–17.

Harris, Susan A. "Reviews: Ed Paschke." *Arts Magazine* 59, 3 (Nov. 1984): 42.

Hawkins, Margaret. "Galleries / Brown's 'Half-Alligator' Snaps Up the Spotlight." *Chicago Sun-Times*, Jan. 10, 1986, p. 62.

Haydon, Harold. "5 'Nonplussed' Artists Exhibit Striking Works." *Chicago Sun-Times*, Feb. 25, 1968, p. 6.

______. "They Arrived Too Late for the Revolution." *Chicago Sun-Times*, Mar. 2, 1969, sec. 3, p. 9.

______. "What a Difference One Woman Makes." *Chicago Sun-Times*, May 3, 1970, sec. 4, p. 6.

______. "Galleries: An 1890 Idea That Still Works in 1970." *Chicago Sun-Times*, May 20, 1970, p. 53.

______. "Galleries: A Mini Preview of the São Paulo Bienal." *Chicago Sun-Times*, Sept. 14, 1973, sec. 2, p. 67.

______. "Chicago Artists Who'll Go Far." *Chicago Sun-Times*, Oct. 7, 1973, sec. 2, p. 2.

______. "Two Shows Based on Local Styles." *Chicago Sun-Times*, Jan. 26, 1977, sec. 1-C, p. 6.

______. "Easel Does It: Painterly Paschke Sets Up Tension." *Chicago Sun-Times*, Oct. 23, 1977, Show sec., p. 17.

Heartney, Eleanor. "Reviews: Ed Paschke." *Arts Magazine* 59, 3 (Nov. 1984): 36.

Hill, June. "Matching Wits with a Strapping Victorian House. . . ." *Chicago Tribune*, Oct. 8, 1979, sec. 3, pp. 3–4.

Hoeksema, Kristopher. "Artists Acclaimed: Chicago School Tour Exemplifies a Provoking Aesthetic." *The Daily Cardinal* (Madison, Wisconsin), Oct. 26, 1988, p. 4.

Homisak, William. "Ed Paschke: Hewlett Gallery." *The New Art Examiner* 11, 4 (Jan. 1984).

Hoxie, Elizabeth. "Ed Paschke." *The New Art Examiner* 7, 3 (Dec. 1979): 13.

Huber, Chris. "Imagists' Exhibition 'Startling.'" *Journal and Courier* (Lafayette, Indiana), Jan. 23, 1977, pp. 12–13.

Hughes, Robert. "Midwestern Eccentrics." *Time* 99, 24 (June 12, 1972): 56–59.

Jackson, David. "Artists by Number." *Chicago Magazine* 33, 5 (May 1984): 170–72.

Januszcak, Waldemar. "Chicago Defies You to Like Its Art." *The Arts Guardian* (London), Dec. 17, 1980.

Jensen, Dean. "Chicago Art Welcome in Own Home." *Milwaukee Sentinel*, July 13, 1984, p. 3.

Kalil, Suzy. "Art: Ed Paschke Selected Works Review." *Houston Post*, Sept. 12, 1982, p. AA2.

Katzman, Lisa. "Saints and Sinners." *The New Art Examiner* 11, 11 (Summer 1984): 17.

Kind, Phyllis. "Speakeasy." *The New Art Examiner* 10, 4 (Jan. 1983): 7.

Kingsley, April. "Chicago, The Look." *Art Express* (Jan.–Feb. 1982): 44–45.

Kirshner, Judith Russi. "Review of Exhibition. Chicago: 'The Science of Fiction / The Fiction of Science,' Video Data Bank." *Artforum* 23, 4 (Dec. 1984): 92–93.

Klein, Frederick C. "Collectors Art: How an Astute Buyer of Surrealist Paintings Acquired His Bargains." *The Wall Street Journal*, Jan. 10, 1978, pp. 1, 17.

Kogan, Rick. "Arts 1977: Chicago's Golden Dozen." *Chicago Daily News*, Dec. 24–25, 1977, Panorama sec., pp. 1, 3.

Kohen, Helen L. "Lowe Gallery's Display: Modernism from A to Z." *Miami Herald*, p. K1.

Kozloff, Max. "Inwardness: Chicago Art since 1945." *Artforum* 11, 2 (Oct. 1972): 51–55.

Larson, Kay. "Caws and Effect." *The Village Voice*, Dec. 31, 1979, p. 66.

Lautman, Victoria. "My Kind of Town." *Art and Auction* 8, 11 (May 1986): cover, 3, 119–29.

Leslie, Rich. "A Meditation on Mediation: Paschke's New Work." *The New Art Examiner* 11, 6 (Mar. 1984): 11.

Linville, Kasha. "New York: Chicago Group, Feigen Gallery." *Artforum* 9, 3 (Nov. 1970): 86–87.

Long Grove, Illinois, Kemper Insurance Companies. *Kemper Art Collection.* Exh. cat. by Joan E. Robertson. Long Grove, 1978.

Lucie-Smith, Edward. *American Art Now.* New York: William Morrow and Company, 1985, pp. 122, 124–25.

Lyon, Christopher. "By Art Possessed." *Chicago Magazine* 33, 5 (May 1984): 174–80, 200.

______. "Coming in from the Cold." *Chicago Magazine* 33, 5 (May 1984): 156–69, 196, 198.

______. "Synthetic Realism: Albright, Golub, Paschke." *Art Journal* 45 (Winter 1985): 330–34.

Madison, Wisconsin, The Madison Art Center. *Contemporary Figurative Painting in the Midwest: An Invitational Exhibition at the Madison Art Center.* Exh. cat. by Gibson Byrd. Madison, 1977.

Marchand, Sabine. "Ed Paschke." *Le Point* (Paris), Nov. 22, 1976.

Martin, Robert. "Painters Get a Perverse Pleasure from These Artworks." *The Tampa Times*, Jan. 19, 1978, Baylife sec., pp. 1, 2.

______. "Eleven Chicago Painters at the University of South Florida (Tampa)." *Art Voice / South*, Mar.–Apr. 1978, p. 41.

"Marvelous Marriage of Matrimony." *Chicago Daily News*, Feb. 7–8, 1970, Panorama sec., p. 3.

McCracken, David. "Exhibits a Cornucopia of Chicago Imagism." *Chicago Tribune*, Oct. 30, 1987, sec. 7, p. 60.

______. "Paschke Takes on Guns, Martyrs, Media." *Chicago Tribune*, Oct. 14, 1988, sec. 7, p. 60.

McGreevey, Linda. "No More Limits: Ed Paschke." *Real Life Magazine* 13 (Autumn 1984): 23.

Micha, René. "Paris: Paschke." *Art International* 21, 1 (Jan. 1977): 43.

Milwaukee, Wisconsin, Milwaukee Art Museum. *American Prints 1960–1980.* Exh. cat. by Gerald Nordland and Verna Posever Curtis. Milwaukee, 1980.

______. *1988 / The World of Art Today.* Exh. cat. by Russell Bowman. Milwaukee, 1988.

Milwaukee, Wisconsin, UWM Art Museum, University of Wisconsin. *Realisms.* Exh. cat. by Frank C. Lewis. Milwaukee, 1988.

Minneapolis, Minnesota, Walker Art Center. *First Impressions: Early Prints by Forty-six Contemporary Artists.* Exh. cat. by Elizabeth Armstrong and Sheila McGuire. New York, Hudson Hills Press, 1989.

Moore, Patricia. "Bizarre 'Weddings' Open Hyde Park Art Show." *Chicago Daily News*, Feb. 7–8, 1970, p. 23.

______. "Artistic Shortcut to 50th Anniversary." *Chicago Daily News*, Mar. 20–21, 1971.

Morrison, C. L. "Fabric and the Man." *Midwest Art* (Milwaukee) 2, 1 (Mar. 1975): 12.

______. "Chicago Dialectic." *Artforum* 16, 6 (Feb. 1978): 32–39.

Moufarrege, Nicholas A. "Intoxication: April 9, 1983." *Arts Magazine* 57, 8 (Apr. 1983): 70–76.

Muchnic, Suzanne. "The Galleries / Santa Monica / Ed Paschke." *Los Angeles Times*, May 20, 1988, sec. 6, p. 12.

Munich, Haus der Kunst. *Amerikanische Malerei 1930–1980.* Exh. cat. by Tom Armstrong, Bernd Growe, Ellen Goldhaar, and Ann Lucke. Munich: Prestel-Verlag, 1981.

New York, American Foundation for AIDS Research, Phyllis Kind Gallery. *Art against Aids.* Exh. cat. by Mathilde Krim and Robert Rosenblum. New York, 1987.

New York, The Art Museum Association of America. *Disarming Images: Art for Nuclear Disarmament.* Exh. cat. by Nina Felshin. New York, 1984.

______. *Focus on the Image: Selections from the Rivendell Collection.* Exh. cat. by Nina Felshin and Thomas McEvilley. New York, 1986.

New York, Independent Curators Inc. *Large Drawings.* Exh. cat. by Elke Solomon. New York, 1984.

New York, The Museum of Modern Art. *An International Survey of Recent Painting and Sculpture.* Exh. cat. by Kynaston McShine. New York, 1984.

______. *Committed to Print: Social and Political Themes in Recent American Printed Art.* Exh. cat. by Deborah Wye. New York, 1988.

New York, The Pace Gallery. *From Chicago.* Exh. cat. by Russell Bowman. New York, 1982.

New York, Whitney Museum of American Art. *Human Concern / Personal Torment: The Grotesque in American Art.* Exh. cat. by Robert Doty. New York, 1969.

______. *Biennial Exhibition, Whitney Museum of American Art, 1981.* Exh. cat. by Tom Armstrong, John G. Hanhardt, Barbara Haskell, Richard Marshall, and Patterson Sims. New York, 1981.

______. *Focus on the Figure: Twenty Years.* Exh. cat. by Barbara Haskell. New York, 1982.

______. *American Art since 1970.* Exh. cat. by Richard Marshall. New York, 1984.

______. *Biennial Exhibition, Whitney Museum of American Art, 1985.* Exh. cat. by Tom Armstrong, John G. Hanhardt, Richard Marshall, and Lisa Phillips. New York, 1985.

______. *Drawing Acquisitions, 1981–1985.* Exh. cat. by Paul Cummings. New York, 1985.

______. *Figure as Subject: The Revival of Figuration since 1975.* Exh. cat. by Patterson Sims. New York, 1988.

New York, Whitney Museum of American Art at Equitable Center. *The Figure as Subject: The Last Decade.* Exh. cat. by Patterson Sims. New York, 1986.

New York, Whitney Museum of American Art at Philip Morris. *The Changing Likeness: Twentieth Century Portrait Drawing*. Exh. cat. by Paul Cummings. New York, 1986.

Newark, New Jersey, Robeson Center Gallery, Rutgers, The State University of New Jersey. *The Political Landscape*. Exh. cat. Newark, 1985.

Nilson, Lisbet. "Chicago's Art Explosion." *Art News* 86 (May 1987): 110–19.

Nye, Mason. "Artists Portray Artists." *The New Art Examiner* 6, 4 (Jan. 1979): 13.

Olegarz, Harold. "Ed Paschke." *Arts Magazine* 53, 3 (Nov. 1978): 29.

Paris, Galerie Darthea Speyer. *Ed Paschke*. Exh. cat. by A. James Speyer. Paris, 1981.

———. *Ed Paschke*. Exh. cat. by Dennis Adrian. Paris, 1983.

———. *Ed Paschke*. Exh. cat. by A. James Speyer. Paris, 1986.

———. *Ed Paschke*. Exh. cat. by Dennis Adrian. Paris, 1988.

Paris, Grand Palais. *FIAC '76: 3ème Foire Internationale d'Art Contemporain*. Exh. cat. by Daniel Gervis. Paris, 1976.

Paschke, Ed. "Speakeasy." *The New Art Examiner* 9, 5 (Feb. 1982): 3.

———. "My Kind of Festival, the Chicago Expo Is." *Chicago Sun-Times*, May 5, 1985, Arts sec., p. 1.

Philadelphia, Institute of Contemporary Art, University of Pennsylvania. *The Spirit of the Comics*. Exh. cat. by Joan C. Siegfried, Philadelphia, 1969.

Philadelphia, Moore College of Art Gallery. *North, East, West, South, and Middle: An Exhibition of Contemporary American Drawings*. Exh. cat. by Peter Plagens. Philadelphia, 1975.

Phoenix, James. "Chicago at the Ackland." *Raleigh Sun*, Feb. 18, 1980.

Pierre, José. *Le Pop Art*. Paris: Fernand Hazan, 1975.

Pincus-Witten, Robert. "New York—Open City." In *Untitled 1984: The Artworld in the Eighties*. New York: Pelham Press, 1984, pp. 80, 88.

Pittsburgh, Pennsylvania, Carnegie Mellon University. *Ed Paschke: New Paintings 1983*. Exh. cat. by Elaine King. Pittsburgh, 1983.

———. *New York Painting Today—A Three River Arts Festival Exhibition*. Exh. cat. by Elaine King and Donald Kuspit. Pittsburgh, 1983.

Plagens, Peter. "The Academy of the Bad." *Art in America* 69, 9 (Nov. 1981): 11–16.

Plath, James E. "Ed Paschke / Interview." *Clockwatch Review* 2. Hartland, Wisconsin: Driftwood Publications, 1983, pp. 46–55.

Poirier, M. "Ed Paschke." *Art News* 86, 6 (Summer 1987): 206.

Powell, Ann. "City Scope—In Focus." *Houston City Magazine*, Aug. 1982, p. 16.

Quinn, Jim. "Third World Art at Marian Locks." *The New Puper* (Philadelphia), Feb. 28, 1976, p. 20.

Raynor, Vivian. "Art: Capturing Essence of a Remote Australia / Ed Paschke." *The New York Times*, Oct. 5, 1984, p. C28.

Richard, Paul. "Galleries: One Glance Isn't Enough." *The Washington Post*, May 29, 1975, p. E9.

———. "Art: Funny, Figurative and Fierce / Contemporary Midwesterners at the Corcoran Biennial." *The Washington Post*, Feb. 2, 1985, pp. 61–62.

———. "Zap! Flash! The New York Look at the Whitney." *The Washington Post*, Mar. 24, 1985, pp. F1, F7.

Richmond, Virginia, The Sydney and Frances Lewis Foundation. *Late Twentieth Century Art: Selections from the Sydney and Frances Lewis Collection in the Virginia Museum of Fine Arts*. Text by Frederick R. Brandt and Susan Butler. Richmond, 1985.

Rickey, Carrie. "Midwest Art: A Special Report—Chicago." *Art in America* 67, 4 (July–Aug. 1979): 47–56.

Rodriguez, Joanne Milani. "Chicagoans' Art Earthy, Energetic." *Tampa Tribune*, Jan. 8, 1978, sec. 4.

Rosenthal, Marshall. "Prize Art Sparkles at the Institute." *Chicago Daily News*, Mar. 28, 1973, p. 28.

———. "The Wonderful World of Prize Art." *Chicago Daily News*, Mar. 28, 1973, p. 27.

Russell, John. "'The Hairy Who' and Other Messages from Chicago." *The New York Times*, Jan. 31, 1982, p. 29.

———. "Art: Ed Paschke." *The New York Times*, May 27, 1983.

———. "Art View: Journeying Back in Time at, Yes, the Whitney." *The New York Times*, June 19, 1983, p. H35.

Russell-Taylor, John. "The Arts—Painting to Challenge the Strongest of Stomachs." *The Times* (London), Dec. 23, 1980.

Sacramento, California, E. B. Crocker Art Gallery. *The Chicago Connection*. Exh. cat. by Wilma Beaty Cox. Sacramento, 1976.

Salvioni, Daniela. "Spotlight / Ed Paschke." *Flash Art* 134 (May 1987): 84.

Saure, Wolfgang. "Pariser Kunstlereignisse: Paris-Berlin, Theimer, Titus-Carmel, Paschke." *Das Kunstwerk*, Dec. 1978, pp. 31, 59–60.

Schjeldahl, Peter. "Letter from Chicago." *Art in America* 64, 4 (July–Aug. 1976): 52–58.

———. "A Doppler Effect: Response to Chicago Artists' Round Table." *Triquarterly* 52 (Fall 1981): 216–21.

———. "Chicagoization: Some Second Thoughts on the Second City." *The New Art Examiner* 12, 8 (May 1985): 28–32.

Schnedler, Jack. "Look Out, Brazil! It's the Hairy Who." *Chicago Daily News*, June 2–3, 1973, Panorama sec., p. 4.

Schreiber, Carol. "Ed Paschke: Beneath the Paint." Master's thesis, The School of The Art Institute of Chicago, 1988.

Schulze, Franz. "New York Cool Meets Chicago Doodly-Scratch." *Chicago Daily News*, Feb. 24, 1968, Panorama sec., p. 4.

———. "Paschke, Master of Monsters." *Chicago Daily News*, Feb. 24, 1968, Panorama sec., p. 4.

______. "The Joys and Wonders of Chicago Art." *Chicago Daily News*, Mar. 22, 1969, Panorama sec., pp. 4–5.

______. "The Daddy of Dada." *Chicago Daily News*, Feb. 28–Mar. 1, 1970, Panorama sec., p. 6.

______. "Powerful Photo-Images." *Chicago Daily News*, May 16–17, 1970, Panorama sec., p. 6.

______. "Hurts and Flowers." *Chicago Daily News*, Feb. 27–28, 1971, Panorama sec., p. 10.

______. "Cooling It with Eyewash in a Generation of Chicago Art." *Chicago Daily News*, Mar. 27–28, 1971.

______. "Art News in Chicago." *Art News* 70, 7 (Nov. 1971): 48–55.

______. "So You Think That's Just a Shoe." *Chicago Daily News*, Nov. 27–28, 1971, Panorama sec.

______. *Fantastic Images: Chicago Art since 1945*. Chicago: Follett Publishing Company, 1972.

______. "Let Plato's Heaven Wait: Chicago Art Is Alive and Defiant." *Chicago Daily News*, May 6–7, 1972, Panorama sec., pp. 4–5.

______. "Yes, That's Chi Funk in São Paulo." *Chicago Daily News*, Oct. 6–7, 1973, Panorama sec., p. 15.

______. "In Chicago No One Owns the Light." *The Chicagoan*, Nov. 1973, pp. 120, 122.

______. "The Gap between Gallery Row and Teeming Chicago Avenue." *Chicago Daily News*, Nov. 24–25, 1973, Panorama sec., p. 13.

______. "The Prodigal Funk Is Home." *Chicago Daily News*, Jan. 11–12, 1975, Panorama sec., pp. 2–4.

______. "Good Vibes of Gallery Row / Ed Paschke at Deson-Zaks Gallery." *Chicago Daily News*, Jan. 18–19, 1975, Panorama sec., p. 15.

______. "Chicago: Bigger and Livelier But. . . ." *Art News* 78, 2 (Feb. 1979): 40–45.

______. "The Art Scene: Vigorous, If Divided, Chicago Takes on Its Own Identity." *Portfolio* 1, 1 (Apr.–May 1979): 114–17.

______. "Venet Exhibit: The Arc Is Mightier than the Pen." *Chicago Sun-Times*, Nov. 18, 1979, Show sec., p. 10.

______. "School for Prominence." *Chicago Magazine* 35, 5 (May 1984): 184–89.

Schwartz, Barry. *The New Humanism: Art in a Time of Change*. New York and Washington, D.C.: Praeger Publishers, 1974.

Seattle, Washington, Henry Art Gallery, University of Washington. *Sources of Light: Contemporary American Luminism*. Exh. cat. by Harvey West and Chris Bruce. Seattle, 1985.

Segard, M., and James Yood. "The Seventy-fifth American Exhibition: Tradition Confronts the Future." *The New Art Examiner* 13, 10 (May 1986): 28.

Shaw, Goldene. *History of the Hyde Park Art Center 1939–1976*. Chicago: Hyde Park Art Center, 1976.

Sheperd, Michael. "Chicago, Chicago. . . ." *Arts Review* (London) 31, 12 (June 22, 1979): 315.

Sherman, Mary. "Ed Paschke Keeps 'Bite' in His Work." *Chicago Sun-Times*, Oct. 23, 1988, pp. E4, E8.

Shirey, David L. "Downtown Art Scene: Celebrities and Horses." *The New York Times*, Apr. 13, 1971, p. 24.

______. "The Butler Institute of American Art / Youngstown: Thirty-ninth Corcoran Biennial." *Dialogue* 8, 5 (Sept.–Oct. 1985): 67–68.

Smith, Roberta. "Munich and Chicago." *The Village Voice*, Feb. 10–16, 1982.

______. "Precise Visions." *The Village Voice*, June 7, 1983, p. 77.

Spector, Buzz, and Leon Upshaw. "Chicago Abstractionists Visually Stunning But. . . ." *The New Art Examiner* 6, 8 (May 1979): 6.

Stewart, Patricia. "Grotesque Reflects Us All." *The Drummer* (Philadelphia), Feb. 28–Mar. 2, 1976.

Stone, Dennis. "Ed Paschke." *Art Scene* 2, 1 (Oct. 1968): 25–28.

Storm, Howard. "Preserving Perversions." *Jester* (Cincinnati), Aug. 2, 1974, p. 3.

Sunderland, England, Ceolfrith Gallery, Sunderland Arts Centre. *Who Chicago? An Exhibition of Contemporary Imagists*. Exh. cat. by Dennis Adrian, Russell Bowman, Roger Brown, and Victor Musgrave. Sunderland, 1980.

Talbot, Linda. "The Bold Beings of Chicago." *Ham and High* (London), Dec. 19, 1980, p. 52.

Tallahassee, Florida, Florida State University Gallery of Art. *Eleven Chicago Painters*. Exh. cat. by Margaret A. Miller. Tallahassee, 1978.

Taylor, Robert. "Who Chicago? Worthy of That Toddlin' Town." *Boston Sunday Globe*, Nov. 22, 1981.

______. "Seurat, A Lasting Impressionist." *Chicago Sun-Times*, June 15, 1986, p. 20.

Taylor, Sue. "Shaping Images for the Video Age / Trio of NU Artists Prove Painting Still Effective." *Chicago Sun-Times*, Feb. 24, 1986, p. 46.

Tully, Judd. "The Chicago Art Scene." *Flash Art International* 103 (Summer 1981): 23–26.

______. "New York Critics on Chicago Imagism." *The New Art Examiner* 12, 3 (Dec. 1984): 44–45.

United States International Communication Agency. *Landfall Press 1970–1980*. Exh. cat. by Joann Moser. Washington, D.C., 1981.

Upshaw, Reagan. "Kind Stable Sets Pace in Manhattan." *The New Art Examiner* 9, 8 (May 1982): 11.

______. "Painting in Chicago: Blue Collar Surrealism Meets Prairie Abstraction." *Portfolio* 4, 3 (May–June 1982): 59–60, 63.

Urbana-Champaign, Illinois, Krannert Art Museum, University of Illinois. *Contemporary American Painting and Sculpture 1974*. Exh. cat. by James R. Shipley and Allen S. Weller. Urbana-Champaign, 1974.

______. *Selections from the Collection of George M. Irwin*. Exh. cat. by Margaret M. Sullivan. Urbana-Champaign, 1980.

Vartanian, Chris. "Collector's Corner." *Chicago Sun-Times*, Feb. 12, 1989, Home sec., p. 1.

Ver Meulen, Michael. "Ed Paschke: The Artist as the Eye of a Storm." *Chicago Life*, June 1975, pp. 20–23.

Virginia Beach, Virginia, Virginia Beach Center for the Arts. *Made in America*. Exh. cat. by Walter Darby Bannard, Jane Kessler, and Lowery S. Sims. Virginia Beach, 1989.

Vishny, Michele. "An Interview with Ed Paschke." *Arts Magazine* 55, 4 (Dec. 1980): 146–49.

Washington, D.C., Corcoran Gallery of Art. *The 39th Corcoran Biennial Exhibition of American Painting*. Exh. cat. by Lisa Lyons. Washington, D.C., 1985.

Washington, D.C., Hirshhorn Museum and Sculpture Garden, Smithsonian Institution. *Content: A Contemporary Focus 1974–1984*. Exh. cat. by Howard N. Fox, Miranda McClintic, and Phyllis Rosenzweig. Washington, D.C., 1984.

Washington, D.C., National Collection of Fine Arts, Smithsonian Institution. *Made in Chicago*. Exh. cat. by Whitney Halstead. Washington, D.C., 1974.

Weiss, Hedy. "Dennis Adrian's Collection / A Tribute to the Art of Aggression." *The New Art Examiner* 9, 7 (Apr. 1982): 9.

Wells, Daniel. "Artful Codgers." *Chicago Tribune*, Apr. 4, 1971, sec. 5, p. 8.

______. "Paschke's Childhood Key to His Paintings." *Art and Artists* 10, 1 (Apr. 1975): 38–39.

Welzenbach, Michael. "Ed Paschke and Dennis Leon." *Artscene* 7, 9 (May 1988): 21–22.

Willis, Thomas. "Art Institute Jury Awards Cash Prizes to 30 at 'Vicinity Show.'" *Chicago Tribune*, Mar. 28, 1973, sec. 3.

Wilson, William. "Chicago Connection Clomps in on Big Feet." *Los Angeles Times*, Feb. 20, 1977, Calendar sec., p. 78.

Yau, John. "How We Live: The Paintings of Robert Birmelin, Eric Fischl, and Ed Paschke." *Artforum* 21, 8 (Apr. 1983): 60–67.

______. "Reviews / Ed Paschke." *Artforum* 25, 9 (May 1987): 144.

Yood, James. "Imagism Revisionism / Chicago Print and Drawing Shows Create a Paper Tiger." *The New Art Examiner* 15, 5 (Jan. 1988): 26–29.

______. "Ed Paschke." *Artforum* 27, 5 (Jan. 1989): 121.

Zimmer, William. "Art / Political Messages." *The New York Times*, Oct. 27, 1985, New Jersey sec., p. 26.

FIG. 1
UNIDENTIFIED PHOTOGRAPH USED BY THE ARTIST

FIG. 2
WILLEM DE KOONING (AMERICAN, B. 1904)
MARILYN MONROE, 1954
Oil on canvas
127 × 76.2 cm (50 × 30 in.)
Neuberger Museum, State University of New York at Purchase, Gift of
Roy R. Neuberger

FIG. 3
ANDY WARHOL (AMERICAN, 1928–1987)
TWENTY-FIVE COLORED MARILYNS, 1962
Acrylic on canvas
226.1 × 175.3 cm (89 × 69 in.)
Modern Art Museum of Fort Worth, Texas, The Benjamin J. Tiller
Memorial Trust
Acquired from the Collection of Vernon Nikkel, Clovis, New Mexico, 1983
© The Estate and Foundation of Andy Warhol, 1989/ARS New York

FIG. 4
ANDY WARHOL
MARILYN MONROE'S LIPS, 1962
Synthetic polymer, enamel, and pencil on canvas
Two parts, 210.7 × 204.9 cm (82¾ × 80¾ in.); 210.7 × 209.7 cm
(82¾ × 82⅜ in.)
Hirshhorn Museum and Sculpture Garden, Smithsonian Institution,
Washington, D.C., Gift of Joseph H. Hirshhorn, 1972
© The Estate and Foundation of Andy Warhol, 1989/ARS New York

FIG. 5
JEAN DUBUFFET (FRENCH, 1901–1985)
**JULES SUPERVIELLE GRAND PORTRAIT MYTHE OR SUPERVIELLE GRAND
PORTRAIT BANNIÈRE, 1947**
Oil and mixed media on canvas
130.2 × 97 cm (51¼ × 38¼ in.)
The Art Institute of Chicago, Gift of Mr. and Mrs. Maurice E. Culberg
(1950.1367)

FIG. 6
GEORGE COHEN (AMERICAN, B. 1919)
EMBLEM FOR AN UNKNOWN NATION #1, 1954
Oil on Masonite
172.7 × 130.2 cm (68 × 51¼ in.)
Museum of Contemporary Art, Chicago, Gift of Muriel Kallis Newman

FIG. 7
LEON GOLUB (AMERICAN, B. 1922)
HEAD I, 1958
Oil on canvas
53.3 × 41.3 cm (21 × 16¼ in.)
The Art Institute of Chicago, Gift of the Estate of Virginia Croon (1973.779)

FIG. 8
ED PASCHKE (AMERICAN, B. 1939)
**UNTITLED ILLUSTRATION FOR "QUEEN DIDO," A MEMOIR BY BEN HECHT,
1962**
Conté crayon
61 × 38.1 cm (24 × 15 in.)
Playboy Collection, Chicago

FIG. 9
GEORGES SEURAT (FRENCH, 1859–1891)
WOMAN WITH A PARASOL, SEEN FROM THE BACK, C. 1882–84
Conté crayon
31.3 × 23.5 cm (12⅜ × 9¼ in.)
Present location unknown
(Formerly in the collection of The Art Institute of Chicago, Estate of
Pauline K. Palmer)

FIG. 10
ED PASCHKE AND SILVESTRI ART MANUFACTURING COMPANY,
CHICAGO
**TEMPORARY FACADE; CARSON, PIRIE, SCOTT AND COMPANY, CHICAGO;
1966**
Paint on hardboard
Collection of the artist

FIG. 11
ED PASCHKE
UNTITLED, 1965
Collaged paper and paint on illustration board
29.8 × 16.2 cm (11¾ × 6⅜ in.)
Collection of the artist

FIG. 12
ED PASCHKE
LARGE ROUND OPEN, 1965
Oil on canvas
40.6 × 81.3 cm (16 × 32 in.)
Collection Dr. and Mrs. Charles Baum, Chicago

FIG. 13
ED PASCHKE
UNTITLED FILM SEQUENCE, 1962

FIG. 14
ED PASCHKE
THE INVISIBLE MAN, 1962
FILM SEQUENCE FEATURING KARL WIRSUM (BANDAGED) AS "THE
INVISIBLE MAN"

FIG. 15
HANDBILL FROM THE AMERICAS THEATER, C. 1968
Collection of the artist

FIG. 16
**COVER OF LIFE MAGAZINE FEATURING LEE HARVEY OSWALD, FEB. 21,
1964**
Courtesy *Life* magazine, © 1964 Time Inc.

FIG. 17
ROBERT RAUSCHENBERG (AMERICAN, B. 1925)
RETROACTIVE II, 1963
Silkscreen and oil on canvas
213.4 × 152.4 cm (84 × 60 in.)
Collection Stefan Edlis and Gael Neeson, Chicago

FIG. 18
ANDY WARHOL
16 JACKIES, 1964
Acrylic and silkscreen enamel on canvas
203.2 × 162.6 cm (80 × 64 in.)
Walker Art Center, Minneapolis
© The Estate and Foundation of Andy Warhol, 1989/ARS New York

FIG. 19
ED PASCHKE
BUDGET FLOORS, 1968–69
Color silkscreen
36 × 27.6 cm (14³⁄₁₆ × 10⅞ in.)
Collection of the artist

FIG. 20
GERHARD RICHTER (GERMAN, B. 1932)
EIGHT STUDENT NURSES, 1971
Photographs
Eight prints, each 95 × 70 cm (37½ × 27½ in.)
Private Collection, Cologne

FIG. 21
**OPENING OF THE EXHIBITION "MARRIAGE CHICAGO STYLE," HYDE
PARK ART CENTER, 1970**
From left: Karl Wirsum, Barbara Anne Rossi, Sarah Anne Canright, Suellen
Rocca, Edward Flood, and Ed Paschke

FIG. 22
ED PASCHKE
HOLY STICK MAN, 1969
Oil on canvas
73 × 62.2 cm (28¾ × 24½ in.)
Jones-Faulkner Collection, Chicago

FIG. 23
ED PASCHKE
PAINTED LADY, 1971
Oil on canvas
177.8 × 55.9 cm (70 × 22 in.)
Collection Gregory Copper, Chicago

FIG. 24
ED PASCHKE
RICHARD (AFTER NIXON), 1975
Graphite on paper
73.7 × 58.4 cm (29 × 23 in.)
Private Collection, Chicago

FIG. 25
ED PASCHKE
JOHN N. (AFTER MITCHELL), 1975
Graphite on paper
73.7 × 58.4 cm (29 × 23 in.)
Private Collection, Chicago

FIG. 26
ED PASCHKE
ADRIA, 1976
Oil on canvas
243.8 × 187.9 cm (96 × 74 in.)
Museum of Contemporary Art, Chicago, Gift of Lewis and Susan Manilow
in honor of Dennis Adrian

FIG. 27
PABLO PICASSO (SPANISH, 1881–1973)
GIRL BEFORE A MIRROR, March 14, 1932
Oil on canvas
162.3 × 130.2 cm (64 × 51¼ in.)
The Museum of Modern Art, New York, Gift of Mrs. Simon Guggenheim

FIG. 28
DAVID SALLE (AMERICAN, B. 1952)
MINER, 1985
Acrylic, oil, table/fabric, canvas
243.8 × 412.1 cm (96 × 162¼ in.)
Collection Phillip Johnson

FIG. 29
PABLO PICASSO (SPANISH, 1881–1973)
LES DEMOISELLES D'AVIGNON, 1907
Oil on canvas
243.9 × 233.7 cm (96 × 92 in.)
Museum of Modern Art, New York, Acquired through the Lillie P. Bliss
Bequest

FIG. 30
JOHN HEARTFIELD (GERMAN, 1891–1968)
**HIS MAJESTY ADOLF—I LEAD YOU ON TO GLORIOUS BANKRUPTCY,
FROM AIZ, 1932**
Offset version of photomontage
36.2 × 27 cm (14¼ × 10⅝ in.)
Akron Art Museum, Museum Acquisition Fund (79.20)

PHOTOGRAPH CREDITS

Illustrations are indicated by page numbers as well as plate numbers in *italics*. Plates 1–59 appear between pages 43 and 106.

abstraction, 19, 111, 113
  vs. naturalism, 36
  New York School, 18, 30
  in Paschke's work, 36, 37, 118, 130, 132
  vs. realism, 37
Academy High School for Performing and Visual Arts (Chicago), 133
Accordion Man, 123, 131, *plate 4*
Adria, 34, 35
Adrian, Dennis, 11, 34, 40
  interview with Paschke, 115–22
Afrique, 126, *plate 42*
Alabama (Robert Indiana), 25
Albers, Josef, 17
Albright, Ivan, 9, 40, 130
Ambrosia, frontispiece, 38, 125, *plate 27*
American Exhibitions, The Art Institute of Chicago:
  62nd to 64th (1957 to 1961), 20, 130
  75th (1986), 133
Ameritech Foundation, 9
Amor, 25, 28, 109, 123, 131, 132, *plate 2*
"Anti-Cultural Positions" (Dubuffet lecture), 18
Armondo, 33, 111, 124, 132, *plate 16*
art brut, 19, 30
"Art by Telephone" (1969 exhibition), 131
"The Artful Codgers," *see* "Chicago Antigua" exhibition
Art in America magazine, 29, 133

Art Institute of Chicago, The, 9, 11, 12, 17, 18, 115, 119, 122, 130, 131
  American Exhibitions, 1957 to 1961 (62nd to 64th), 20, 130
  American Exhibition, 1986 (75th), 133
  "Artists of Chicago and Vicinity" exhibitions, 17, 131, 132, 133
  Logan Prize, 132
  Raymond Foreign Traveling Fellowship, 21, 130
  Society for Contemporary Art exhibitions (1970, 1977), 131, 132
  see also School of The Art Institute of Chicago
"Artists of Chicago and Vicinity" exhibitions, 17, 131, 132, 133
Artner, Alan G., 132
Art News magazine, 29
"The Art of Playboy from the First 25 Years" (1978–79 exhibition), 133
Arts Club of Chicago, 18, 24, 40
Arts Magazine, 133

Bacon, Francis, 32
Bag Boots, 30, 111, 124, *plate 10*
Bahamas, 126, *plate 38*
Barat College (Lake Forest, Ill.), 31, 131–32
Barr, Alfred, 17
Baselitz, Georg, 31
Bataille, Georges, 107
Baum, Don, 28, 131, 132
Beckmann, Max, 131
Bibutsu, 125, *plate 34*
blacks, Paschke's paintings and drawings of, 32, 38
Blackshear, Kathleen, 19
Blackstone, 38, 127, *plate 56*

Blume, Peter, *The Rock*, 130
Bowman, Russell, 133
Brettell, Richard R., 9
Brooks, Mel, 122
Brown, Roger, 29, 30, 119
Budget Floors, 27–28, *28*, 131
Business Committee for the Arts, 133

Caliente, 38, 126, 133, *plate 45*
Campoli, Cosmo, 17, 40
Canright, Sarah, 28, 29, 131, 132
Carson, Pirie, Scott and Company, 21, 131
Centre d'Art Contemporain (Geneva), 133
Centre Pompidou, Paris, *see* Musée Nationale d'Art Moderne
Ceoltrith Gallery, Sunderland Arts Centre (England), 133
Chaplin, Charlie, 24
"Chicago: Self-Portraits" (1978 exhibition), 133
"Chicago: The City and Its Artists 1945–1978" (1978 exhibition), 133
"Chicago and Vicinity" exhibitions, 17, 131, 132, 133
"Chicago Antigua" (1971 exhibition), 28, 132
"Chicago Collects Chicago" (1978 exhibition), 133
Chicago Council on Fine Arts, 133
Chicago Daily News, 132
Chicago environment for artists, 17–20, 40
  Imagism, 17, 19, 28–30, 40
"Chicago Imagist Art" (1972 exhibition), 132
"Chicago International Art Exposition" (1983), 133

Chicago Public Library, 24, 133
Chicago Tribune, 132
"Chicago White Sox Baseball Cards Portraits," 133
Cho Chan, 35, 112, 125, 133, *plate 25*
Cohen, George, 17, 18, 19, 40
  Emblem for an Unknown Nation # 1, 18, *18*
Cohn, Daniel, 132
Cohn, Nancy (Nancy Cohn Paschke), 28, 31, 131, 132
Colbert, Claudette, 32
collages, 22–23, 130
  film, 24
color, use of, 16, 23, 25, 34, 36, 37, 38, 112, 113, 119–20, 133
Columbia College (Chicago), 133
Commutism, 130
Conner, Bruce, 20, 24, 130
Conté-crayon drawings, Seurat and Paschke, 20, *20*, 130
Contemporary Arts Center (Cincinnati), 132
"Contemporary Chicago Painters" (1978 exhibition), 133
Cosmetica, 38, 127, *plate 51*
couples series of paintings, 115
Culberg, Maurice, 40

Dallas Museum of Art, 9, 11, 122
Davis, Stuart, 20, 131
"Death and Disaster" paintings of Warhol, 109
Deerpath Art League (Lake Forest, Ill.), 132
Degas, Edgar, 130
  The Millinery Shop, 130
de Kooning, Willem, 15–16
  Marilyn Monroe, 15–16, *16*

de Marco (Richard) Gallery (Edinburgh), 132
Les Demoiselles d' Avignon (Picasso), 107, 108, *108,* 111–12, 113
Deson-Zaks Gallery (Chicago), 29, 131, 132
diptych format, 36
Disney, Walt, 19, 129
Dominant Nurse, 34, 112, 124, *plate 20*
"Don Baum Sez 'Chicago Needs Famous Artists'" (1969 exhibition), 131
Dos Criados, 123, 131, *plate 3*
drawings, 119, 130
    Conté-crayon, 20, *20,* 130
Dubuffet, Jean, 17–18, 19, 40
    "Anti-Cultural Positions" (lecture), 18
    Jules Supervielle grand portrait mythe, 17–18, *18*
Dunning Psychiatric Center (Chicago), 21, 130
Duro-Verde, 35, 125, 133, *plate 26*

Eight Student Nurses (Richter), 28, *29*
Eisendrath, Bill, 40
Electalady, 38, 126, *plate 43*
electronic media art, 16, 17, 31, 34–39, 112, 116, 132
"Eleven Chicago Painters" (1978 exhibition), 133
Emblem for an Unknown Nation #1 (Cohen), 18, *18*
Europe, trip to (1965), 22, 130
European expressionism, 17
Execo, 133
exhibitions, 131
    first museum, 131
    group, selected, 135–39
    Imagist groups, at Hyde Park Art Center, 28–29, 131
    one-person, 134
    one-person, first, 29, 131
    one-person, first in Europe, 132
    one-person, first in New York, 30, 132
    one-person, first museum, 132
    reception abroad, 121
Exley, Frederick, 133
expressionism, 17–18, 19, 130, 133

Fabion, John, 19, 130
Falconer, James, 28, 131
"The False Image," 29
Fantastic Images (Schulze), 132
Fernsehen, 36, 125, *plate 35*
Field Museum of Natural History (Chicago), 17, 19
"The Figure as Subject: The Last Decade" (1986 exhibition), 133
figure paintings and drawings, 111–13, 117
    multifigure compositions, 34–38, 113, 115
    single-figure works, 31–35, 37, 38
filmmaking, 22, 23–24, 36, 130
Flavin, Don, 131
"Flip! Flash! Pinball Art!" (1982 exhibition), 133

Flood, Edward C., 29, *29,* 131, 132
folk art, 29, 30
formalist theory, 20, 34, 108, 110
Fort, Jeff, 38
Francine, 31, 124, *plate 11*
Freud, Sigmund, 107, 108
Frio, 38, 126, *plate 46*
"From Chicago" (1982 exhibition), 133
Fuller-Goldeen Gallery (San Francisco), 133
Fumar, 38, 112–13, 125, 133, *plate 28*

Galerie Darthea Speyer (Paris), 12, 132, 133
"Gauguin" (1959 exhibition), 20
Gestalt art, 19
Girl before a Mirror (Picasso), 36, *36*
Goldeen (Dorothy) Gallery (Santa Monica, Calif.), 133
Gold Marilyn (Warhol), 131
Golub, Leon, 17, 18, 19, 20, 40, 130
    Head I, 18, *19*
Gordon, Stuart, 119
Green, Art, 28, 131
Greenberg, Clement, 17
Grooms, Red, 41, 131
Guinan, Robert, 28, 131
Guston, Philip, 31

Hairy Shoes, 31, 111, 124, 132, 133, *plate 9*
"Hairy Who" exhibitions (1966–68), 28, 131
"Hairy Who" group, 28, 29, 131
Haldeman, H. R. (Bob), 33, 132
Halstead, Whitney, 19
Hamilton, Richard, 131
handbill from the Americas Theater, 25
Hanson, Philip, 119
Hat, 132
Head I (Golub), 18, *19*
Heartfield, John, 109
    His Majesty Adolf—I Lead You on to Glorious Bankruptcy, from Aiz, 109
Hefferton, Phillip C., 40
Hellman, Lillian, 38
His Majesty Adolf—I Lead You on to Glorious Bankruptcy, from Aiz (Heartfield), *109*
Hitler, Adolf, 38, 121–22
Hofmann, Hans, 19, 130
Holy Stick Man, 30, *30*
Hophead, 115, 123, *plate 7*
Hubert, 132
Hughes, Robert, 132
"Human Concern/Personal Torment: The Grotesque in American Art" (1969–70 exhibition), 131
Hundred Acres Gallery (New York), 30, 132
Hyde Park Art Center (Chicago), 12
    Imagist exhibitions, 28–29, 29, 131, 132
"Hyde Park Art Center Retrospective Exhibition: Historic Panoramic Abra Cadabra" (1976), 132

iconic heads series of paintings, 38, 113, 121–22, 133
Illinois Institute of Technology (Chicago), "Phalanx 3" (1965 exhibition), 131
Imagism, 17–19, 28–30, 40
    exhibitions, 1966–72, 28–29, 131–32
L'Impression, 36, 125, *plate 32*
Indiana, Robert, *Alabama,* 25
Ingres, J.-A.-D., 130
"An International Survey of Recent Painting and Sculpture" (1984 exhibition), 133
Interview magazine, 133
Invisible Man, The, 24, *24*

Janis, Sidney, 17
Jeanine, 31, 124, *plate 12*
Joella, 31, 111, 124, *plate 13*
John N. (After Mitchell), 33
Johns, Jasper, 20
Jules Supervielle grand portrait mythe (Dubuffet), 17–18, *18*

Kalmbach, Herbert, 132
Kennedy, Jacqueline, 25, 110
Kennedy, John F., 25–26
Kennedy, Robert F., 110
Kind, Phyllis, 12
Kind (Phyllis) Gallery:
    Chicago, 121, 133
    New York, 12, 133
Kingston Mines Theater (Chicago), 41, 132
Klaus, 132

Landfall Press (Chicago), 132
Large Round Open, 22–23, 24, 25, 131
Leaf, June, 17
Levine, Jack, 20, 130, 131
    The Trial, 130
Libredo, 38, 127, *plate 52*
Lichtenstein, Roy, 40
Life magazine cover, 26
Lincoln, Abraham, 38, 113, 122
Lindner, Richard, 20, 32, 130
Locks (Marion) Gallery (Philadelphia), 132
Logan Prize, The Art Institute of Chicago, 132
Lowe Art Museum, University of Miami, 133
Luce (Henry) Foundation, 9
Lucy, 34, 111, 124, 132, *plate 14*
Ludlum, Charles, 41, 118, 132
Luhring, Augustine and Hodes gallery (New York), 133

McGinnes, Mac, 34, 41, 132
Machino, 34, 124, *plate 18*
MacKinnon, Isobel Steele, 19, 130
McLuhan, Marshall, 34–35, 131
"Made in Chicago" (1973–75 exhibition), 132
Magritte, René, 27, 131
M.A. Lady, 132
Malibu, 126, *plate 44*
Mandrix, 34, 124, *plate 21*

Manet, Edouard, 130
man series of paintings and drawings, 115, 132
Marilyn Monroe (de Kooning), 15–16, *16*
Marilyn Monroe's Lips (Warhol), 16, *17*
"Marriage Chicago Style" (1970 exhibition), 28, 131
    opening of, 29
Martin, Jean-Hubert, 9
masks and masking devices, 27, 34, 35, 38, 112
Matinee, 38, 127, *plate 53*
Mechanique, 36, 125, *plate 36*
Medium Is the Message, The (film), 35, 131
Melon-Lamé, 34, 35, 124, *plate 22*
Meramec Community College (Kirkwood, Mo.), 30, 131
Metal de Bleu, 125, *plate 23*
Mexico, fellowship trip to, 21, 130
Mid American, 111, 121, 123, 131, *plate 5*
Millinery Shop, The (Degas), 130
Miner (Salle), 36, *37*
Minimalism, 30, 110
Minnie, 132
mirror motif, Picasso and Paschke, 36
Mitchell, John, 33, 132
Modernism, 107, 113
"Momentum" exhibitions, 17
Mona Lisa (Leonardo da Vinci), 39, 113, 116
Mondrian, Piet, 113
Monroe, Marilyn, 15–17, 28
"Monster Roster" group, 40
Motherwell, Robert, 17
multifigured paintings, 35–38, 113
Munch, Edvard, 37
Musée Nationale d'Art Moderne (Centre Pompidou, Paris), 9, 11, 115, 122
Museum of Contemporary Art (Chicago), 12, 131, 132
    "Art by Telephone" (1969 exhibition), 131
    "Chicago Imagist Art" (1972 exhibition), 132
    "Don Baum Sez 'Chicago Needs Famous Artists'" (1969 exhibition), 131
    "Violence in Recent American Art" (1968–69 exhibition), 25, 131
    Warhol retrospective of 1970, 131
Museum of Modern Art (New York):
    "An International Survey of Recent Painting and Sculpture" (1984 exhibition), 133
    "Recent Painting and Sculpture Acquisitions" (1965 exhibition), 130–31

National Collection of Fine Arts, Smithsonian Institution (Washington, D.C.), 132
naturalism, 36, 37
Negrette, 38, 127, *plate 57*
"neon" paintings, 112, 132.
Nervosa, 38, 113, 125, *plate 30*

Newsweek magazine, 22
New York City, 21, 22–23, 30, 130, 132
New York School, 18, 30
New York Times, The, 30, 133
Niemann, Leroy, 19
Nilsson, Gladys, 28, 29, 131
"1958 Chicago Artists Exhibition," 130
Nixon, Richard M., 33, 132
"Nonplussed Some" (1968 exhibition), 28, 29, 131
"Nonplussed Some Some More" (1969 exhibition), 28, 131
non-Western tradition, 17, 19, 29, 30
Northwestern University (Evanston, Ill.), 133
   "Painting at Northwestern: Conger, Paschke, Valerio" (1986 exhibition), 133
Nutt, Jim, 28, 29, 30, 131

O'Keeffe, Georgia, 9
Oldenburg, Claes, 9, 19, 131
Olivier, Laurence, 38
Organic Theater (Chicago), 119
Oswald, Lee Harvey, 25–26, 110
Oz Park, 40

Pace Gallery (New York), 133
Painted Lady, 31–32, *32*
"Painting at Northwestern: Conger, Paschke, Valerio" (1986 exhibition), 133
painting techniques, 23, 119–20, 121
Palazzolo, Tom, 131
Papal Lunacy, 127, *plate 54*
Parsons, Betty, 17
Paschke, Ed:
   art training of, 19–21, 25, 28, 36, 130, 131
   background of, 19, 129
   MFA, 30, 131
   military service of, 22, 130
   at opening of "Marriage Chicago Style" exhibition, 29
   in his studio, *114*
   teaching positions, 30, 31, 131–32, 133
Pazzo, 16–17, 126, *plate 48*
Pedifem, 127, *plate 55*
"Phalanx 3" (1965 exhibition), 131
Phillips, Bert, 21, 130
Photo-Realism, 109, 110
Picasso, Pablo, 36, 107, 108
   Les Demoiselles d'Avignon, 107, 108, *108*, 111–12, 113
   Girl before a Mirror, 36, *36*
   scarification marks used by, 108, 111, 112, 113
   "Picasso: 75th Anniversary Exhibition" (1957), 20, 130
pimps and prostitutes paintings of Paschke, 32–33, 37, 111–12
Pink Lady, *14*, *15*, 16–17, 28, 111, 117, 123, *plate 8*
Playboy magazine, 12, 20, 21, 40, 118, 130, 133
plus-minus paintings of Mondrian, 113
politicians series of drawings, 33, 132
Pollock, Jackson, 17

Pop Art, 16, 17, 22, 25, 29, 30, 32, 40, 109, 130
portraiture, 34, 38, 118
Post-Impressionism, 20
Postmodernism, 113
Presley, Elvis, 38, 113, 116, 121
Prima Vere, 38, 126, *plate 49*
printmaking, 16, 17, 27, 40, 131, 132, 133
Producers, The (film), 122
Purisma, 126, *plate 50*
Purple Ritual, 25–26, 28, 33, 110, 123, 131, *plate 1*
Pyramid Gallery (Washington, D.C.), 132

Queen Dido illustration, 20, *20*, 130

Race Riot (Warhol), 25
Ramos, Mel, 40
Ramrod, 26–27, 28, 30, 32, 109, 110, 111, 115, 123, *plate 6*
Rauschenberg, Robert, 17, 20, 22, 40, 130, 131
   "Retroactive" paintings of, 25
   Retroactive II, 27
Raymond (Anna Louise) Foreign Traveling Fellowship, 21, 130
realism, 37, 130; *see also* Photo-Realism
Red Ball, 129
Red Sweeney, 33, 34, 111, 124, 132, *plate 17*
Rembrandt van Rijn, 130
Renaissance Society, University of Chicago, 133
repainted works of Paschke, 121, 131
"Retroactive" paintings of Rauschenberg, 25
Retroactive II (Rauschenberg), 27
Richard (After Nixon), 33
Richter, Gerhard, *Eight Student Nurses*, 28, 29
Rivers, Larry, 20, 22, 130
Rocca, Suellen, 28, 29, 131, 132
Rock, The (Blume), 130
Rodin, Auguste, *The Thinker*, 113
Rosenquist, James, 16, 40, 131
Rosofsky, Seymour, 18
Rossi, Barbara Anne, 29, 132
Rothko, Mark, 133
Rubens, Peter Paul, 36
Ruby Jo, 132
Rufus, 33, 34, 111, 124, 132, 133, *plate 15*
Russell, John, 133

Sabreena, 34, 111–12, 124, *plate 19*
Sac, Le, 126, *plate 39*
"Saint Gloria and the Troll" (Exley), 133
Salle, David, 36
   Miner, 36, *37*
"Salon de Mai," Grand Palais (Paris), 133
Santa Caballo, 127, *plate 58*
Sao Paulo Bienal, XIIth, 132
Sauganash, 133
scarification marks, used by Picasso and Paschke, 108, 111–12, 113
Scharres, Barbara, 40

School of The Art Institute of Chicago, 9, 11, 12, 19, 20–21, 22, 25, 28, 29, 116, 130, 131
   Paschke as teacher at, 132
   Ponte del Arte Fellowship, 131
Schulze, Franz, 29, 30, 132
Seurat, Georges, 20
   Sunday Afternoon on the Island of the Grande Jatte, 20
   Woman with a Parasol, Seen from the Back, 20
   "Seurat: Paintings and Drawings" (1958 exhibition), 20, 130
Sheridan, Sonia, 40, 131
Shirey, David L., 30
shoe paintings, 30–31, 111, 115, 132
show-girl (stripper) paintings, 31–33, 34, 132
Signaturo, 132
silkscreening, 131
   Warhol, 23, 110
Silvestri Art Manufacturing Company, 21, 131
16 Jackies (Warhol), 25, 27
Smithsonian Institution, 132
Society for Contemporary Art exhibitions (The Art Institute of Chicago, 1970, 1977), 131, 132
Speck, Richard, 27–28
Speyer, Darthea, 12
Speyer (Darthea), Gallery (Paris), 12, 132, 133
Steinem, Gloria, 133
Strangulita, 125, *plate 29*
stripper (show-girl) paintings, 31–33, 34, 132
Suburban Fine Arts Center (Highland Park, Ill.), 133
Sullivan, Louis, 131
Sunday Afternoon on the Island of the Grande Jatte (Seurat), 20
Sunderland Arts Centre (England), 133
Surrealism, 17, 18, 19, 27, 29, 40, 131

Tanz, Der, 37, 126, *plate 37*
Tappy Toes (film), 41, 131
Taylor, Elizabeth, 110
television, 35, 112
Televismo, 37, 125, *plate 33*
Temporary Facade; Carson, Pirie, Scott and Company, Chicago (Paschke and Silvestri Art), 21
Terminale, 125, *plate 24*
theater design, 34, 41, 118–19, 132
Thinker, The (Rodin), 113
"30th Society for Contemporary Art Exhibition" (1970), 131
"35th Society for Contemporary Art Exhibition: Drawings of the 70's" (1977), 132
This Is Marshall McLuhan: The Medium Is the Message (film), 35, 131
Time magazine, 22, 132
Titian, 36
Towanda, 37, 126, *plate 40*
Trial, The (Levine), 130
tribal arts, 17, 107, 108
Troika, 37, 126, *plate 47*
Tropicale, 132

Tudor, 132
Turds in Hell (Ludlum and Vehr), 41, 118, 119, 132
XII Bienal de São Paulo (Brazil), 132
Twenty-five Colored Marilyns (Warhol), 16, *16*

underpainting and drawing, 23, 119–20
Understanding Media: The Extensions of Man (McLuhan), 34
University of Chicago, 133
Untitled (1965), 22, *23*
Untitled Film Sequence, 24, *24*
Untitled Illustration for "Queen Dido," A Memoir by Ben Hecht, 20

Velázquez, Diego Rodriquez, 36
"Violence in Recent American Art," (1968–69 exhibition), 25, 131
Violencia, 37, 41, *106*, 113, 125, 133, *plate 31*
Viseon, 133
Vosotros, 37, 41, 126, *plate 41*

Warhol, Andy, 16, 17, 22, 30, 40, 109–10, 131, 133
   "Death and Disaster" paintings of, 109
   Gold Marilyn, 131
   Marilyn Monroe's Lips, 16, *17*
   Race Riot, 25
   shoe renderings of, 41
   silkscreen paintings of, 23, 110
   16 Jackies, 25, 27
   Twenty-five Colored Marilyns, 16, *16*
Washington, George, 38, 113, 122,
Watergate drawings, 33, 34
Wesselmann, Tom, 40
Westermann, H. C., 9, 19, 20, 130
Wetzel, Richard, 28, 131
Whitney Museum of American Art (New York):
   "The Figure as Subject: The Last Decade" (1986 exhibition), 133
   "Human Concern/Personal Torment: The Grotesque in American Art" (1969–70 exhibition), 131
   1981 Biennial Exhibition, 133
   south gallery at Equitable Center, 133
"Who Chicago? An Exhibition of Contemporary Imagists" (1981 exhibition), 133
Wilding Studio (Chicago), 23, 131
Wiley, William, 20
Wirsum, Karl, 21, 24, 28, 29, *29*, 119, 130, 131, 132
woman series of paintings, 31–32, 115, 132
Woman with a Parasol, Seen from the Back (Seurat), 20
Wood, Grant, 9
"Works on Paper: 77th Exhibition by Artists of Chicago and Vicinity" (1978), 133
wrestler paintings, 26–27

Yin and Yang, 38–39, 127, *plate 59*